Homestretch

Homestretch

by Nancy Stout

With a Foreword by Jerry Cooke

COURAGE
BOOKS
AN IMPRINT OF RUNNING PRESS
PHILADELPHIA · LONDON

Cover photo: Affirmed v. Alydar, 1978 Belmont Stakes
Title page photo: Monmouth Park

© 2000 by Running Press
All rights reserved under the Pan-American
and International Copyright Conventions
Printed in China

9   8   7   6   5   4   3   2   1
Digit on the right indicates the number of this printing

Library of Congress Cataloging-in-Publication Number 98-68520

ISBN 0-7624-0298-9

Cover and interior design by Frances J. Soo Ping Chow
Edited by Greg Jones
Typography: Perpetua

This book may be ordered by mail from the publisher.
But try your bookstore first!

Published by Courage Books, an imprint of
Running Press Book Publishers
125 South Twenty-second Street
Philadelphia, Pennsylvania 19103-4399

Visit us on the web!
www.runningpress.com

Contents

Foreword

by Jerry Cooke

In the old days, horse racing was known as the "Sport of Kings." Alas, there aren't too many kings around anymore; the only royalty left in racing are Queen Elizabeth II of Britain and a handful of Middle Eastern princes and emirs. Still, horse racing has survived and is thriving around the world, and actually is doing a lot better than the kings are.

As a horse racing photographer, I have been to all of the fifteen North American tracks that Nancy Stout talks about in this book, plus just about every other important racetrack in the world. Each of them has its own character and has left me with lasting memories.

I know of no one who doesn't have a tear in their eye when the Derby horses come out onto the track at Churchill Downs and the band plays "My Old Kentucky Home" as they get ready for the Run for the Roses. I've heard it forty-two times and it never fails. "Sidewalks of New York," played just before the Belmont Stakes at Belmont Park, will soften up even the toughest New York horseplayer. And "Maryland, oh Maryland," struck up just before the Preakness Stakes at Pimlico, never fails to pull a few heartstrings.

The British are right in tune, also. Queen Elizabeth and Prince Phillip arrive at Ascot (in England) in a horse-drawn carriage which delivers them right to the track, while the tune of "God Save the Queen" plays in honor. (*My Fair Lady* can't beat that.)

At all of these places the ghostly sound of the hooves of Man o' War, Secretariat, War Admiral, Seabiscuit, Whirlaway, Native Dancer, and Citation thunder along the empty stretch when you stand trackside and relive their past glory. In your mind, Affirmed and Alydar (forever joined together), Seattle Slew, Spectacular Bid, Forego, Kelso and John Henry, Sunday Silence, and Easy Goer and Cigar, are all racing to the wire. Their stories are forever playing out on the dirt and turf of America's greatest racetracks.

The great filly Ruffian is buried in the Belmont Infield. You can still hear the 83,000-plus fans in the Belmont Grandstand cheering on Canonero II as he tried in vain to win the Triple Crown on the long course.

There are people ghosts, too. The jockeys—Arcaro and Shoemaker, Longden and Pincay, Angel Cordero and Bill Hartack, Pat Day and Jerry Bailey, and many others. Some are gone, some retired, some very much with us still.

The trainers—Ben and Jimmy Jones, Max Hirsch, Woody Stephens, Mac Miller, Elliot Burch, Le Roy Jolley, Charlie Whittingham, Mr. Fitz, D. Wayne Lukas.

The great names of American racing—the owners

who started it all—the Whitneys, the Vanderbilts, the Phippses and the Mellons, the Woodwards and the Wideners, the Morrisses and the Bradys. You see Diamond Jim Brady and Dutch Schultz dining at Saratoga, with caviar and champagne at the Gideon Putnam.

These are the things that stay in the mind of the horse-racing fan. But when you photograph horse racing, you forget all that. The photographer's view of the track is totally different from that of the racing fans, racing writers, or, in fact, anyone else. You need to get as close as possible to the horses, jockeys, trainers and owners, exercise riders, stablehands, and backstretch help. You get a lot of dirt on your feet and, sometimes, on your face.

Modern camera equipment, developed over the last forty years or so, has made things a lot easier for us. Remote-controlled cameras can be put under the rail, so you can get a head-on look at the horses without getting run over. Auto-focus lenses and electronic devices let you take photographs that you could only dream of before the late '50s.

I photographed my first Kentucky Derby in 1956, with a small spring-wound hand-held camera. After the race, in the winner's circle, there was Needles, the jockey, the trainer, the groom, the owner, an Associated Press photographer, and myself.

Jerry Cooke at Saratoga.

That made seven of us (including the horse).

Nowadays, at rough count, there are several hundred photographers, dozens of TV cameras, hundreds of reporters, TV commentators and technicians, the Governor of Kentucky, all the hangers-on, and God knows who else. You need binoculars to see the winning horse. Such is progress.

Nancy Stout gives us a lot of valuable information about racetrack architecture, racing history, the horses and people involved, and how it all came together. Her photographs are elegant. Her words are evocative. When you read it, you'll hope for a long future for the Sport of Kings.

Acknowledgments

My first introduction to a racetrack came in the 1980s, when I photographed La Gavea track in Rio de Janeiro. There, located in the middle of the city, the famous statue of Christ on Sugar Loaf Mountain overlooks the horses as they come down the homestretch. I began to look for an opportunity to study American racetracks immediately upon returning to the United States. This came in 1989, when I received a National Endowment for the Arts (Design Grant to Individuals) grant to document racetrack architecture. Jerry Cooke, America's preeminent racing photographer, had no trouble listing the "great" tracks for me. For two years, I traveled across the country visiting racetracks, and produced a book in 1991.

It has been with great pleasure that I have returned to our great American racetracks in order to write this book. I made sure that I was never far from a telephone

that would link me to Cathy Schenck, Librarian, Keeneland Association in Lexington, Kentucky, and Tom Merritt, Director, Thoroughbred Communications, Inc. in New York City. Cathy helped me discover racing history, and Tom assisted me in contacting people in the Thoroughbred industry. I've never experienced anything less than complete encouragement and assistance from either of them.

During 1998, I revisited many racetracks and saw one for the first time, the beautiful Woodbine in Toronto. I am grateful to many people at those tracks who provided assistance that contributed to my understanding of their facilities. Cindy Duebler (Pimlico), Jane Goldstein (Santa Anita), Myra Lewin (Fair Grounds), Glen Mathes (Belmont and Saratoga), Mac McBride (Del Mar), Mike Mooney (Hollywood), Karl Schmidt (Churchill Downs), John Siscos (Woodbine), and Jim Williams (Keeneland).

I'd like to thank members of the racing press who shared information and insights: Joe Hirsch, Bill Mooney, Neil Milbert, Muriel Lennox, and John Crittenden; and historians Charlene Johnson and Edward Hotaling. I am grateful for the recollections of several distinguished men of racing: W. Cothran Campbell, Odgen Mills Phipps, Alfred Gwynn Vanderbilt, and James E. Bassett III (who kindly read this manuscript).

Finally, during the years when I worked on other projects or was out of the country in the racing season,

Michael Amoruso always kept me informed as he traveled to racetracks to photograph horses. He has been photographing racing since 1984 and has been a breeder of Thoroughbreds since 1993. It is a pleasure to include his work in this volume. It more than fills the gaps.

Publisher's Acknowledgments

The publisher would like to thank Kim Brown for providing the inspiration to create this book.

The editor gratefully thanks the public relations officers for providing rare and wonderful photographs: Fran La Belle, Mac McBride, Mike Diliberto, Bill Denver, Kathleen Bishop, Scott Mordell, Allison Byczbnski, Joe Savage, Chris Esslinger, Phyllis Rogers, Cathy Schenck, Mike Mooney, Sandy Baze, Michael Burns, Richard Sacco, Jim Williams, Terry Wallace.

Opposite: **Start of the New Orleans Handicap at the Fair Grounds, 1930.**

Introduction

Thoroughbred horse racing came to America in the eighteenth century. Within a short time, races were organized and recorded, and bloodlines were carefully charted. By the late 1800s, several major Thoroughbred racetracks had been founded and their legends had begun to take shape. Geographic areas like Saratoga, New York; Lexington, Kentucky; and Baltimore, Maryland, became famous for their breeding and racing, and national racing periodicals like the *Daily Racing Form* were firmly established. In short, Thoroughbred racing became a major sport in the States by the turn of the twentieth century.

In the early parts of the twentieth century, however, horse racing across America was crippled by a governmental backlash against gambling in general, and a handful of tracks around the country were forced to close down—temporarily, or for good. When the antigambling sentiment eventually subsided—between the 1920s and 1940s—the old guard of racing tracks continued or resumed their status, and a new wave of tracks was built. Overall, the fifteen tracks that are included in this book represent the best of the old and the new. They cover the entire country geographically (and include Canada), and

offer a wide array of intriguing stories of fascinating horses and horse people. Together, they tell the story of Thoroughbred racing in America.

The tracks included in this book are Saratoga Race Course, Pimlico Race Course, Fair Grounds Race Course, Churchill Downs, Oaklawn Park, Belmont Park, Arlington International Racecourse, Hialeah Park, Santa Anita Park, Keeneland Race Course, Del Mar Fairgrounds and Thoroughbred Club, Hollywood Park, Gulfstream Park, Monmouth Park, and Woodbine. Because the development of Thoroughbred racing in North America has been such an organic process that has grown over time, the tracks are presented in chronological order based on the year they were established. It is important to understand each track in this context.

The history of the Thoroughbred horse breed is itself an interesting story. Thoroughbred horses can be traced to three stallions from Arabia, Persia, and the Barbary States—these horses were named Darley Arabian, Godolphin Arabian, and Bylery Turk. These stallions were purchased by Englishmen (circa 1700) and bred to about fifty English mares. This was done to produce offspring for racing that would have two essential qualities—speed from the Arabian horses and stamina from the English horses—thus establishing the breed now known as the "Thoroughbred." Most notable for the purposes of this book, the seventeenth-

and eighteenth-century English settlers of the southern United States (Virginia, South Carolina, Kentucky, and Tennessee, in particular) brought progeny of these important horses to the New World. These settlers—mostly from aristocratic backgrounds—established Thoroughbred stud farms for breeding, and built tracks for racing the new breed in America.

America as a nation relied on horses for many years before Thoroughbreds were ever brought here. The horse was a substantial part of early American existence: it worked the land, provided travel resources, and was part and parcel of daily livelihood. Especially in colonial days, owning a fine horse that ran faster than others' horses was a matter of pride among people. The very fact that a horse was exceptional made the owner exceptional. But racing a horse was just one of its duties, and usually not its most important job. When the Thoroughbred suddenly entered the scene in the late eighteenth century, however, a new demand for horses was created. With only one job to perform—racing—a Thoroughbred's training regimen was given much time and devotion by its owner. Thoroughbred owners developed the sport of Thoroughbred racing to test the speed and improve the breed. Almost two centuries later, Thoroughbred racing is a full-fledged entertainment operation.

In America today, people who gather to organize a racetrack are called sports developers. But in earlier days, these groups called themselves "jockey clubs." The jockey clubs of old purchased suitable land, created the track for the horses to run on, and either erected a tent or constructed a wooden grandstand for the spectators. They also put up the money for the prize (called the "purse," because the money was placed inside a silk purse that dangled in front of the judges' stand). Jockey clubs usually consisted of men with money, a competitive spirit, and a keen business sense.

The European counterparts of American jockey club members have usually been members of the royalty in their countries. Very little has changed to this day. For example, the Queen of England sponsors racing at Ascot, while the Duke of Norfolk presents three days of racing each year at Goodwood (these are two of England's finest racetracks). There are not many races run at European meets—compared to American racing meets—but European meets are astounding as both sporting and social events. In short, going to the races in Europe is a majestic experience. Perhaps that is why it is called the "Sport of Kings."

During the development stages of Thoroughbred racing in England, races were run on a course usually made of grass, or "turf." The courses were often established on the king's land and were set up along a well-chosen route that followed the contours of the land. America, meanwhile, was a virtually untamed land covered with forests; therefore, racing venues would spring up in clearings. In order to maximize racing distances within these clearings, jockey clubs built tracks around the edges of the clearing. Since then, American Thoroughbreds have raced around a track (while English and European Thoroughbreds still race over irregularly shaped courses). These tracks cover distances from 1 mile to 1½ miles, and oval courses around the world today are copies of the original American designs.

Watching races in America can be a magnificent experience, too, although American racetracks are generally more about business, and prefer to hold as many races as possible. For this reason, the American Thoroughbred community has continued to embrace and improve their own invention—the indestructible dirt track. The dirt track can accommodate many races per day, every day. And although American racing remains committed to the relatively small dirt track, many of the venues in this book have added spectacular turf tracks to their facilities—for both aesthetic and practical reasons.

As the racing business has grown, each state has created a racing commission to control it. Today's tracks have full-time stewards from the racetrack and at least one steward from the state commission on hand to ensure that the rules are always upheld. These commissions regulate many aspects of the business of racing, including racing dates and legalized gambling. Each state's racing commission decides on the dates and length of each track's racing season so there are no overlapping or excessive seasons, and so there are enough horses and people to go around. Most tracks have had the same racing dates for years and years. Because any given track is only open for a relatively brief period, many trainers follow a circuit—they shift their horses from track to track, depending on where the best races

are held. Fans in all areas of the country can count on seeing at least some of the very best Thoroughbreds in America each year.

Because weather has always been a consideration, racing meetings in most parts of America are held in the spring and the fall. The Kentucky Derby is held the first Saturday in May, and has practically become the definition of springtime. Winter racing (December to March) is a phenomenon of southern and western states like Florida, Louisiana, Arkansas, and California. In fact, much of the winter racing in these states (by many top trainers' estimation, at least) is geared toward preparing horses for the Kentucky Derby. However, each track is a business in itself, and every stakes race is important in its own right.

To put on a day of racing, a racetrack must offer money for the winning horses. The bulk of this money comes from owner nominations and patrons' gambling dollars, while more money is generated through sponsorship and other means. Horse owners pay to nominate their horses to run in the races. This financial requirement helps to ensure that the best Thoroughbreds run in the most expensive stakes races, since no owner would pay a nomination fee for a horse that has no chance to win.

A large portion of the purse is collected via the track's patrons, otherwise known as the "$2 bettor." Thousands of bettors generate the money—known as the "handle"—that tracks have come to rely on to fill their purses. With a good handle, a track can offer a purse that is big enough to attract owners of quality horses. It is impossible to estimate an average handle of a typical racetrack, but the amount of money generated by the tracks included in this book is staggering. You will read more about that later.

You will also read about the fabulous "aristocracy" that makes up the Thoroughbred world: every horse in every Thoroughbred race in America (and around the world, for that matter) has a genealogy that can be traced back to horses registered in the *English General Stud Book* (published in 1791), the *French Stud Book* (1838), the *American Stud Book* (1896), or a Thoroughbred stud book of another country (Italy and Argentina come to mind). This emphasis on bloodlines is why Thoroughbreds are called "blooded" horses. It is always fascinating to trace the bloodline of a champion Thoroughbred, and to follow the careers of a champion's offspring.

Present, too, are the wonderful racing personalities—the owners, trainers, and jockeys—who people the Thoroughbred world. They are a breed apart! Thoroughbred racing is about owners who have invested in breeding an animal that is faster than all the others, a trainer who conditions that animal to perform at its optimum level, and a jockey who guides that animal through the race according to the particular track, the distance, the competition, and the conditions of the day. Never underestimate the spectacle of the sport; good racing is pageantry and drama. And this drama is a direct result of the perpetuation of quality people and horses—only the best survive.

Once all the races are run, and all the results are in, one question remains: Which is the best horse? For years, the *Daily Racing Form,* the National Thoroughbred Racing Association (NTRA), and the National Turf Writers came up with separate answers. Recently the three groups, voting by ballot, have moved to a consensus. This consensus is translated into horse racing's annual Eclipse Awards.

Eclipse Awards are given to the best horses (there are several categories, based on age and gender) and horse people (owner, breeder, trainer, jockey, apprentice jockey, and media persons). Each year, the best all-around horse is given the title "Horse of the Year." Less frequently, really outstanding people are given recognition, called the "Lifetime Award of Merit." Racing has much to thank them for. You'll find many of these award winners throughout the pages of this book. Their stories, and the stories of many others who have made Thoroughbred racing a big part of their lives, are what make the sport great and this book possible.

Saratoga
Race Course

Saratoga Springs, New York
(Established 1864)

Saratoga Race Course is considered to be the nation's oldest Thoroughbred racetrack. It wasn't the first Thoroughbred track to be built in America (the oval course at Fair Grounds in New Orleans dates from 1851), but Saratoga is the oldest track that has continued nonstop since its inception. Several tracks operated in New York City during the nineteenth century—one was on what is now the campus of Columbia University; another was in Greenwich Village—but they all shut down long ago. Saratoga, on the other hand, was always embraced for its summer racing—so much so that summer racing at Saratoga became an institution.

The Saratoga racing season takes place during the month of August, which is always humid and brutally hot in most Eastern cities (less so at Saratoga). Still, none of the racetrack's facilities have ever been air conditioned. There is no administration office, in the usual sense of such places, but rather there is a small cottage that houses the racing secretary's office downstairs and the press office upstairs. During the first week of each season, business and serious socializing are conducted. The Jockey Club meets in a large clubhouse at the edge of the racetrack, called the Reading Room, and parties are held in sprawling Victorian summer houses called "cottages." The wind blows through tall pine trees, and lightning and thunderstorms often break the heat and monotony. This type of weather, though, has always been a welcome change from the still, sticky heat of the city.

The quaint custom of moving an entire household from the city to a cooler place in the country during the hottest month of summer brought racing fans to Saratoga from its earliest days. People flocked to Saratoga for the cool pine forests of the Adirondack Mountains and the therapeutic mineral springs. The bubbling, slightly sulfurous spring water won over many families in the nineteenth century. (It has even been written that George Washington tried to buy the springs at some point.) Early in the century, a Saratogan named Gideon Putnam built a small inn beside one of the springs. (There is still a Gideon Putnam Hotel, and Saratoga remains a quaint village—until racing day, that is.)

Hotels—truly grand hotels the length of a city block—sprouted in the little village. Each August, racetrack patrons filled the small town, arriving in carriages and on trains, accompanied by their Saratoga trunks. The

Opposite: **The post parade viewed from the infield.**

serious patrons—mostly owners and breeders of Thoroughbreds—built opulent summer houses for their August racing holiday. Racing was serious business and sometimes a forum for national political discussion, drawing fans from all over the country.

The first racing meeting at Saratoga Race Course was held in August of 1864 and lasted only four days. The Travers Stakes, run at the very first meeting at Saratoga, is North America's second-oldest continuous Thoroughbred event. Only the Queen's Plate, first run at Carleton, Ontario, in 1860 (and still run today at Woodbine, Toronto) predates it. During those four days in August of 1864, just as the Union Army marched into Atlanta, William Travers' horse, Kentucky, won the first Travers Stakes race.

In 1872, the Saratoga Cup race drew three starters but became a virtual match race between Longfellow (representing the North) and Harry Bassett (representing the South). It was a true test of endurance—the length of the race was an amazing 2½ miles. In spirit, the race provided redemption for the South, as Harry Bassett won by a length.

The earliest owner of Saratoga Race Course was a boxer-turned-gambler named John Morrissey. Morrissey developed the track for a specific crowd, making it attractive to the high rollers—he even camouflaged the gambling that was present by naming the casino the "Club House." (Since the Club House couldn't accommodate all the gamblers, several smaller gaming houses were also built.)

Many of Morrissey's early racing patrons were New York City tycoons. Leonard W. Jerome (grandfather of Winston Churchill), John R. Hunter, and William R. Travers were three prominent figures at Saratoga. After the Civil War, General Ulysses S. Grant joined Commodore Cornelius Vanderbilt at the racecourse's gambling house.

It is said that Morrissey died a bitter man because he was not accepted by the top echelon of Saratoga society, remaining only a facilitator to the compulsive gamblers and nouveau riche.

By 1894, after the turreted grandstand was constructed, the racetrack changed hands. August Belmont, James B. Haggin, and William K. Vanderbilt were now the

Clubhouse entrance on Travers Day.

16

owners, and William C. Whitney was among its racing patrons. The names Carnegie, Phipps, Woodward, Widener, Mellon, The King Ranch, Greentree Stables, and Calumet Stable would become Saratoga's racing royalty. They all shipped their horses to Saratoga every August for end-of-summer racing after having competed in all the major races of the late winter, spring, and early summer around the country. The very presence of these families helped to establish a grand social scene in Saratoga. It also helped to establish Saratoga as one of the country's great Thoroughbred racetracks.

Ceiling fans—not air-conditioning—cool the summer air in the grandstand.

These families and farms, and many others like them, continue to ship their Thoroughbreds to Saratoga every August after the big racing events of May and June. Saratoga is a much deserved and much anticipated celebration at the end of a long racing season, with plenty of parties filling the summer nights. Nothing really has changed since the racecourse opened in 1864—good racing and good socializing remain to this day.

The Grand Buildings

Saratoga Race Course (as we know it today) was built about twenty years after the first racing meeting. The roof of the grandstand, which fills the skyline with sweeping diagonal planes, was constructed in 1892. The image of the heavy roof of the grandstand has come to symbolize racing at Saratoga. The big turrets at the center, covered in slate shingles, shelter the oldest part of the grandstand. This little central portion measures about 585 feet and is constructed of wood posts and beams. Hundreds of wood trusses support the heavy slate-shingle roof and the three towers that stand on top of it—one at the center and one at each end.

Even though a big clubhouse was added on one end (in 1941) and an extension was added to the other (in the 1960s), the old 1892 building is still the heart of the racecourse today. In keeping with the simple elegance that Saratoga is famous for, the grounds crew calls the area in front of the grandstand (known as the "infield" at every other track) the "front yard," and the grounds behind it, the "backyard," as if the massive grandstand were their summer "cottage."

This oldest part of the grandstand contains the best box seating, "ownership" of which is passed down from generation to generation, and is greatly coveted. These boxes are spare enclosures made of tongue-and-groove paneling; they feature bentwood chairs for sitting. Ceiling fans hang from the trusses and turn the air a bit, but generally the patrons are cooled by the shade of the roof and the wind that agitates the tall pines trees behind the grandstand. While other tracks may put up plate glass panels and install air-conditioning, Saratoga would not think of it. These are true racing fans who try to match, step for step, the aristocratic owners, trainers, and horsemen who step out into real weather each day. No one ever misses the racing meet due to discomfort.

Sportswriter Heywood Hale Broun describes the Saratoga phenomenon as "a mixture of bucolic simplicity and gilded sophistication. . . . Unlike the false-fronted fantasy of reconstructed Americana—those places where actor-blacksmiths and actress-cookiemakers mimic ancestral trades—this place is real, functional, and fun."

A simple stroll around the grounds at Saratoga gives one the feeling that it is a most venerable locale, even in a sport that is steeped in tradition. The combination of seasoned buildings and timeless traditions conjure up a tactile spirit that can bridge the past with the present.

The clubhouse is a big building covered in snowy white clapboard; it is attached to the old grandstand. Completed in 1941, it is mostly a collection of dining rooms. At ground level, the building ends with an ellip-

tically curved portico decorated with carved horses' heads. Flower boxes with red geraniums and white petunias line every ledge. Red- and white-striped canvas awnings and curved copper roofing cover porches and sidewalks—spaces that are often enclosed by picket fences.

The clubhouse, at trackside, is still the favorite place for racing fans to enjoy their early morning breakfast. After the melon and eggs Benedict are cleared away, patrons study their racing sheets until the races begin. Until fairly recently, tables were located on both sides of the "gap" (the path on which the horses walk between the paddock and the track). Jockeys walked the horses

Bettors planning their day at Saratoga.

Top: **The 1890's-era saddling shed now houses betting windows.**
Bottom: **Horses go for a workout on the Oklahoma Track.**

ting windows. There used to be stalls inside where horses were saddled and paraded on rainy days (in 1963, the stalls were enclosed to create outdoor pari-mutuel windows). Many people recall the mysterious dark interior, smelling of straw and horses, with triangular shafts of light coming through louvered windows in diamond-shaped dormers in the roof. Some traditionalists even dream of restoring that building—it's a dream that may not come true, but a pleasant dream nonetheless.

A similar building (now demolished) was called the betting ring. It also had an enormous shingle roof and was almost as large in plan as the saddling shed, rectangular in shape with a hipped roof low at the eaves rising to a peak as tall as the grandstand. Several bookmakers had their headquarters in this building—Mark Costello, a former resident manager, remembers eight as late as the 1950s—each with a slate man to write up the bets.

This betting ring, along with the field stand that stood next to it, was demolished in 1963 in order to construct the present grandstand extension. The field stand, also built in 1892, was really just another grandstand, large in scale but set apart from the main grandstand. In reality, this field stand was built to accommodate African-American jockeys, trainers, grooms, and stable hands, as well as black track patrons and owners.

across this path, between tables, bringing with them the smell of horse sweat, the squeak of leather, the roll of big tense muscles, the twitching of tails, and a brief sense of danger. One was, after all, sitting quite close to highly wrought animals. It was exhilarating. That, of course, was its undoing (thanks to ever-increasing liability insurance costs). The bridle path, or gap, is now located just outside the building.

Another beautiful old building from the 1890s is the oval saddling shed, which has been converted into bet-

Throughbreds are led to the paddock where they will be saddled "under the trees," a tradition at Saratoga.

Sports are a reflection of our nation's history, and segregation, unfortunately, existed even in the racing world. Most every racetrack had a similar stand for African-Americans, usually located on the stretch furthest away from the clubhouse. Most tracks, including Saratoga, demolished these buildings in the 1960s as a positive reaction to the civil rights movement.

Saddling Horses Under the Trees

The reputation of Saratoga Race Course for saddling horses under the trees is still strong. For a century, the paddock was an area of vast lawn where anybody could gather to look at the horses. Each stable had a group of trees that served as an outdoor stall and exercise area where the horse is saddled before a race. Everybody convened in the paddock—the horse and groom came from the barn area, the jockey from the jockey's quarters, the trainer and owner from the clubhouse, and any patron interested in closely observing the horses also went there. It was an ideal world. But over time, two major changes occurred: the paddock area was decreased, and patrons were disallowed admittance to the area.

Today, horse, jockey, owner, trainer, and entourage still assemble under the trees in the paddock, but within a fenced area. Only persons connected with a particular racing stable, or members of the media, are allowed within the fence. The fenced-in area is necessarily smaller than the immense paddock area of old. As far as admitting patrons to the paddock, insurance costs eventually prohibited the public from being so near to the horses. This change was not without reason, though, since horses do have the tendency to kick people from time to time and the average person nowadays may not understand this fact. Before the 1940s, horses were in Americans' everyday consciousness—they were in neighborhoods with milk and produce wagons, they pulled trolleys, and they were part of street cleaning and garden agriculture. But these days, average Americans don't interact with horses as much and have largely forgotten how and when to steer clear of them.

Every August, people line up in vast numbers by the paddock, now safely behind the fence among the pine trees. Currently the racing season has been extended from the last week in July through Labor Day because of popularity. Patrons still bring picnics. They also bring their children, teaching them to sit under the old pine trees, drink mineral waters from the "Big Red" Spring, and keep an eye on the jockeys.

At no other track are the jock-

eys' quarters so accessible. Indeed, since racing regulations keep the quarters off-limits, they are usually hidden from view. But, at this eccentric old track, the jockeys are quartered in a house located in the middle of the backyard, just outside the grandstand. Here they sit on the porch, play horseshoes in a little area behind the house, and sign autographs and chat with their fans.

The Backstretch

Another aspect of the entertainment package is an early morning visit to the backstretch. The word "backstretch"—besides being the name of the far side of the track itself—is also used to refer to the area where the barns and stables stand. It is an interesting little

The backstretch at Saratoga is known for its bucolic beauty.

community—it's where many of the horse people live and work during a track's racing meet or season.

The stables on Saratoga's backstretch are truly bucolic. Old wooden barns are painted dark green. Flower boxes, buckets, and leg wrappings hang from window ledges, rafters, and rails. Chickens search amid straw dust for bits of oats and hay; goats and ponies keep the Thoroughbreds company; and dogs hang at the heels of the people who feed and exercise the horses and keep the place clean.

There are a group of barns located at the far turn known as Millionaire's Row—a name reflecting the income of the owners. During the first fifty years of the racetrack, the stable owners erected their own barns, apparently building them in their favorite spots, for they are in several locations. One group, called Claire Court, is located on the backstretch across from the grandstand; yet another is located in barns at Oklahoma Track located across Union Avenue. This portion of the racetrack is even older than Saratoga Race Course and also known as "Horse Haven." It was the site of the first season of racing, in 1863, before the track was created. There are eighty-six barns in all, spread over 350 acres.

Saratoga Traditions

Saratoga is famous for upholding tradition. For example, there is a pair of joined poles that form an information tower where, by a rope-and-pulley system, a signboard is hoisted and includes such information as jockey changes or horses withdrawn from the race. For many years this was the only source of up-to-the-minute information for bettors to use in their deliberations. There is now an electronic tote board that provides important race information instantly, but the tower has not been abandoned and is still used today to display certain messages.

The infield lake has a canoe tied at its bank—this is an allusion to the past, suggesting that somewhere out there in the infield, among the hydrangeas, hides an

The canoe on the infield lake is a tribute to local Native American tradition.

Another great tradition at Saratoga is the preparation of a new winner's circle for each race.

Indian maiden. The story comes from local legend, and the Saratoga area has an interesting Native American tradition. Saratoga's traditions are respected and imitated throughout the racing community, and many other American tracks have borrowed from it. (Gulfstream also keeps a canoe on its infield lake, and Keeneland saddles horses under the trees.)

Saratoga keeps the old kind of winner's circle, too—it is a circle drawn in the dirt with a mixture of chalk and flour after each race. (Nearly an obsolete tradition, Keeneland was the last to use it regularly besides Saratoga.) Each circle is fresh; each is unique. Why were they replaced with cement at most tracks? Because the new breed of owner doesn't like to get his or her shoes dirty and because the media likes the winner's circle to be in a predictable place. But not at Saratoga, at least not all the time. For stakes races, which are heavily covered by the media, the track uses a designated platform for the winner's presentation. At all the other Saratoga races, victory is celebrated in heat and dust (at best), and often in ankle-deep soil and rain (at worst).

The Travers Stakes

In 1864, a crowd of 10,000 made their way west of the village of Saratoga to the new Saratoga Race Course for the first day of a four-day meet. William Travers had been named president of the racing association, and a new race, the Travers Stakes, was named in his honor. This was Saratoga's first big race, and it was a success.

Holy Bull defeats Concern in the 1994 Travers on his way to the 3-year-old championship and the Horse of the Year honors.

The Travers Stakes is still the biggest race at Saratoga, and it is also one of the most important events in American racing. Since this stakes race is run late in the summer—after the horses have gained fame throughout the country all year long at many other important races—most of the horses are entered with the expectation of winning. Saratoga, then, because of the understandable anticipation it creates among owners and trainers, has become a racecourse notorious for its upsets. Racing writers charmingly call it the "Graveyard of Favorites."

The great Man o' War lost only once in a career of twenty-one races (in the 1919 Sanford Memorial Stakes at Saratoga). He placed behind a horse named Upset, from whom the sports term "upset" comes. The 1930 Triple Crown winner, Gallant Fox, lost the Travers to a 100–1 shot named Jim Dandy. Saratoga, to be sure, is not only hot for the people in attendance, but is also a test to any horse's stamina.

One of the greatest Travers tests was between Alydar and Affirmed in 1978, in front of a record crowd of 50,359. Affirmed had won the Triple Crown that year, but by no more than a length in any of the three races—and Alydar ran second each time. It was noses and necks apart all spring and summer as the two great horses raced against each other nine times—the Travers would be their tenth meeting. These two young horses were the country's greatest rivals, and the crowd at the Travers Stakes responded to the drama with great emotion and anticipation.

Affirmed with trainer Laz Barnena.

Again, the competitors found themselves in a very tight race. When Affirmed crossed the finish line first, it was apparently the perfect ending to a marvelous season. On the backstretch, however—according to the judges—Affirmed had bumped into Alydar and cut him off. Affirmed was disqualified and Alydar ended up in the Travers winner's circle.

Affirmed's jockey, Laffit Pincay Jr., protested that that kind of thing happens all the time, while Alydar's rider, Jorge Velasquez, said, "I didn't want to win it that way." Score another victory for Saratoga's famous "graveyard."

In 1993 owner Paul Mellon and trainer MacKenzie "Mack" Miller teamed up to accomplish something that hadn't been done in fifty-one years—win the Travers Stakes with the same horse that won the Kentucky Derby (in this case, Sea Hero).

Edward Hotaling, author of *They're Off! Horse Racing at Saratoga*, tells his version of the event. "I remember it was one of those Saratoga afternoons. Like some movie star, the Derby winner was there, about to stroll through the pines.

"But could Sea Hero, so close I could touch him, do the deed? Lots had made the trip up, but no Derby winner had captured this midsummer derby after Shut Out did it fifty-one years earlier. Even Paul [Mellon] admitted he wasn't any more confident than us average racegoers, who made his colt six to one, the bettor's favorite.

Mackenzie "Mack" Miller

"And Mack Miller [Sea Hero's trainer], he went and changed Sea Hero's bridle and shoes, then sat and fidgeted in the clubhouse. That would help about as much as feeding Sea Hero a Saratoga melon.

"And that [jockey] Jerry Bailey. He was even less sure of winning this than he had been about the Derby. But hey, [in the Travers] Bailey took a very relaxed Sea Hero into the stretch four horses wide, bushed but not the least bothered by Miner's Mark in front of him. Sea Hero was running just beautifully, well within himself, overtaking Colonial Affair and Devoted Brass, Miner's Mark and Kissin' Kris, and doing that Derby-Travers double by two lengths.

"There was even more to it than that, though. For one thing, Paul already had become the first owner to win the most prestigious races of three countries. The Kentucky Derby, the Epsom Derby, and the Prix de l'Arch de Triomphe," Hotaling wrote, referring to America's, England's, and France's major races, respectively. "Now he just tied George Widener with a record five Travers wins. And to celebrate, all he had to do was walk across the street to the neatest museum in sports." (The National Museum of Racing, which Mr. Mellon has abundantly funded.)

The next day, after beating the odds to win the first Derby and Travers in the same year in fifty-one years, Mellon, Miller, and Bailey (Rokeby Stables) won another race, this time with a filly named You'd Be Surprised.

Well, they were!

Horses leaving the starting gate.

Milestones

1863, August 3–6—The first Thoroughbred meet is held in Saratoga at the Horse Haven course. An association comprised of William R. Travers, Leonard Jerome, and John Hunter buys 125 acres of land across the street from John Morrissey's Horse Haven track and builds Saratoga Race Course.

1864—A crowd of 10,000 fills the stands at Saratoga Race Course during the inaugural four-day meet. William Travers is named president of the racing association and a new race, the Travers Stakes, is named for him.

1872—The Saratoga Cup draws three starters, but becomes a virtual match race between Longfellow, representing the North, and Harry Bassett, representing the South. Harry Bassett wins the unusually long 2½-mile race by a length over Longfellow.

1900—Saratoga is purchased by a syndicate headed by William C. Whitney.

1911—The Agnew-Hart Bill shuts down New York racing for two years.

1913—Because of a loophole in the law, the New York tracks reopen and betting is permitted.

1918—Samuel D. Riddle purchases the yearling Man o' War for $5,000 in a sale of August Belmont II's bloodstock at Saratoga.

1919—Man o' War suffers his only career defeat in twenty-one starts to a horse named Upset in the Sanford Memorial Stakes.

1930—Jim Dandy, a 100–1 longshot, upsets Triple Crown winner Gallant Fox in the Travers Stakes; it was and is one of the greatest upsets in racing history.

1940—Bookmakers are replaced by pari-mutuel machines.

1943–45—Because of World War II, racing is shifted to Belmont Park. Trains between New York City and Saratoga now carry war supplies.

1951—The National Museum of Racing and Hall of Fame opens in Congress Park at Saratoga Springs.

1954—Native Dancer concludes his twenty-two-race career with a victory in the Oneonta Handicap, a nonbetting exhibition race at Saratoga Race Course that he wins by nine lengths while carrying 137 pounds. He is voted Horse of the Year.

1965—Renovations and an extension of the grandstand are completed for $3.5 million.

1966—Ogden Phipps's horse Buckpasser, ridden by Braulio Baeza, becomes racing's first 3-year-old millionaire after he wins the Travers Stakes.

1972—Secretariat wins his first stakes race, the Sanford Stakes, at Saratoga Race Course. The time for the six-furlong race is 1:10, the fastest time for that distance at Saratoga in that year.

1973—Furthering its reputation as a "graveyard of favorites," Ionion, trained by Allen Jerkens, defeats the mighty Triple Crown winner Secretariat in the Whitney Handicap at Saratoga.

1976—Jockey Angel Cordero Jr. wins the first of eleven straight riding titles at Saratoga.

1977—Jockey Steve Cauthen rides Affirmed for the first time, winning the Sanford Stakes at Saratoga Race Course by 2¾ lengths.

1978—In front of a then-record crowd of 50,359, Alydar and Affirmed race against each other for the tenth and last time. Alydar is placed first upon the disqualification of Affirmed.

1982—In the Travers Stakes, jockey Jeffrey Fell runs Runaway Groom to victory over Gato Del Sol, Aloma's Ruler, and Conquistador Cielo in another upset. (The last three were winners of 1982's three Triple Crown races.)

1987—Jose Santos breaks Angel Cordero Jr.'s eleven-year riding-title streak.

1988—Cordero Jr. regains his Saratoga riding crown.

1989—Cordero Jr. wins his thirteenth title as most successful jockey at Saratoga.

1990—While earning top-track status in the country in attendance, this year's meet also establishes a record on-track handle of $89,297,389. Jockey Chris Antley takes the riding title from Cordero Jr.

1991—The successful Saratoga season is extended to five weeks for the first time. Corporate Report defeats Hansel (that year's Preakness and Belmont winner) in the Travers. Attendance and handle records continue to set records.

1993—Paul Mellon and trainer MacKenzie Miller team up to win the Travers with Sea Hero, who becomes the first Kentucky Derby winner to take the Travers in fifty-one years.

1994—Holy Bull defeats Concern (the eventual Breeders' Cup Classic winner) in the Travers. Eclipse Award winners Holy Bull, Flanders, Sky Beauty, Heavenly Prize, Cherokee Run, and Paradise Creek all run in stakes races at Saratoga.

1995—Kentucky Derby and Belmont winner Thunder Gulch dominates the Travers. Saratoga sets a record handle on Travers Day, when $20,336,681 is wagered.

1998—Attendance reaches a daily average of 24,660—the largest on-track attendance rate of any track in the U.S. Also, the daily average handle of $12,697,170 sets a new Saratoga record.

Top: **The Saratoga grandstand, viewed from the turn.**
Bottom: **The horses pass the grandstand, the heart of the racecourse.**

Pimlico
Race Course

Baltimore, Maryland
(Established 1870)

The Maryland Jockey Club considers itself to be the nation's oldest sporting organization, tracing its origins to 1743 when it conducted races in Annapolis, Maryland. Regarding racing in Maryland, the United States' first president, George Washington, dispassionately wrote in his diary that he was a consistent and persistent loser.

In 1830 the Maryland Jockey Club moved to Baltimore and asked President Andrew Jackson (incidentally the American president most consistently pictured on a horse) to be an honorary member. He replied, "Having once taken an interest in associations calculated to improve the breed of the American horse, I am enabled to appreciate the efforts which you are now devoting to the same object, and do not object to give it the sanction of my name."

A track at Baltimore flourished under the club until 1860, then closed during the Civil War and remained closed after the war ended. Legend has it that the idea of reviving Baltimore racing originated at a dinner party in Saratoga, New York, in 1868. There, at the illustrious Saratoga spa, Maryland's Governor Olden Bowie and his friends discussed opening a new Baltimore track and planning a racing season to open in 1870. The main race, they decided, would be called the "Dinner Party Stakes" to commemorate the meal they were having together. Governor Bowie made a stunning offer: he would offer $15,000 for a stakes race. At the time, this purse was greater than any stakes race in the country.

The Saratoga party was hosted by Milton H. Sanford, a wealthy man who had earned part of his money by selling blankets during the Civil War. When Pimlico did open in 1870, under the auspices of the Maryland Jockey Club, Sanford entered his horse, Preakness, in the Dinner Party Stakes race. The new racecourse was off to an auspicious start.

Opening Day at "Old Hilltop"

October 25, 1870, was a warm day. Thousands arrived to watch the races on opening day at the new Pimlico Race Course. The name, Pimlico, comes from the part of Baltimore where the new track was located. (The popular name of the track in the nineteenth century, however, was "Old Hilltop.") The track itself was a 1-mile oval that was built around a low hill that made up a good part of the infield. The hill gave a perfect view of

Opposite: **Secretariat outruns Sham to win the 1973 Preakness Stakes at Pimlico.**

the racetrack. The infield served as a parking lot for the carriages and as a picnic location. The picnics at Pimlico were traditionally champagne lunches, and the atmosphere around the track was festive.

About opening day, *The Baltimore Sun* reported: "There was a dazzling array of toilettes, and enough of the Maryland beauties were present from Baltimore and vicinity to consolidate all the jockey clubs in America, and the interest and excitement displayed during the racing by four thousand ladies present was the most intense ever witnessed at a similar scene. . . . In the field there were hundreds of teams, and below the quarter-stretch about seven hundred carriages, dregs, and other turnouts."

The main race of the day was the Dinner Party Stakes, the third of a four-race program that began at 1:00 p.m. There were seven starters in the Stakes, among them Sanford's colt, Preakness. A purse of $18,500 (the original $15,000 from Bowie, plus nominations) was at stake; it was the richest race ever run in this country at the time.

The Dinner Party Stakes was a 2-mile race—it covered the 1-mile oval twice. The racers started from a standing position on a roll of the drums. The jockeys rode straight-legged, copying the English style which had been popular for more than a century. Preakness quickly raced off the pace and staged a powerful move that carried him past the rest of the field, with a mile-and-a-half to go, and then on to victory. On his return, the victorious jockey performed a tradition of the day by riding back to the finish line and untying a silk bag filled with gold pieces—the "purse"—that was hanging on a wire strung over the judge's stand.

Preakness was a Kentucky colt sired by the great racing horse Lexington. In this race, as a 3 year old, he was ridden by white English jockey Billy Hayward. All the other jockeys in the race were African-Americans. It was the colt's only start in 1870, but he continued to race for five more years, winning the Baltimore Cup and finishing in a dead heat in the Saratoga Cup at 2¼ miles, both in his eighth year. He then was purchased for breeding by the Duke of Hamilton and shipped to England, where he became one of the first American horses to be given recognition by the British. Unfortunately, Preakness became an aggressive horse (as stud horses sometimes do), and the Duke shot him in a fit of anger.

The Preakness Stakes

The first official Preakness Stakes race, named after the top-winning horse on Pimlico's opening day, was run on Tuesday, May 27, 1873. The stands were painted violet. The blue-and-white pennants of the Maryland Jockey Club flew around the big Italianate-styled clubhouse that stood at the track's edge. Entertainment was provided by Itzel's Fifth Regiment Band, which played operatic airs and popular tunes of the day. The weather was warm and muggy. The crowd arrived by horse-drawn carriage and by omnibus. Some fans arrived via the Northern Central Railroad to the East and walked a mile uphill to the track. The crowd was estimated at 12,000.

The first Preakness Stakes drew a field of seven starters for a race of 1½ miles. The favorite horse, Catesby, belonged to former Governor Oden Bowie who had done so much to establish Pimlico and to popularize this race. Bowie's horse, unfortunately, came in fourth. A horse named Survivor, owned by John Chamberlain, won by ten lengths.

Pimlico Race Course prospered for the next fifteen years, then came upon hard times. In 1885, the track closed. Exactly why Pimlico declined is unclear, although competition with other tracks is usually cited among the reasons. (Another possible reason, cited in the 1924 Preakness Day program, was that Pimlico "for a while fell into disreputable hands.") During Pimlico's closure, The Preakness Stakes race was run at other tracks in Baltimore and elsewhere. The Maryland Jockey Club continued its involvement in racing, and even presented some steeplechase events, but the Preakness did not

Parade to the post at the 1940 Preakness Stakes. The race is won by Bimelech, who placed second in the Kentucky Derby and later won the Belmont Stakes.

return to Baltimore until 1909. In its absence from Pimlico, the Preakness was run most often (fifteen years) at the Gravesend track in Brooklyn, New York.

The Preakness was reestablished at Pimlico on May 12, 1909. From that day forward the Preakness has been run without a break at Pimlico. In 1918, eager to attract the best horses, the Preakness purse was increased to $15,000-added (from a previous $5,000), and the race was scheduled to run five days after the Kentucky Derby at Churchill Downs (which didn't offer as big a purse). Because of the Preakness's big prize and the small amount of time between the two races, Easterners opted to stay home and run their horses in the Preakness instead of going to Kentucky. Twenty-six horses entered the 1918 Preakness race; there were so many entrants that the field had to be split into two races. Wisely, the officials didn't split the purse. War Cloud and Jack Hare Jr. took home $15,000 each.

The following year, in 1919, the Preakness carried $25,000 in added money, again topping the Kentucky Derby, which then offered $20,000. (The Belmont Stakes—the third jewel in the Triple Crown—guaranteed $10,000.) That spring, Commander J. K. L. Ross entered a colt named Sir Barton into the Preakness Stakes. Sir Barton, who had already won the Kentucky Derby, won the Preakness and then went on to win the Belmont Stakes, making him the first Triple Crown winner. (The term "Triple Crown," however, did not become widely used until the 1930s.)

The real milestone for the Preakness Stakes came in 1920, when Man o'War appeared in the race. At the time, he was the most popular horse in the East. By passing up the Kentucky Derby for the Preakness, Man o'War helped establish the Preakness as a great classic race in America, and one that many other owners and trainers began to set their sights on.

Man o'War had won nine races as a 2 year old, all by wide margins, and was the 2-year-old champion for 1919. When his owner, Samuel D. Riddle, announced in early 1920 that Man o'War would pass up the Kentucky Derby for the Preakness, Pimlico became elevated in everyone's eyes. Thousands of racing fans went to Pimlico the Saturday before the race to see Man o'War work out over the track. He was going to race against his rival, appropriately named Upset, the horse that had beaten Man o'War at Saratoga as a 2 year old in his only loss. On Tuesday, May 18, 1920, Man o'War raced before a crowd of 23,500.

Newspaper accounts of the day note that it was doubtful if so many people ever crowded so close together to watch a race. For some reason, the infield was closed and everyone had to crowd into the grandstand. Man o'War set a terrific pace and, although Upset made a run in the stretch, Man o'War won by 1½ lengths over Upset. He raced twenty-one times during the 1919 and 1920 seasons, and set five American records.

History has been kind to Pimlico. Most of the so-called "lost" Preaknesses were officially incorporated into the race history of the classic in 1948. By the 1960s, all of the Preaknesses that had been run outside of Pimlico were added to the official record.

The Pimlico Environment

Although the best vantage point for race watchers may have been the infield at Old Hilltop, Pimlico's clubhouse, located at the edge of the first turn, was where everyone wanted to be.

The Maryland Jockey Club built the large building for opening day in 1870. It was more or less square and constructed of wood, with a deep, wraparound porch. What distinguished it most was the Victorian decor. The main floor contained the dining room and numerous sitting rooms. A wide stairway led from the ground level to the second story and its wide porches—the favorite spot, of course, to watch the races. The third floor, beneath the cupola, contained a number of guest rooms where the most prominent trainers stayed during the meets (these were removed during the 1950s and replaced with dining areas, a library, and a reading room). On Preakness Day, tables in the dining room, on the porch, and on the lawn were the best seats at the track.

The peak of the hip-roofed clubhouse building was finished off with a tower topped by a cupola. The cupola was fitted with a weather vane shaped in the form of a horse and rider. Each year, as soon as the Preakness winner is declared official, the weather vane is changed: a worker climbs to the top of the cupola to paint the weather vane horse the color of the winning horse's coat; he removes the silks of the previous year's winner from the weather vane jockey and replaces them with those of the new winner's silks; finally, he adds the winner's post-position number to the saddle blanket of the weather vane. This practice started in 1909 when a standard arrow-shaped weather vane was struck down by lightning and the Maryland Jockey Club commissioned an ornamental vane in the form of a horse and a rider to replace it. The new weather vane was christened that spring by coating it with the colors of the silks carried by Effendi, the winner of the 1909 Preakness. When the old members' clubhouse burned down in 1966, the only thing saved from the ruins was the iron weather vane. The weather vane is now on top of a little replica of the old cupola, at ground level. Painting the new winner's colors still occurs as soon as the Preakness is over.

Seabiscuit vs. War Admiral

For the generation who watched racing in the 1930s, what eventually became known as the "Race of the Century" was clearly the event of the decade. The date was November 1, 1938; the place was Pimlico Race Course. Only two horses were entered in the race—Seabiscuit and War Admiral. The matched race was called the Pimlico Special.

Like crafty old boxers, these were seasoned horses. Four-year-old War Admiral had won the Triple Crown and was named Horse of the Year in 1937, and won nine more races the following year. He had proven himself beyond question, and was considered the leading horse in the East. His breeding was impeccable: War Admiral was the son of the great Man o' War.

Seabiscuit (number 1) and War Admiral parade to the post in the "Dream Race" of 1938.

Seabiscuit, on the other hand, was Man o' War's grandson. A 5 year old racing mostly in the West and Midwest, he was recognized for his greatness in breeding and stamina. As a 3 year old, he was first in nine of twenty-three races. By 1937, as a 4 year old, he came in first in eleven of fifteen races and was the year's leading money-winner, with earnings of $168,642. In 1938, as a 5 year old, he became the Horse of the Year.

Everyone in the Thoroughbred racing world had heard of the race long before it actually went off. For almost two years, several tracks had tried to schedule the race for their venue. Numerous offers were made that involved incredible sums of money (perhaps for that reason, when it was finally arranged, it was called the "Dream Race"). In fact, the race had been scheduled to go off at Belmont in 1937, with a purse of $100,000,

Alfred G. Vanderbilt

but War Admiral developed a temperature and the race had to be canceled.

Then, Alfred Gwynne Vanderbilt, the president of the Maryland Jockey Club, finally made the deal. And his was not even the highest bid! Vanderbilt managed to secure the race for Pimlico for a purse of $15,000. Sixty years later, Vanderbilt recalled the circumstances that led to this historic event.

"I was a kid. I was twenty-six years old," Vanderbilt said.

"I'd boosted Pimlico up so that it was the only track in America where we had a stakes race every day. Those real good sports writers covered our races. And that meant at lot. You had seven or eight daily papers in New York. They all had turf writers.

"Everybody was selling horses, I was buying horses. They [the Maryland Jockey Club] put me on the board because I was running races."

Vanderbilt says he knew he wanted to be involved with horse racing since the age of twelve, when his mother would take him to the track. Vanderbilt's maternal grandfather had owned Sagamore Farm, and when he died he left the farm to Vanderbilt's mother. (Upon her death, she left the farm to Vanderbilt.)

Legend has it that War Admiral's owner, Samuel D. Riddle, was very finicky and critical about many of the details of the race.

"Mr. Riddle was a sorry, pompous old guy," Vanderbilt said. "He disliked the way the starter had started the year before. He said he wouldn't start his horse with that starter.

"Riddle wanted a fast track. Said he wouldn't run [War Admiral] if it wasn't a fast track. The Commissioner was to come out on the morning of the race and walk the track. Well, as you know, it didn't rain. The track wasn't slow or muddy."

The gates opened at 10 a.m.; by race time there were 30,000 people in attendance. The race was run at the Preakness distance (1$\frac{3}{16}$ miles), 120 pounds carried, and with a walk-up start. After three attempts to start, the barrier finally dropped and the race began. Seabiscuit took an early lead.

One of the best accounts of the race was given by a well-known sportswriter for the *Baltimore Sun*, Grantland Rice:

"The Admiral's supporters were dazed as the 'Biscuit not only held this lead, but increased it to two lengths before they passed the first quarter. . . . The

'Biscuit was moving along as smoothly as a southern breeze. And then the first roar of the big crowd swept over Maryland. The Admiral was moving up. . . .

"The Admiral looked Seabiscuit in the eye at the three-quarters—but Seabiscuit never got the look. He was too busy running with his shorter, faster stride. . . . For almost a half mile they ran as one horse, painted against the green, red, and orange foliage of a Maryland countryside. They were neck-and-neck, head-and-head, nose-and-nose. . . . It was a question now of the horse that had the heart. Seabiscuit had lost his two-length margin. His velvet had been shot away. He was on his own where all races are won—down the stretch. He had come to the great kingdom of all sport—the kingdom of the heart."

Finally, War Admiral started to tire and Seabiscuit moved ahead to win by a length-and-a-half. Rice wrote, "War Admiral might just as well have been chasing a will o' the wisp in a midnight swamp. He might just as well have been a fat poodle chasing a meat wagon. He had been outrun and outgamed—he had been run off the track by a battered 5 year old who had more speed and heart."

Nicholas Zito, Trainer

For most world-class trainers, the heart of the matter is competition. Trainer D. Wayne Lukas's horses won six straight Triple Crown races (1994–96), but his stupendous winning streak ended when trainer Nicholas Zito's Louis Quatorze, ridden by Pat Day, won the Preakness in 1996. Zito, a New Yorker, is younger than Lukas, respectful, modest, and hard-working. Stopping Lukas was a victory in itself. He is a competitor worthy of such an accomplishment—in other words, when Lukas was finally defeated, it was not a fluke.

"Yeah, it was good." Zito says. "The thing was, we had finished second so many times to him.

"I'd won two Derbies, but Louis [Quatorze] broke the streak." (Louis Quatorze is one of the speedy grandsons of Northern Dancer.)

Nicholas Zito

Louis Quatorze winning the 1996 Preakness, jockey Pat Day aboard.

Zito went to the races with his father, who once exercised horses for the well-known New York trainer Max Hirsch. Zito's father may have passed on a sense of romance about being around horses. After working as a hotwalker as a teenager, Zito got a job as a groom for Buddy Jacobson, a respected New York trainer, then worked as an assistant trainer for Johnny Campo and later for LeRoy Jolley, also in New York. At the age of 26, Zito saddled his first winner, and from there he has worked his way up.

In person, Zito, a self-proclaimed "street kid," does not strike one as tough. However, two of his clients (whom he conditions horses for) are some of the biggest self-styled street kids in America: George Steinbrenner, owner of the New York Yankees, and Rick Pitino, former head coach of the extremely successful Kentucky University Wildcats basketball team and current head coach of the NBA's Boston Celtics.

"I started very young, at fifteen and a half. Once I got the taste of it, I knew that was it. But I paid my dues. I started as a hotwalker, then a groom, and just worked my way up," he says.

Go for Gin prepares for the 1994 Kentucky Derby (above) **and the Preakness** (left)**. He won the Derby but placed second at Pimlico.**

"I came from a home with two hardworking parents, and they taught me that if you are willing to apply yourself to what you want, you can get it," he has said. "I keep trying."

And he keeps winning races. In 1990 Thirty-six Red won the Gotham and the Wood Memorial, both New York stakes races; in 1991 Strike the Gold won the Kentucky Derby; and in 1996 he trained an exceptional filly, Storm Song, for the Frizette and the Breeders' Cup Juvenile. She became his first Eclipse champion. In that year he finished fourth nationally in earnings. In 1994 he won the Kentucky Derby again with Go for Gin. He is clearly here for the long haul and is still relatively young for the business; so he is sure to have many more Thoroughbreds in the winner's circle.

Skip Away

"There's a special place in my heart for Cigar, but maybe Skip Away's better," jockey Jerry Bailey told the *New York Times*. "Surely there's a place in my heart big enough for the two of them."

Through 1995 and 1996 Bailey had consistently ridden Cigar—an exceptional horse that was named Horse of the Year for two consecutive seasons. Then another horse—Skip Away—came into the picture. Bailey had the good fortune of going from one great champion to another.

The beginning of Skip Away's career was fairly ordinary, but he grew stronger as he got older. In the fall of 1997 Skip Away won the Jockey Club Gold Cup, which is run at Belmont over 1¼ miles, with Bailey as jockey. (One year earlier, he beat Cigar with such authority that people were stunned when he failed to win seven of his eleven starts in 1997.) Less than a month later he won the Breeders' Cup Classic, held at Hollywood Park. With a purse of $4 million it was the richest race in the nation. By 1998, his superiority was clearly established. Seven months after his Breeder's Cup victory, Skip Away won the $1 million Hollywood Gold Cup. It was the thirty-fourth race of his career, and his seventh consecutive victory.

Jockey Jerry Bailey

Joe Hirsch, the grand old reporter for the *Daily Racing Form*, noted, "Over the years, many outstanding Eastern-based horses have flown to California to try their luck. Few have been successful and, offhand, we can't think of another horse who has won two races of this caliber."

Many people in racing consider Hirsch to be "a walking encyclopedia," and so will be hard pressed to offer an alternative opinion.

Skip Away's owners are a married couple—Carolyn and Sonny Hine. Carolyn is the owner, Sonny the trainer. They call their horse "Skippy," as if he were a big dog.

Left: **Skip Away winning the Pimlico Special in 1998 en route to Horse of the Year. Jockey is Jerry Bailey.**

Right: **The winner's circle in the 1998 Pimlico Special. Owner Carolyn Hine is a native of Baltimore. Her husband, Sonny Hine, is the trainer.**

They love the horse. When Skip Away beat Cigar, "It was a lifetime in a year," said Sonny. "We're just so grateful to have a horse of this magnitude. I've spent a career winning big races for other people, and it was great to be able to do it for my wife."

Milestones

1743—The Maryland Jockey Club (MJC) is created in Annapolis, Maryland.

1830—The MJC opens the Central Course in Baltimore. Admission is twenty-five cents for patrons on foot, and seventy-five cents for customers on horseback.

1869—The MJC leases land northwest of Baltimore for ten years at $1,000 annually.

1870, October 25—Pimlico Race Course opens. A horse named Preakness (a son of the great Lexington) wins the Dinner Party Stakes on opening day. The race is renamed the Preakness Stakes three years later.

1873, May 27—A bay colt, Survivor, wins the first Preakness Stakes by ten lengths, the largest margin in the race's history. The entire field of Preakness Stakes horses—three—is owned by a single family, the brothers George and Pierre Lorillard.

1881—The Western Maryland branch of Arlington and Pimlico Railroad is founded to connect Pimlico with the city of Baltimore. The trip from Hillen Station to the track is twenty-five minutes; the round-trip fare is fifty cents.

1888, June 11—Willie Simms becomes the only African-American jockey to win the Preakness Stakes when he rides Sly Fox to victory.

1889—The MJC abandons Pimlico until 1904. During this period, several Maryland racing groups hold abbreviated meetings at Pimlico—some are "outlaw" affairs; some are sanctioned.

1890, June 10—The Preakness Stakes is run this one time at Morris Park in New York under the auspices of the New York Jockey Club. Suspended for three years, the Preakness is moved to the Brooklyn Jockey Club's Gravesend Course, where it is held from 1894 to 1908.

1894, September 2—Fire destroys Pimlico's grandstand.

1898, April 26—The First Maryland Brigade goes into training at Camp Wilmer, which is set up on Pimlico's infield.

1902—Within forty-eight hours after Spain declares war on the United States, crowds line the march route from Paca Street to the track at Pimlico to watch troops begin training for active duty in Cuba.

Previous Preakness Stakes winners are honored on plaques affixed to the grandstand.

1903, May 30—Flocarline becomes the first filly to win the Preakness. Fifty-one fillies have contested the Preakness, and only three other fillies have won it—Whimsical (1906), Rohine Maiden (1915), and Nellie Morse (1924)—but none has won at the present distance of 1³⁄₁₆ miles. The best recent showing by a filly was by Genuine Risk, who finished second to Codex in 1980.

1904—A young James E. (Sunny Jim) Fitzsimmons is the leading trainer at the seven-day fall meeting—he has three winners. William P. Riggs, a New Englander, is the leader in bringing racing back to Pimlico in this year.

1908—New world automobile time record for a mile on a circular track is established at Pimlico when Italian driver Emmanuele Cedrino speeds the mile in :51, shaving 5⅗ seconds off the world standard. Upon completing the mile, Cedrino's car goes out of control, throwing and fatally injuring its driver.

1909—The Preakness returns to Pimlico—after sixteen runnings in New York—where it has since been run annually without interruption. As part of the celebration that marks the return of the Preakness, the colors of the race's winner are painted onto the weather vane for the first time. This becomes a tradition that remains to this day.

1919—Sir Barton is the first Kentucky Derby winner to also win the Preakness and the Belmont Stakes, becoming America's first Triple Crown winner. The J. K. L. Ross-owned colt captures the Preakness four days after his Derby victory. The Preakness purse was increased to $25,000 for the race.

1920—Man o' War begins his unparalleled 3-year-old season with a victory in the Preakness.

1925—The Preakness is run at a distance of 1³⁄₁₆ miles for the first time. The Preakness has been run at seven different distances:
1½ miles—1873–88 and 1890
1¼ miles—1889
1¹⁄₁₆ miles—1891–1900 and 1908
1 mile, 70 yards—1901–07
1 mile—1909–10
1⅛ miles—1911 to 1924
1³⁄₁₆ miles—1925 to present

1930—After winning the Kentucky Derby, Gallant Fox (with Earle Sande up) wins the 55th Preakness. He goes on to win the Belmont Stakes and becomes the second Triple Crown winner.

1935—Omaha captures the 60th Preakness by six lengths and later becomes the third Triple Crown winner by taking the Belmont.

1937—War Admiral wins the Derby, Preakness, and Belmont to become the fourth Triple Crown champion.

1938—The infield hill, which has long identified Pimlico as "Old Hilltop," is leveled.

1938—Alfred G. Vanderbilt, who, over a period of two years, secured control of the stock, is elected president of the MJC, succeeding Charles E. McLane.

1941—Whirlaway easily wins the 66th Preakness and later becomes the fifth Triple Crown winner.

1943—With many of the country's young men joining the war effort, women exercise riders are employed at Pimlico for the first time.

1943—Count Fleet wins the 68th Preakness by eight lengths in a four-horse field—the smallest since 1908. He becomes the sixth Triple Crown winner. Pimlico runs a five-day National War Fund meeting and contributes $267,142 from the receipts to various war charities.

1946—Assault wins the 71st Preakness by a neck over Lord Boswell, then takes the Belmont Stakes to become the seventh Triple Crown winner.

1947, May 17—Seabiscuit, owned by Charles S. Howard, succumbs to a heart attack at Ridgewood Ranch in Willit, California. He is fourteen.

1948—CBS Television Network first televises the Preakness Stakes to Baltimore, Washington, and Philadelphia. Citation wins the Preakness and goes on to become the eighth Triple Crown winner.

1951, November 16—The first Thoroughbred race to be televised nationally is the Pimlico Special (CBS Network). The Special is won by Bryan G.

1953—The Preakness and Belmont Stakes are won by Native Dancer, who is bred by Alfred Gwynne Vanderbilt.

1954—The new multimillion-dollar grandstand opens.

1955—The National Jockeys Hall of Fame is founded at Pimlico. Eddie Arcaro, Earl Sande, and George Woolf are enshrined by votes from more than 1,000 sportswriters.

1956—The members' clubhouse, built for Pimlico's opening in 1870, is completely restored to its original grandeur in a major remodeling project.

An undercard race on Preakness Day.

1957, May 18—Eddie Arcaro sets the record for most Preakness Stakes wins (six) by a jockey when he rides Bold Ruler to victory for Wheatley Stable.

1957—Vice President and Mrs. Richard M. Nixon attend the Preakness Stakes and present the Woodlawn Vase to the winning owner, Mrs. Henry Carnegie Phipps, whose Bold Ruler defeats Kentucky Derby winner Iron Liege by two lengths.

1960—The ultramodern clubhouse is completed in the 176-day interval between the spring and autumn meetings. The new building contains a dining room, theater-type seats, indoor paddock, jockeys' quarters, and administrative offices.

1966, June 16—Fire destroys Pimlico's Victorian-styled members' clubhouse (built in 1870), reducing racing's oldest edifice to ashes. It also housed the National Jockeys Hall of Fame.

1968, May 18—Calumet Farm sets the record for most number of wins in the Preakness Stakes by an owner (seven) when Forward Pass wins the race by six lengths.

1973, May 19—Secretariat's winning performance in the Preakness Stakes is marred by a controversy over the timing of the race. The original teletimer time was 1:55 for the 1³⁄₁₆-mile race. Pimlico amends it to 1:54⅖ two days later. However, clockers for the *Daily Racing Form* had Secretariat at 1:53⅗. The controversy remains to this day.

1975—Laffit Pincay is elected to the National Jockeys Hall of Fame; he is the first inductee since 1965. Musician Eubie Blake, 92, is honored at Pimlico. The Baltimore-bred celebrity exercised horses at Pimlico at age 12 (he said he was 14) in 1895.

1983—The Woodlawn Vase, emblematic of victory in the Preakness Stakes, is appraised for $1 million. The vase, created by Tiffany and Co. in 1860, is considered the most valuable trophy in American sports. It is on display at the Baltimore Museum of Art and is brought to Pimlico Race Course under guard at Preakness time each year. Each year, a half-size reproduction, valued at $25,000, is given permanently to the owner of the Preakness winner.

1985, May 18—Patricia Cooksey becomes the first female jockey to compete in the Preakness Stakes. Her mount, Tajawa, finishes sixth in a field of eleven.

1990, May 12—D. Wayne Lukas becomes the first trainer to top $100 million in purses when he sends Calumet Farm's Criminal Type to win the Pimlico Special. D. Wayne Lukas leads trainers with twenty-one all-time starters in the Preakness.

1995—A new single-day wagering record at Pimlico is established as betting totals $15,910,405 on Preakness Day.

1996—Jockey Pat Day establishes a Preakness Stakes record by winning his third straight classic at Pimlico.

1998—Real Quiet, trained by Bob Baffert, takes the Preakness after having won the Kentucky Derby (but goes on to lose the Belmont Stakes by a nose). The year before, Baffert's Silver Charm met the same fate.

1998—An all-time on-track attendance record is set when 91,122 fans visit Pimlico for the 123rd running of the Preakness Stakes.

1999—Charismatic wins the Preakness Stakes after having won the Kentucky Derby. He is the third horse in as many years to earn a shot at the Triple Crown.

Fair Grounds Race Course

New Orleans, Louisiana
(Established 1872)

The city of New Orleans has been the home of a wide variety of people through the years. With a complicated mix of French, Spanish, Germans, Irish, Africans, Native Americans, and Caribbean islanders, it is a bayou melting pot. With a lush tropical climate and lively cultural diversity, the people in New Orleans have always shared a love for great food, great fun, great music, and great horse racing.

New Orleans was a rich city; it was the biggest port in the South. Like New York, Lexington, and Baltimore, the Crescent City was known for its horses. There were several important Thoroughbred tracks in New Orleans early in the nineteenth century—a time when New Orleans was the fourth largest city in the nation and the biggest port in the South. The most important courses were Eclipse Course, Metairie Course, City Park, and Union Course.

Metairie Course survived the longest of these major nineteenth-century tracks—it held its last race on April 12, 1872. Basically, Metairie's management had upset everyone in the city save an exclusive few who belonged to the racing club (the reason being that they always kept the races expensive and private). In fact, the management even upset some of the members. Eventually, the disgruntled members of the group overthrew the old guard. They soon formed the Louisiana Jockey Club and bought the Metairie Course, which they turned into a cemetery!

The Union Course's facilities were used in the 1850s for the Mechanics and Agricultural Fair, and it appears on earlier maps as "Fair Grounds." During the first year after the Civil War, 1866, the Union Course was the site of an important event known as the Southern States Agricultural and Industrial Exposition. For this event, red-brick gate houses on Gentilly were

Top: **The Louisiana Jockey Club, Fair Grounds, 1882.**
Middle: **The Fair Grounds, circa 1904.**
Bottom: **The Fair Grounds in 1931.**

One of the gatehouses on Chantilly which were built in 1862 and still stand today.

built and the statue on Esplanade and Bayou Road was erected. (These structures are still standing today.)

The same Louisiana Jockey Club that obliterated Metairie refurbished and reopened the Union Course in 1872. They gave it a new name, reminiscent of its recent past: Fair Grounds. The club planted new flowers and rebuilt the clubhouse. Most importantly, they made sure that all people—no matter what their race, status, or sex—could attend the races for the first time in years. It was cause for celebration!

The first racing season at the newly formed Fair Grounds officially began on Saturday, April 13, 1872.

The initial meeting consisted of four racing days. The opening of the course was so widely anticipated that New York turf writers were sent all the way to New Orleans to cover the grand opening events.

"The day opened beautifully; the sun shed its bright effulgent rays. . . . At an early hour in the afternoon the avenues leading to the course were thronged with motley vehicles—from the stylish brougham and jaunty drag . . . to rickety express wagons. . . . The three lines of [mule-drawn trolley] cars leading to the Fair Grounds were uncomfortably packed," a New York turf writer reported in *Turf, Field, and Farm*.

By 3 p.m., more than eight thousand people were reportedly inside the gates. "The grandstand," the New York writer wrote, "when viewed from the field, presented a picture teeming with life and beauty. On all sides of the stand and fringing the green fields, hundreds of carriages dotted the scene, forming as it were a framework to the picture.

"As the time approached . . . the clubhouse, grandstand, quarter stretch, and surroundings generally, were alive with busy people of all sexes and color."

The Fair Grounds, it seems, has had more grandstands than there are steamboats on the Mississippi! Well, at least six have been erected—each replacing the one that came before it—since the course officially opened in 1872. The first was a two-story, wood-frame structure with decorative millwork topped by a cupola. This was replaced in 1882 by a larger grandstand equipped with electric lights. The third was a very grand iron-and-wood structure moved from St. Louis following the abolition of horse racing in Missouri in 1907. It had domed towers and was exotic with a Middle Eastern quality; it burned in 1918. A fourth, but temporary, grandstand was erected in three days in order to open the 1919 season. The fifth grandstand (which lasted until 1993) was designed by local architect Rathbone De Buys for another racetrack in 1905, and the entire structure was moved to the Fair Grounds in 1919. This old grandstand from 1905 had sash windows that worked on pulleys and is featured in Oliver Stone's film, *JFK*.

KEENELAND-COOK

The second grandstand at Fair Grounds, built in 1882.
Photographed in 1903 when the races were run by the Crescent City Jockey Club.

Pan Zareta and Black Gold

It was in front of the fourth grandstand—the exotic Middle Eastern-looking structure—that a mare named Pan Zareta made her racing debut at the Fair Grounds. A member of the National Racing Hall of Fame, she finished in first place seventy-six times during her racing career in the early part of the twentieth century. Today, she is still the winningest race mare in the history of the American turf!

Pan Zareta was very well traveled and very hard-raced from 1912 through 1917. She ran in the days when horses were transported by train or were walked to their destination, "on shanks mare" (or, by foot). She raced in Mexico, Canada, New York, Kentucky, Arkansas, Idaho, Montana, Texas, Utah, and Louisiana. She died at the Fair Grounds, in her stall, in 1918. The people of New Orleans wept openly at her death. She is actually buried at the Fair Grounds, under one of two whitewashed obelisks that stand in the infield, wreathed at the base by boxwood hedges.

Every year the Fair Grounds runs the Pan Zareta Handicap in her honor. The winning jockey takes a wreath of flowers, tied in gold, to her grave. Perhaps New Orleans was her destiny. Her racing silks were gold, and there was always a myth that she raced with a gold bit in her mouth. In New Orleans they called her the "Queen of the Turf." And now, each year at the start of the new racing season, a tribute is read over the loudspeaker:

Left: **The obelisks at right mark the graves of Pan Zareta and Black Gold.**

Right: **Pan Zareta, the winningest race mare in history.**

48

Under the other whitewashed obelisk in the infield lies another famous horse: Black Gold. Notable winner of four derbies—the Louisiana, Kentucky, Chicago, and Ohio—this horse was also inducted into the National Racing Hall of Fame (in 1989). Always the local favorite at the Fair Grounds, Black Gold's story has a sad ending. Still, the fans at the Fair Grounds have never forgotten the great old horse.

Unfortunately, Black Gold's owner and trainer had knowingly run the horse when he was lame. For some reason, the track stewards didn't step forward, even though everyone was aware of the situation. The *Times-Picayune* actually made the situation clear to the public before what became the horse's final race, stating, "Black Gold has worked well but his bad leg makes it look hopeless for him."

"The bustling life of the racetrack was all Pan Zareta ever had known, and she was destined to never know another. Thus, she receives a sort of memorial tribute . . . as the ground in which she lies buried begins to vibrate to the tempo of pounding hooves, and another Fair Grounds race season begins."

Then, everyone in the clubhouse and grandstand raises their glasses in a toast to the greatest mare in Thoroughbred history.

Such a tribute isn't considered odd in New Orleans, however, since perhaps nothing is more New Orleans than speaking about the dead. As a matter of fact, a cemetery (the St. Louis Cemetery III) lies just outside the racetrack walls and sanctifies the barn area.

Top: **The backstretch at the Fair Grounds abuts the St. Louis Cemetery III.**
Bottom: **Black Gold, winner of the Louisiana Derby and Kentucky Derby in 1924.**

49

Black Gold's last race at the Fair Grounds was on January 18, 1928, when he broke a bone in his foreleg as he neared the finish line in front of the grandstand. All accounts more or less express the following quote from an old Fair Grounds program: "With all the stamina that had made him famous, he ran courageously on three legs until his jockey mercifully pulled him up. With his head held high, Black Gold was led to the paddock for the last time." There, he was destroyed.

The next day Black Gold was buried in the infield. Following the burial, the *Picayune* wrote: "Black Gold's death has plunged the racing colony here in mourning." The *Picayune* goes on to reveal the reason and the futile comments and excuses offered by the horse's trainer.

Many people who visit the Fair Grounds put flowers on the grave of Black Gold. After the Black Gold Handicap, the announcer calls out, "As game a horse as ever stood on plates and answered the bugle's call," and racetrackers raise their glasses and toast the memory of the old horse.

The Louisiana Derby

The origins of the Louisiana Derby—the Fair Grounds' biggest race—can be traced back to 1894. That year the Fair Grounds was used under the auspices of the Crescent City Jockey Club for the 1-mile-long Crescent City Derby, which guaranteed $1,500 to the winner (the winner was a gelding named Buckwa). The Crescent City Derby wasn't renewed in 1895 or '96, but was run at the Fair Grounds in 1897. There, the race was held annually until 1908.

In 1920, the Crescent City Derby was revived under the name "Louisiana Derby," but it was run at Jefferson Park in Shrewsbury, Louisiana—about eight miles from the Fair Grounds. Jefferson Park hosted the race until 1930 when it transferred to the Fair Grounds, home to the annual derby ever since.

Although the Louisiana Derby is a preparation race for the Kentucky Derby, it is a rare occasion when a horse wins both. (Black Gold won the Louisiana Derby at Jefferson Park in 1924, and went on to win the Kentucky Derby that year, as well.) The last horse to do so was Grindstone, in 1996. Owned by Overbrook Farm and trained by D. Wayne Lukas, Grindstone's Louisiana Derby victory, run at a distance of 1$\frac{1}{16}$ miles, paid $350,000. His victory in the Kentucky Derby paid $869,800.

It's difficult to think of such a high-paying race as a prep race for anything, but the Louisiana Derby is a prep race for a variety of reasons. There is always much excitement in New Orleans leading up to this big race, and it is an important race in its own right. Each year, some of the top contenders for the Triple Crown events start the Louisiana Derby. People from all over the country attend this race, and many more watch it on television. It is in the Louisiana Derby (and several other major prep races) that fans become attached to specific horses as the horses prepare for the Crown—from here they will follow a particular horse as the one they will root for—and maybe even place a wager on—in the

Grindstone winning the Louisiana Derby in 1996.

Kentucky Derby. Trainers use the opportunity to monitor their horses' progress as an athlete and competitor. Jockeys have a chance to further develop a bond between themselves and their horses. The horses themselves get a chance to experience a big-time race. And the owners have a chance to experience a nice payday.

Louie J. Roussel III and Risen Star

In the 1980s the people of New Orleans found another horse to love: Risen Star. A son of Secretariat, Risen Star in 1988 won the Louisiana Derby, the Preakness Stakes, and the Belmont Stakes, and became the national champion 3 year old. His owner (together with Ronnie Lamarque) and trainer was Louie J. Roussel III, whose father owned the Fair Grounds. Louie and Risen Star *were* New Orleans.

Roussel has skin that is very white, like a camellia, and jet black hair and eyes. His speech is filled with French phrases like *mon cher* and he might, if he likes you and is explaining something, call you "Mama." His conversation always seems to have a little Zydeco music somewhere in the background. A devout Catholic, Louie managed to acquire a chair that the Pope sat in on a trip to New Orleans. Also, he has said that he made a deal with his guiding angels, should he have a winning horse. Risen Star turned out to be that winner.

Perhaps in no other city do racing fans revere their hometown horses with such fervor and love as they do in New Orleans. Risen Star became a great symbol of New Orleans, carrying Roussel's black silks with a gold cat in silhouette and three stars on the sleeve. He was cheered heartily as he won the 1988 Louisiana Derby, and the fans hoped and prayed that he would fare well in the Triple Crown events later that year. Risen Star did not disappoint them. In fact, after accomplishing so much on the track, the horse and his owners proved to be winners off the track, as well. Risen Star brought money and fame and delight to the city when it was disclosed that part of his $3 million earnings were tithed to The Little Sisters of the Poor, one of the city's Catholic charities. (Fair Grounds is a racetrack with religion. During the racing meet, Sunday Mass is held in the grandstand and broadcast over loudspeakers to the barn area.)

Trainer Clifford Scott

From the 1940s through the '80s, the Fair Grounds had a favorite trainer: Clifford Scott. Scott was recently inducted into the Fair Grounds Hall of Fame. A Chicagoan who spent his summers working at Arlington Park, Scott spent the winter seasons with his wife, Renette, in New Orleans. They lived and entertained their friends in her family house on St. Anthony Street. (Among their friends was the great bandleader and race-tracker Cab Calloway.)

Scott galloped horses in Cuba, Louisiana, and Illinois before becoming a trainer. He got his trainer's license in 1935 at the old Aurora Race Track in suburban Chicago. He was one of the few successful black trainers

Hall of Fame trainer Clifford Scott.

in the twentieth century. Mervin Muniz Jr., Racing Secretary at the Fair Grounds, says that there were three or four other great trainers at the Fair Grounds but that "[Scott] was a pioneering kind of guy. He opened a lot of doors for other people. Scotty was the kind of guy that was raceless.

"He was well respected as a horseman, but he earned everything he got. He was very well-off financially." Muniz says, "He wasn't cheap, but didn't throw his money away. You'd always see him out at a good restaurant in town. He was pretty sharp. A credit to his profession."

From all reports, Scott had an individual style—he often wore a mask while watching his riders work the horses. He didn't do so to remain incognito, but rather for a more practical purpose.

"He was a health bug. Wore a surgical mask to keep dust from his throat. Looked like the Lone Ranger. He kept himself in good condition," said Muniz. "[He was] from the old school. Arrived at four-thirty a.m. Now you can't get on (the course) before six because of insurance and safety regulations." And, Muniz says, "He was a great ballroom dancer."

The racing season sure is fun in New Orleans.

The Fair Grounds Environs Today

One of the best things about the Fair Grounds is its location—there is no city in America, or in the world for that matter, quite like New Orleans. And the area near the Fair Grounds offers plenty in the way of a fine

The statue at Bayou and Esplanade.

Palmettos, crepe-myrtle trees, and iron benches surround the fancy statue, which was commissioned as a beautification project for the 1866 Agricultural Exposition. On Bayou, the street pavement isn't covered in blacktop. It is dark-red brick, the kind called ox blood. This is the historic route to the Fair Grounds, and is in the process of restoration.

Along Bayou, just past the triangle, is the elegant Benachi-Torre House, which stands behind a high iron fence. It was built in 1859 by the consul of Greece to New Orleans. So many campaigns were discussed in this house, a plaque says that it was known as the "Rendezvous des Chasseurs" (loosely translated as "meeting place of the sportsmen"). The next house, at 2275 Bayou, is a former Creole plantation house set in a garden of oak trees and banana plants. Both of these are private houses, carefully restored with the help of

taste of the city, past and present. The history, culture, and atmosphere of N'awlins is a real treat, and one that is best experienced on foot.

Today, if you walk up Esplanade from the French Quarter, you come to a triangular park where Esplanade meets Bayou (Road). The little triangle is called Gayarre Place and is marked by a statue of a goddess in white stone mounted on an elaborate dark-red tile base with wreaths and cherubs.

The former Creole plantation at 2275 Bayou.

the landmarks commission, and are available for travelers who want to stay for "bed and breakfast."

If, at the Gayerre Place triangle, you continue about one hundred feet along Esplanade to No. 2306, you'll stand in front of the house where the great Impressionist painter Edgar Degas lived in 1872 while visiting the American side of his mother's family. It has recently been turned into a small museum, but also doubles as a bed and breakfast.

On Bayou at the corner of Dorgenois Street is a Fragrance Shop—with a heavy, curved-tile roof—that is also an African-American bookshop, with titles by such authors as Maya Angelou, Langston Hughes, Ralph Ellison, and James Baldwin. Up Bayou a ways, a crayfish vendor may be out selling his catch. Then suddenly, Bayou becomes Gentilly Boulevard. Here the corner

newspaper shop sells the Fair Grounds programs and *Daily Racing Form*, and Gentilly follows a curve of single-story "shotgun" houses before it widens into four lanes at the Fair Grounds. Just beyond the Pretty Filly Beauty Shop is the entrance to the racetrack at 1751 Gentilly Boulevard.

The public gate at 1751 Gentilly is a big iron fence. A bar called "The Big Easy" lies directly opposite. The Horseman's Gate, used by owners, trainers, horse vans, and jockeys, is located down the street—its Gothic Revival gatehouses have been designated as city landmarks. A traditional cast-iron jockey with painted silks and an outstretched arm marks the entrance.

Left: **The Fragrance shop on Bayou.**
Right: **Incredible architecture and design are found in the neighborhood surrounding the Fair Grounds.**

The New Grandstand and Clubhouse

When a fire destroyed the long-standing grandstand and clubhouse on the night of December 17, 1993, the folks in the neighborhood—as well as those around the city—felt great concern for the outcome of their old racetrack. That old grandstand was the center of the neighborhood for a long, long time—a friendly, reassuring silhouette—and the people were afraid of what might become of the track when a new grandstand was built. Luckily, the new structure didn't disappoint anyone.

"We didn't want to change the neighborhood," said track owner Bryan Krantz.

The new grandstand—the sixth to hold court at the Fair Grounds—is two stories tall (instead of one, like the old grandstand) and features walls comprised almost entirely of windows. The plates of glass are stacked and are supported by glass posts, and all are held together by small metal clips. It is possible for all patrons to see every part of the race course. And, since the building is a celebration of glass, you can also see the skyline of downtown New Orleans from the balconies that line the rear of the grandstand.

Left: **The old grandstand, erected in 1919, burnt down in 1993.**
Middle: **The new grandstand as seen from the turf course.**
Right: **Fair Grounds owner Bryan Krantz.**

The new grandstand is truly a gem. It is unadorned except for its line of cupolas, and undecorated except for its fine design. All the parts—grandstand, clubhouse, walking ring, saddling shed, jockeys' quarters, administration offices, restaurants, gift shop, and off-track-betting parlor—fit together. It's like a jigsaw puzzle, with every piece carefully in place. One Fair Grounds architect, Morio Kow, is the grand master when it comes to racetrack architecture. His hand has touched nearly every Thoroughbred racetrack designed or modified in the world over the last thirty years. The founder of his firm, Arthur Froehlich, has influenced track design for fifty years. A local architect, Eskew Filson, gave it a regional flavor. Remember, in New Orleans a racetrack isn't just a racetrack. When the horses leave, the jazzmen arrive. The place has to swing!

The New Orleans Jazz Festival

The track is located so near the French Quarter that, even today, it has the ambiance of a country fairgrounds. In fact, thousands of people don't even think about the Fair Grounds in terms of racing—they only know the Fair Grounds as the host site for the annual New Orleans Jazz Festival. Hundreds of thousands of people from all over the world make their way to "Jazz Fest"—which follows the racing meeting each year. It is arguably the best event of its kind in the entire world. And why wouldn't it be? After all, New Orleans is the birthplace of jazz.

Fair Grounds has always had great music. Al Hirt—a

Jazz Fest, 1998.

world-famous New Orleans trumpet player—had his first job as a paid musician at the racetrack. He played the bugle for the call to the post (to bring the horses out onto the track). According to an old racing program, the Crescent City Jockey Club also presented music by Prof. Wolff's Crescent City Orchestra. On one particular day in 1903 they presented fourteen pieces of music, including a cake walk, "Big Foot Lou"; a rag, "The Rag-Time Laundry"; and a medley, "Under the Bamboo Tree." We know the music selection from this event because the actual program—printed on silk, especially for the ladies—has lasted all these years. Apparently, the Fair Grounds has always had a place in its heart for the ladies.

Today, Jazz Fest has grown into a two-weekend event (held every April) that features some of the best jazz and blues musicians in the world, along with musical acts from a variety of other genres. Because the Fair Grounds is so vast, the festival is able to erect more than a dozen separate stages, and each stage has nonstop music. Tens of thousands of music lovers converge to help create one of the most entertaining experiences one will ever have. And the Fair Grounds is considered by all to be a wonderful host for this internationally attended musical gathering.

Jambalaya, Red Beans and Rice

And you can't forget the cuisine. Only in New Orleans is the track announcer also the host of a popular television cooking show. Tony Bentley, Fair Grounds' inimitable track announcer, also interviews New Orleans chefs on a local television program. This is serious stuff in a city of restaurants where, it is calculated, it would take four-and-one-half years to eat at all of them.

The good food at many other tracks owes its genesis to the kitchen at Fair Grounds. Turf Caterers, a company still in existence, cooked there during the 1920s. And when the racing season ended, they traveled north. With around one hundred waiters, cooks, and kitchen boys, they went up to Oaklawn in Hot Springs, to Lexington

The picturesque new grandstand as seen from the infield.

for the spring meet at Keeneland, on to Arlington for the summer, then back to Lexington for the fall racing meeting. Lexington was home, but by Thanksgiving everybody was back in New Orleans—time for Christmas, good racing, and, soon enough, Mardi Gras.

It was a nomadic life for the food staff, with tuxedos, white linen, and cooking pots in the luggage. But wherever they went, the cook always sent to the Gulf for shrimp, oysters, filé, and spices. White beans were served in Arkansas, corned beef in Kentucky, and fruit pies in Chicago, but the obsession with good food began in New Orleans. A platoon of waiters, trained in the great dining cars of the Baltimore & Ohio Railroad and the restaurants of New Orleans, made temporary homes in all the racing cities.

At Fair Grounds the menu is largely Creole: jambalaya, red or white beans with rice, seafood gumbo, and po'-boys (sandwiches on soft rolls with any variety of fillings). Oysters, of course, and grilled chicken breast are also standard fare. Bread pudding and apple cobbler are the basic desserts.

But at the heart of it all is the versatile "gumbo," a stew made of ham, poultry, shellfish, tomatoes, onions, and green peppers, cooked with rice and simmered in spices. Dark, spiced with filé powder, and filled with okra, it is real food from the bayou.

Attending races at the Fair Grounds is more than a trip to the track. It is a cultural experience set in an historic district with well-appointed facilities and great racing.

Milestones

1872, April 13—Inaugural day of racing of the Louisiana Jockey Club at the Fair Grounds. The fall meeting is beset by a horse epizootic.

1879—The Louisiana Jockey Club disbands due to financial problems.

1880—The new Louisiana Jockey Club forms and buys the Fair Grounds. Retired President of the United States Ulysses S. Grant attends the spring meeting.

1893—First 100-day meet. Pat Garrett—the capturer of Billy the Kid—races a stable of horses at the meeting.

1898—Fair Grounds is converted to Army Camp Foster during the summer for Spanish-American War maneuvers.

1905—City Park—a competing track in New Orleans—runs a racing meet at the same time as Fair Grounds.

1907—Matt Winn (from Churchill Downs) helps resolve the conflict between the two tracks for the American Turf Association. The public, however, is disgusted with racing and the influence of bookmakers.

1907—After betting is outlawed in Missouri, a grandstand from a track in St. Louis is dismantled and shipped to the Fair Grounds. It is the largest auditorium in New Orleans.

1908—Louisiana legislature places a six-year ban on racing.

1915, January 1—Legal racing resumes.

1916—Pan Zareta makes her local debut at the Fair Grounds.

1918—Pan Zareta dies of pneumonia on January 19 and is buried in the infield.

1919—Fire destroys the grandstand. Workmen build a temporary facility for the racing meet. Later in the year, the grandstand is moved from the now defunct City Park race track to the Fair Grounds.

1924—Black Gold—in his second year of racing—wins the Louisiana Derby.

1926—Colonel E. R. Bradley becomes owner of the Fair Grounds and builds new stables and a clubhouse.

1928, January 18—Black Gold breaks down during the running of the Salome Purse. He is destroyed and is buried in the infield the next day.

1932—Colonel Bradley retires and the track is leased to a group from Chicago headed by J. C. Schank. Purses drop.

1934—A syndicate of men including Robert S. Eddy Jr. and Joseph Cattarinich, who operate Jefferson Park, buys the Fair Grounds.

1940—The Louisiana legislature sanctions racing in Louisiana. The Louisiana State Racing Commission is established.

1941—Fair Grounds is auctioned. It is bought by a group of New Orleans horsemen and businessmen which forms the Fair Grounds Corporation.

1942—More than 20,000 spectators watch Calumet Farm's Whirlaway in a benefit race that is part of a war relief effort developed by the newly formed Thoroughbred Racing Association.

1945—The War Mobilization Department calls for all racetracks to close down by January 3.

1950—Willie Shoemaker rides the final month of the year at Fair Grounds on his way to receiving his first national riding title.

1969, March 29—Diane Crump becomes the first female jockey to win a stakes race when she takes the Spring Fiesta Cup at the Fair Grounds aboard Easy Lime.

1977–78—John Henry makes nine starts at the Fair Grounds and places twice during the meeting, earning just $2,663. He would later go on to become Horse of the Year in 1981 and 1984.

1988—Roussel and Lamarque's Risen Star wins the Louisiana Derby on March 13. He later wins the Preakness and Belmont Stakes.

1990—Fair Grounds is sold to the Krantz family, owners of Jefferson Downs.

1993, December 17—Fire completely destroys the grandstand. Tents are erected and the racing meet is held.

1994—Construction begins on a new grandstand and clubhouse.

1996—Overbrook Farm's Grindstone wins the Louisiana Derby and the Kentucky Derby (the first since Black Gold to win these two races).

1998—The new grandstand and clubhouse is in operation.

Horses at the finish, the May 12, 1989 Louisiana Derby.

Churchill Downs

Louisville, Kentucky
(Established 1875)

The Kentucky Derby is a racing event so fundamental to American popular culture that the site, Churchill Downs, has been designated a National Historic Landmark. The twin spires that grace the top of the grandstand produce the signature image of this hallowed institution, and the name itself has inspired memories of legendary races for more than a century. In the world of Thoroughbred racing, Churchill Downs (and the Kentucky Derby) is the ultimate destination.

The Derby is a social as well as a racing event. From the beginning it has been festive, with picnics in the infield and more than 10,000 spectators attending. Reports from a variety of newspapers in the early years of the event echo the same sentiments present at the first: the grandstand was crowded, the weather good, the women attractive, and the track fast. These features together remain a common and successful formula (only the weather changes). Each year, on the first Saturday in May, in front of a live capacity crowd and a television audience of millions, the best 3-year-old horses in America compete in a race run over what is perhaps the world's most famous 1¼-mile dirt track—Churchill Downs. The Kentucky Derby is considered by many to be the greatest two minutes in sports.

The History of Churchill Downs

In Kentucky, Thoroughbred horse racing started around 1789 and never stopped—it even continued throughout the Civil War. The war, of course, brought destruction to many prize horses of the South. Union troops demolished whole stud farms, wiping out many early Thoroughbred bloodlines. In Virginia, South Carolina, and Tennessee, racing never fully recovered. Kentucky, however, fared a little better.

Although Thoroughbred racing did survive in Kentucky, the state's post-Civil War economy was so bad that many horse breeders were forced to close their farms when they could not get decent prices for their Thoroughbred yearlings. A measure of how bad things had become was the closing of the famous old Louisville track, Woodlawn. Because many of the Louisville-area Thoroughbred farms closed, Woodlawn lost its means of survival.

Soon after Woodlawn closed, however, a group of prominent Louisville businessmen came up with a plan: they would create a new racetrack featuring the best

Opposite: **Breeders' Cup Day,**
November 5, 1988, at Churchill Downs.

racing in America. It was a move designed to revive racing in Kentucky and help stimulate the Thoroughbred breeding industry. This group became the Louisville Jockey Club.

The first thing the group did was to seek the involvement of Colonel Meriwether Lewis Clark—a prominent Louisville Thoroughbred breeder and the grandson of William Clark of the famous Lewis and Clark expedition. Financed by the group, Clark traveled to Europe in 1873 to observe racing. Among the famous tracks Clark visited was Epsom Downs in England, where the Epsom Derby was (and still is) held. Clark decided to model the new Kentucky track after Epsom Downs, and to call it Churchill Downs, since it was to be built on land belonging to his great-grandfather, Armstead Churchill.

Clark was also influenced by the way the English organized races. Each race was designated for particular ages and classes of Thoroughbreds. Based on these races, Clark devised the Kentucky Derby as a stakes race for 3-year-old horses. (The theory being that most horses reach their peak at the age of three.) Since that time, the Derby has become the ultimate test for spirited young American horses of 3 years old.

The first Kentucky Derby was run on May 17, 1875, at a distance of a mile-and-a-half. (The length of the race was reduced to 1¼ miles in 1894, a distance that has remained constant to this day.) A surprising amount of information about this inaugural race was documented in accounts of racing writers and the track's official records.

For instance, there were fifteen horses chosen (out of forty-two nominations) to start in the race. Existing records indicate the names of the horses, the names of the jockeys, the position of the horses at the starting line (post position), and the weight the horses carried. The betting records indicate which horses were the favorites, and accounts from New York papers of the day offer even more information.

Often called the best racing paper of its time, *The Spirit of the Times*, on May 22, 1875, offered this account: "The inaugural meeting of the newly organized Louisville Jockey Club commenced on Monday, May 17 and continued over six days. A more brilliant opening was never witnessed, and the anticipations of the most sanguine and enthusiastic Kentuckian were more than realized. . . . Delightful weather favored the Jockey Club on this opening day, and the presence of a dazzling array of female loveliness, representatives of Kentucky's proverbially beautiful daughters, enhanced the attractiveness of the occasion."

The winner of the first Kentucky Derby was Aristides, bred in Kentucky by H. P. McGrath and trained by Ansel Williamson. Genealogy, an important factor in determining which horses would even be admitted into the race, favored Aristides (he was sired by Leamington, and his dam's sire was Lexington).

Aristides' racing history also came under scrutiny, and it was certainly a factor in his acceptance in the field of fifteen horses. As a 2 year old, he had run nine races, winning only three, but in his last appearance as a 2 year

Aristides, winner of the first Kentucky Derby, in 1875;
(left) **Aristides' owner, H.P. McGrath;**
(right) **Aristides' jockey, Oliver Lewis.**

old he ran a mile in 1:44¾ seconds at Baltimore, which set the record for 2 year olds at that track.

Williamson, Aristides' trainer, was born a slave in Virginia circa 1806. He had worked as a trainer since the 1850s and had important victories in New Orleans, Charleston, Atlanta, and Mobile. (Williamson died in 1881, leaving no descendants. He was inducted in the Hall of Fame in 1998.)

Although the Kentucky Derby was a very successful social event right from the start, nearly fifty years passed before it became an important horse race. The main problem was competition. The Kentucky Derby was run each year on more or less the same day as the Preakness Stakes (another important race for 3-year-old horses, held at Pimlico Race Course in Baltimore). The races were sometimes scheduled as many as eleven days apart, but that was rare—usually they took place only a few days apart. (In fact, in 1917 and 1922 they were held on the same day!) It was nearly impossible to ship a horse from Louisville to Baltimore in a few days and expect it to race well. Because of the distance between the tracks and also because the horses needed rest, no owner felt comfortable entering a horse in both of these races.

Through the 1880s and 1890s, the Kentucky Derby ran neck and neck with the Preakness, so to speak, in terms of importance, but by the turn of the century Pimlico began to establish an advantage. Many New York and Maryland horse breeders preferred to run their horses in the nearby Preakness rather than travel out to Kentucky. Others chose the Preakness simply because they were attempting to revive Maryland racing. (In the 1890s, Pimlico itself had floundered a bit due to competition with other tracks which had the same May racing season.)

Around the turn of the century, the Derby appeared to be in deep trouble. According to the late Jim Bolus, historian of the Kentucky Derby for Churchill Downs, the final blow came when James Ben Ali Haggin, a New Yorker with a large racing stable, felt personally insulted by something that was said to him when he ran his horse in the Derby in 1910. He proceeded to mount a full Eastern-establishment boycott of the Kentucky Derby, which lasted nearly two decades.

After years of boycott by the East, the brain trust at Churchill Downs decided to employ charm and compromise in order to turn things around. The manager of

Churchill Downs, Matt J. Winn, traveled to New York to promote his biggest race. He sweet-talked racing writers into covering the race by assuring them it was a great social event as well as a great race. Then, the country's best horses were needed to complete the formula. Finally, in 1922, Winn convinced the owner of the year's leading horse (Morvich) to enter the Derby. This was very instrumental in helping the race become an important event once again. The Derby and the Preakness were held on the same day that year: May 13. It was a showdown by which the Derby definitely gained some ground when, in fact, many of the best horses were transferred from the Preakness to the Derby.

By 1930 Churchill Downs and Pimlico finally realized that they needed to work together to ensure that the best 3-year-old Thoroughbreds in America would be able to race at each track's grand event, guaranteed. That year, the Preakness was run on May 9, followed by the Derby on May 17. These dates were set specifically to allow Gallant Fox—the year's leading horse—to compete in both races. From that point forward, the Derby was finally on course toward its present state of world and financial renown. After that, neither track tempted fate by forcing owners to choose one race or the other.

Another key to Churchill Downs' burgeoning success was the addition of two modernizations that would change the distinguished race course forever: the starting gate and the public address system.

"The Kentucky Derby, a race born during the horse-and-buggy days of 1875," Bolus writes, "moved out of the Dark Ages, so to speak, in 1930. That year, for the first time in the annals of the historic event, a stall machine was used to start the Derby and a public address system was in operation at Churchill Downs."

Earlier, during the 1920s, net webbing was stretched across the track and then pulled up and away at the start of the race. But now, there was a starting gate (pulled into place by draught horses) designed to create an even and exciting start. To keep the horses in place, a tape was stretched across the front of the gate. The horses were set, the tape was released, and the announcer cried "They are off!"

Amplifiers carried out the cry to the tens of thousands of people attending the race. Gallant Fox was ridden by Earl Sande, a veteran jockey making a comeback. (Sande had won the Derby in 1923 on Zev and in 1925 on Flying Ebony. He had retired to become an owner of race horses, but lost too much money in the stock-market crash and returned as a jockey.) That day he won his third Derby, tying a nineteenth-century jockey, Isaac Murphy, for the most Kentucky Derby victories.

Gallant Fox—having won the Preakness Stakes two weeks earlier—went on to win the Belmont Stakes and, consequently, the Triple Crown with it. He was the second horse in history to win the three prized races. (In 1919, Sir Barton became the first horse to win the Triple Crown. The term itself started becoming popular around 1930.) Gallant Fox raced for Belair Stud Farm and was trained by Hall of Famer James "Sunny Jim" Fitzsimmons.

The Winningest Jockeys

Winning the Kentucky Derby is the dream of every jockey's life. Winning several of them guarantees a place in sports history. Half a century following Isaac Murphy (who had won three Derbies in the nineteenth century), Eddie Arcaro (1916–1997) won the race five times. Arcaro loved the track that brought him glory.

"A special word about Churchill Downs," said Arcaro, "where I rode my five Kentucky Derby Winners: it has more atmosphere than any other track in this country. You just look at it and your mind drifts back to some of the great horses and great Derbies of the past: Whirlaway, with his long tail flapping behind him as he wins by eight lengths; Native Dancer, roughed at the first turn and beaten by a head by Dark Star, the only loss of his career; and

Seattle Slew, bursting between horses after a moderate start and charging to a lead he never relinquished."

Arcaro's greatest Derby win was on Calumet Farm's great horse, Citation, in 1948. The victory came just weeks after Arcaro jockeyed Citation to victory in the Preakness Stakes. Then, a few weeks after the Derby, Arcaro rode Citation to victory in the Belmont Stakes to take the triple Crown. Arcaro—one of the greatest jockeys in Thoroughbred racing history—has said that Citation was the greatest horse he ever rode.

Jockey William Hartack (b. 1932) also won five Derbies. A difficult personality, known to use a harsh crop on horses, his reputation and ego became bruised by uncomfortable brushes with the press. He withdrew, saying nothing, and the press returned the favor. Little is known about him except that he was a consistently winning rider.

Left: **Jockey Isaac Murphy.**
Right: **The great Citation.**

On the other hand, Willie Shoemaker (b. 1931), who won the renowned race four times, was a popular figure. To date, he is the most successful rider in racing history. Winning more than two hundred races during his first year as a professional jockey, he created much excitement in the racing world, and also drew crossover crowds of fans who weren't normally racing fans. Affectionately nicknamed "The Shoe," he set a season record of 485 wins in 1953, and has a lifetime total of 8,883 winning races. His Derby winners were Swaps in 1955, Tommy Lee in 1959, Lucky Debonair in 1965, and Ferdinand in 1986 (when Shoe was fifty-four years old).

Three-time Kentucky Derby winners are also scarce. They are: Isaac Murphy on Buchanan (1884), Riley (1890), and Kingman (1891); Earl Sande on Zev (1923), Flying Ebony (1925), and Gallant Fox (1930); Angel Cordero Jr. on Cannonade (1974), Bold Forbes (1976), and Spend a Buck (1985); and Gary Stevens on Winning Colors (1988), Thunder Gulch (1995), and Silver Charm (1997).

The Twin Spires

If there is one image that evokes Churchill Downs more than any other, it is the grandstand. In the Thoroughbred racing world, the twin towers of Churchill Downs are as famous as the New York City skyline—they are its most enduring image.

"The rambling Churchill Downs stands look like they were put together by a committee," said Arcaro, "but somehow they capture the spirit and tradition of the 'Run for the Roses,' America's greatest race. And if you're lucky enough to be sitting on one of the [horses] when they come out onto the track, and the band plays 'My Old Kentucky Home,' and you hear one hundred thousand spectators join in with 'Weep No More My Lady' . . . you get a jolt in the heart, whether you're riding in your first or your twenty-first. And that comes from personal experience."

The first grandstand and clubhouse buildings—built in 1875—included towers which were used as observation posts. The location of the grandstand was a major mistake, though, since the late afternoon sun shone directly into the faces of the patrons. In 1894–95, a new grandstand was constructed on the track's opposite side. The design wisely kept the idea of the towers, and elongated them to form eight-sided spires. (This grandstand has stood for more than a century.) The section under the spires facing the paddock contains the old Jockey Club. It is made of brick and has equine decorations on the front of the building. The downstairs rooms of the grandstand are paved in brick. There are so many turns and curves between hallways and rooms—constructed over the course of the years—you feel that you are in an old village with brick streets.

From the infield, the grandstand looks like a riverboat with church spires stranded on a grassy field. It may look like it was put together by a committee, as Arcaro said, but Churchill Downs has such character that it clearly stands alone. It is a place of great hopes and dreams. Utmost, of course, is the spirit of the place,

The back of the grandstand viewed from the paddock on Breeders' Cup Day, November 5, 1998.

which shines through in the memory of the horses—Churchill Downs is haunted wonderfully by champion Thoroughbreds. Their names appear everywhere. The name of the first Derby winner, Aristides, is written on the saddling shed; the names of all the other Derby winners are found around the paddock. The greatest horses' portraits hang on the walls of administrative offices and clubrooms. Churchill Downs has the air of a shrine.

The Kentucky Derby Experience

For this most popular of all horse races, Derby Day in Louisville has become "Derby week." The week begins with an event called "Thunder over Louisville," a fireworks display that is billed as the world's largest. More than a thousand fireworks are set off all at once, and when they are finished, are followed immediately by an air show that provides such great overhead noise as to seem a continuation to the fireworks. The U.S. military each year sends guest-appearance aircraft that range from helicopters to the stealth bomber.

The week also includes a hot air balloon race and "The Great Steamboat Race"—a matched race between the Belle of Louisville and the Delta Queen—which goes six miles up the Ohio River and six miles back. The Belle always wins this event, edging out Cincinnati's Delta Queen in typically "dramatic" fashion. Perhaps chagrined that it is a fixed race, the local media refer to the Queen as a "Yankee cart," and their own boat as the Belle. A Dixieland band greets the riders at the end of the race. Neither of these races, however, can compare to the Derby itself.

Since the invention of television, each running of the Kentucky Derby has had such wide appeal that, annually, it is considered by many to be the greatest two minutes in sports. People all over the world watch the Kentucky Derby. In America it is a cultural as well as a sporting event. It appeals to everyone. People who never watch Thoroughbred racing and who know absolutely nothing about the sport, tune in. In terms of widespread popularity, the Kentucky Derby has many of the same qualities of the NFL's Super Bowl.

The Kentucky Derby allows many people to indulge in things they rarely experience throughout the year. Upstanding citizens who never gamble and know nothing about horses, place bets and cheer on their horses with vigor. The enthusiastic abandon of these "Derby-day aficionados" makes the race a bookmaker's dream. (Derby-day aficionados are racing fans who can name

Racing fans, Kentucky Derby Day

every horse in the race but, a week later, will forget about Thoroughbreds until next year.) There are many more Derby-day aficionados than there are regular racing fans, since millions of people watch the Derby each year on television and many of them decide to attend the Derby as a result.

Another strange thing about the Derby is that teetotalers can often be seen sipping Kentucky's other great product, bourbon whisky, on Derby Day. This strong, sweet spirit is taken by many on Kentucky's famous racing day in a delicious manner: the mint julep. To make a mint julep, one must stir some fresh mint and sugar together, sharply, in a pitcher with a small amount of cold

water. This mixture becomes a syrup that is set aside for a few hours before the drink is served. Then, in a frosted silver glass, pour plenty of bourbon over crushed ice and add a few tablespoons of the mint and sugar mixture. Also add a sprig of mint to sharpen the senses and tickle the nose. The silver julep cups, which originally were little racing trophies, keep the drink chilly.

On race day, the festivities begin early. Breakfasts are held all over the city and around the state. Perhaps the most democratic one—open to everyone—is held at the governor's mansion in Frankfort. At 7:00 a.m., on the lawns leading up to the Capitol building, Southern belles in long flowing chiffon dresses over hooped petticoats hand out official invitations. Politicians line the route to the breakfast tent, shaking hands with potential voters. Each year, the governor expects 10,000 people to attend the breakfast.

The drink of choice at this breakfast—other than some orange juice thrown back as a starter and maybe a little coffee to sharpen the wits—is bourbon. Since parties are held all over Kentucky the night before, there's little doubt these morning drinks are considered a necessary antidote on Derby Day.

Besides drinks, hats are probably the most important accoutrements of the day. Some wear earnest straw hats with a silk band and a spray of flowers; others carry on a far more ironic dialogue with the public through their hats. Some hats are a modern collage of the history of Churchill Downs; others seem to be nostalgic for a former era. Once, a pair of friends in the infield wore hats banded with roses and surmounted with small piles of horse manure! But no matter what hat you wear, Derby Day is always a wonderful experience.

The Kentucky Derby is always a spectacle—unfortunately, many in attendance never get to see the race! This includes most of the people who buy tickets for the infield. Fortunately, many of these people have no expectation of actually seeing the entire race—in fact, they're just happy to be there!

The infield, which holds the greatest number of Derby attendees compared to all other spectator areas, is also the location of giant digital monitors called "jumbotrons." Unfortunately, their electronic images are usually whited-out by the sun. Attending the Derby in the infield is not quite a graceful or nostalgic experience these days. There are no Dixieland bands or even guitar and fiddle ensembles playing famous Kentucky bluegrass music. Nowadays there is usually a band playing loud rock-and-roll music among hundreds of beer stands. Because they can't really see most of the race, folks in the infield are mostly there for a good time.

Only the photographers on the roof, the several hundred hand-picked sports writers in the press box, and people sit-

ting in a few select boxes can actually see the whole race. The start of the race (just like in 1875) originates on the side of the track opposite the grandstand. The buildings, concession stands, and giant balloons in the

JERRY COOKE

Seattle Slew (right) racing to victory in the 1977 Kentucky Derby

Press photographers from around the world prepare to shoot the Derby.

inclement weather because umbrellas are not allowed) and divided into sections by dark-green painted metal railings, these chairs offer a view to two-thirds of the track. By 10:00 a.m. on Derby Day these seats begin to fill up steadily. There are rumors stating that seats for the Derby are passed down in wills. Another rumor is that, in Louisville, Derby seats are one of the most hotly contested items in divorce proceedings.

On Derby Day, the flower beds are covered with tulips. Besides the tulips there are petunias, scarlet sage, marigolds, dusty miller, achyranthes, and lantana. There are urns filled with flowers throughout the grounds, including several in the infield dating from the 1893 Chicago Exposition. The most celebrated flowers of the day, however, are red roses—the signature symbol of the great American race. Today, a blanket of red roses is woven, much like a saddle blanket, to drape over the winning horse in the winner's circle after the race.

This tradition of honoring the winning horse with flowers began more than one hundred years ago. The first Derby-winning horse to have flowers draped over him was Ben Brush, ridden by Willie Simms, in 1896. He wore a collar of roses, lilies, and some other spring flowers. Eventually, roses became the flower of choice. When sports writer Bill Corum in 1925 called the race "the run for the roses," the phrase stuck. While owners of the winning horse get one of racing's most beautiful trophies—an urn made of gold—to keep forever, the horse and jockey are swathed in red roses for one precious moment.

infield hinder the sightlines of people sitting in what are normally the best seats in the grandstand. In fact, besides the people in the select seats mentioned above, only those with the cheapest tickets in the infield can see the start of the race. The rest of the infield crowd has to watch the jumbotrons.

For those who prefer to sit in the stands, finding tickets for the price and location you prefer is nothing less than a longshot. One of the best views of the race is from the boxes along the clubhouse turn to the right of the grandstand. Open to the sky (these are bad seats in

Milestones

1875, May 17—The first running of the Kentucky Derby. The race is won by Aristides, who is ridden and trained by African-Americans Oliver Lewis and Ansel Williamson, respectively. The day marks the opening of Churchill Downs.

1891, May 13—Kingman, owned and trained by Dudley Allen, becomes the only African-American-owned horse to win the Kentucky Derby. He does so with African-American jockey Isaac Murphy up. The win gives Murphy back-to-back Derby wins and makes him the first jockey to win three Derbies.

1902, May 3—Jockey James Winkfield, the last African-American rider to win the Kentucky Derby, wins his second consecutive Derby aboard Alan-a-Dale.

1904, May 2—Laska Durnell becomes the first woman to own a Kentucky Derby starter and winner when longshot Elwood wins the thirtieth Derby. Elwood is also the first Derby winner to be bred by a woman, Mrs. J. B. Prather.

1915, May 8—Regret becomes the first filly to win the Kentucky Derby.

1919, May 10—Sir Barton wins the Kentucky Derby. Four days later he wins the Preakness Stakes, and on June 11, he becomes the first Triple Crown winner after capturing the Belmont Stakes.

1943, May 1—Count Fleet wins the "street car" Kentucky Derby, for which no tickets could be sold to out-of-town spectators due to wartime travel restrictions.

1948, May 1—H. A. "Jimmy" Jones, son of Ben A. Jones, steps aside as the trainer of Citation, allowing his father to be named the colt's official trainer in the Kentucky Derby.

1952, May 3—Hill Gail wins the Derby, giving his jockey Eddie Arcaro a record fifth Derby victory, and his trainer, Ben A. Jones, the record for most Derby wins at six. (Jones's record has not been equaled.)

1953, May 2—Native Dancer suffers his only defeat in twenty-two career starts. He finishes second in the Kentucky Derby as the 7–10 favorite, beaten by a head by a 25–1 longshot named Dark Star.

1969, May 3—Jockey Bill Hartack wins his fifth Kentucky Derby aboard Majestic Prince, tying Eddie Arcaro's record. Majestic Prince is trained by Hall of Fame jockey John Longden, the only person to have trained and ridden a Kentucky Derby winner.

1970, May 2—Diane Crump becomes the first female jockey to ride in the Kentucky Derby. Her mount, Fathom, finishes fifteenth in a field of seventeen.

The infield on Derby Day is one of the wildest venues in all of sports.

1973, May 5—Secretariat becomes the first horse to complete the 1¼-mile course for the Kentucky Derby in less than two minutes when he wins the ninety-ninth Run for the Roses in a record 1:59⅖ to set a track and stakes record (beating Northern Dancer's 1964 mark of 2:00) that still holds. He runs each successive quarter-mile of the race faster than the previous one, with split times of :25¼, :24, :23⅘, :23⅖, and :23.

1980, May 3—Diana Firestone's Genuine Risk becomes the second filly to win the Kentucky Derby.

1986, May 3—Charlie Whittingham, at age 73, becomes the oldest trainer to win his first Kentucky Derby, with Ferdinand. Ferdinand's rider, Willie Shoemaker, is the oldest jockey (age fifty-four) to take the "Run for the Roses."

1988, May 7—A filly, Winning Colors, becomes just the third filly to win the Kentucky Derby.

1989, May 6—Whittingham tops himself, winning the Derby a second time (at age seventy-six) with Sunday Silence.

1990, May 5—Frances Genter, at age ninety-two, becomes the oldest winning owner in Derby history when Unbridled wins the 116th Kentucky Derby.

1996, May 4—Trainer D. Wayne Lukas wins his third Kentucky Derby (and second in a row) with Grindstone.

1998—Trainer Bob Baffert wins his second consecutive Derby with Real Quiet. (Real Quiet would go on to win the Preakness, but then lose the Belmont Stakes by a nose, to Victory Gallop.) He won the 1997 Derby with Silver Charm.

1999—D. Wayne Lukas's Charismatic wins the Derby as a 31-to-1 longshot. He pays $64.80 to win; it's the third largest payoff in Kentucky Derby history.

Oaklawn Park

Hot Springs, Arkansas
(Established 1904)

Hot Springs, Arkansas, is a very unusual place. It is named for the nearly fifty natural hot springs that exist in the area. For centuries, the Ouachita mountains and plains in the region were home to various Native American tribes. All the tribes utilized the springs since they all recognized the universal medicinal importance of the mineral waters. The region was first discovered by Europeans when explorer Hernando de Soto came upon it in 1541—by the 1800s, it was considered prime real estate.

Shortly after the Louisiana Purchase in 1803, President Thomas Jefferson commissioned a report on the valuable springs. The first permanent house in the valley around the hot springs is credited to Jean Emanuel Prudhomme, a Louisiana planter who was guided to the spot in 1807 by Natchitoches Indians. The region lay within the territory of Louisiana until 1812, and then within the jurisdiction of Missouri until 1819. The first hotel opened at the springs in 1820, and the first bathhouse in 1830. In 1836, Arkansas became a

state, and the hot springs were part of it. People traveled north from Louisiana and south from Illinois to visit the springs. When a railroad line from Chicago was built in 1875, tourists began to pour into the area, and within a few years there were at least ten bathhouses at the spa—they were located on a street known as Bathhouse Row.

By the turn of the century, Hot Springs was a bustling town, trading center, and tourist destination.

Founding of Oaklawn Park

Although Oaklawn Park didn't really begin to function as a major track until 1934, the track originally opened in 1904. The earliest owners were brothers Louis and Charles Cella, and businessmen John Condon, Dan Stuart, and C. B. Dugan. The park was closed in 1907 when wagering on horse racing was declared illegal in Arkansas. (This was a phenomenon that affected racing throughout the United States in the early part of the century.) Oaklawn Park was revived for racing by the city of Hot Springs in 1916, then closed again in 1919 due to antigambling sentiments and religious objections. It reopened in 1934 when the Business Men's Racing Association decided to support racing at Oaklawn in order to generate business. Mayor Leo P. McLaughlin and leading businessmen sanctioned "spa racing"—called that because the temperature in Hot

Top: **The entrance to Oaklawn Park.**
Bottom: **The grandstand from the infield.**

Springs from February through April was warmer than usual in that area, and therefore offered a great alternative for spring racing.

In 1935, pari-mutuel wagering was made legal thanks to new legislation. The racetrack provided a good deal of tax revenue for the city and state government, which probably secured racing's place in the local economic community. Pari-mutuel gambling at Oaklawn proved to be a sort of monopoly, as Oaklawn was the only place for this kind of legal gambling for thousands of miles around. The track has remained open and successful ever since 1934.

At one time or another, the Cella brothers owned successful racetracks in various parts of the country, including: Latonia (Cincinnati); Douglas Park (Louisville); Fort Erie (Buffalo); Del Mar Park, Kinloch, and the St. Louis Fair Grounds (St. Louis); Oaklawn Park (Hot Springs); Highlands Park (Detroit); Cumberland Park (Nashville); and Montgomery Park (Memphis). After Louis Cella died in 1918, Charles Cella managed Oaklawn while it was being reformed. He developed Oaklawn into an attractive alternative to Florida for winter training and racing. For owners of horses who did not go to Florida, Oaklawn became the place to go. Many of the Chicago stables, in fact, went to Oaklawn each spring.

Parade to the post, circa 1940's.

Bathhouses and Casinos

Hot Springs in the 1930s had become an amazing place. It was filled with gangsters, socialites, pleasure seekers, and lots of other characters. The Arkansas Works Projects Administration (WPA) guide to the state offered this entry, published in 1941, for Bathhouse Row: "Canes and monocles pass without a second glance from farmers in . . . overalls. The sight of a prominent motion picture star, prize fighter, or major league baseball player 'down for the baths' starts only a ripple of comment."

During the 1930s, the leading stable at the racetrack was owned by Emil Denemark, owner of a prominent Cadillac dealership in Chicago. Denemark, the father-in-law of gangster Al Capone, kept his racing stable in Capone's Sportsman's Park in Chicago (Capone owned two racetracks in Chicago—Hawthorn and Sportsman's). Capone and his men often went to Hot Springs for the spring season. (Capone himself, according to reports, preferred going to Hialeah, Florida.) During the '30s, the Hot Springs city administration tolerated casinos and the police tolerated all visitors to the resort; only Federal authorities made arrests there, and apparently rarely.

In his book *Arkansas Odyssey*, Michael Dougan sums it up this way: "Hot Springs prospered despite [its] reputation. Some major league baseball teams trained there, but horse racing at Oaklawn and illegal gambling were central to its prosperity. With local officials readily for sale and state authorities willing to look the other way, Hot Springs was a neutral ground where top criminals, including Al Capone, visited peacefully."

The town needed the racetrack for tourists. The state needed the racetrack for its own revenue from

Annual handicappers seminar at the historic Arlington Hotel. Arkansas Derby Day, April 22, 1989

legalized gambling. The mob, on the other hand, ran their own clubs—which were actually casinos—in Hot Springs, and they didn't want anything to do with legalized gambling. It is generally thought that they were content with what they had.

Where did the Cellas fit in the middle of all this? Tough guys themselves, they apparently knew where and how to draw the line. For example, Emil Denemark constructed his own shed-row barn near the backstretch at Oaklawn, but not actually within the property. (Today, this barn is located on part of the backstretch and has been renamed the Count Fleet barn.) Denemark ran his horses freely at the track, but he had no other involvement in the operation of the track.

Oaklawn Park was a melting pot for racing fans and gamblers for hundreds and hundreds of miles. It was the only track in the vicinity of Oklahoma, Texas, Mississippi, and Tennessee that offered pari-mutuel wagering. The racetrack drew approximately 15,000 people on weekdays, and up to 30,000 or more on the weekends. On major race days, crowds of more than 50,000 spectators commonly attended—on these days, the population at the racetrack was greater than that of the town!

The Arkansas Derby

In 1936, Oaklawn Park established the Arkansas Derby as a prep race for the Kentucky Derby. With racing dates from

Owners and their families go to the infield for the saddling of horses for the Arkansas Derby, April 22, 1989.

"The better your horse quality, the greater the racing and the entertainment it provides," Charles Cella once said. "We are in show business. To put on good theater, the best horses are necessary. To bring in quality runners and stables, there must be good purse money to attract them."

When Charles Cella died in 1940, his son John inherited Oaklawn Park. He also inherited the racetrack at Fort Erie in Buffalo, but sold this track to Woodbine in order to concentrate on business at Oaklawn.

In 1942, John Cella made Oaklawn Park a charter member of the Thoroughbred Racing Association, a national organization which was established to legitimize and promote racing (i.e., get organized crime out of racing), and which operates the Thoroughbred Racing Protective Bureau (TRPB), a bureau which investigates all matters in the racing world. The TRPB, with the help of FBI Chief J. Edgar Hoover, began the process of cleaning up racetracks across America.

John Cella chose to live at the racetrack during the race meetings, and built a ranch-style house at the edge of the racing strip opposite the ⅛-mile pole. His physical closeness to the Park suggests his emotional closeness to it—he did all he could to make the Park the best it could be. (His son, Charles J. Cella, who assumed own-

February to April, Oaklawn's timing couldn't have been better—it opened just after the Fair Grounds (New Orleans) closed for the season, and closed before the Kentucky Derby on the first Saturday in May. In time, the Arkansas Derby was to become a very important race.

The first Arkansas Derby was run for a purse of $5,000—not a ton of money, but at least a good start. Also in 1936, the typical month-long racing meet was extended one week, and the meet would now run until early April. This last week of the season became the biggest part of the meet, and eventually was dubbed the "Racing Festival of the South." The Festival features one big stakes race each day. (By 1974, the Arkansas Derby had become the final race—the climax—of the Festival of the South each season.)

ership of Oaklawn Park after John's death in 1968, replaced this house with a much larger version.)

John Cella's method of management was described accurately in *Blood-Horse Magazine*, on October 19, 1968: "He relied entirely for the actual operations on the track [officials] and racing officials he engaged, but mixed with horsemen on the backstretch and with track employees engaged in various duties, then circulated among patrons during the afternoon racing, thus exercising close supervision while seeking additional ways to improve the plant and the general operation."

Charles J. Cella took over Oaklawn in 1968.

The purse of the Arkansas Derby has climbed steadily over the years, from $5,000 in 1936 to $10,000 in 1943 to $50,000 in 1965. In 1972, track president Charles J. Cella increased the purse to $100,000, making that year's prize Oaklawn's first six-figure purse. In 1982, Oaklawn experienced its first million-dollar handle for a single race, when fans bet $1,020,098 on the Arkansas Derby. In 1984, Oaklawn upped the Arkansas Derby purse to $500,000 and expanded its racing season to sixty-two days.

The Racing Festival, and especially the Arkansas Derby, still attracts the best horses. With apple blossoms in bloom and spring in the air, the town of Hot Springs in early April turns into a big social event, with plenty of gatherings, horse races, and parties.

The Oaklawn Atmosphere

Oaklawn Park is unique from all other major racetracks in America in that it seems to be like a small town, filled with a variety of people and an exceptional choice of restaurants. Located in an area bounded by busy residential and commercial neighborhoods, Oaklawn Park offers very little parking space and has virtually no room for expansion. The entire facility seems to be constructed of every possible material: prefabricated logs, steel, glass, local rusticated sandstone, cement block, clapboard, brick, and painted tin. No master plan seems to have been behind the construction of this track, nor does there appear to be any focused plan for its further development. Instead, it seems to

Oaklawn Park's entrance lies in the middle of a busy residential and commercial neighborhood.

have always been added to or subtracted from based on the whims of its owners.

The infield is a good example of this nebulous direction. During the off season in the early years of the racetrack, the infield was used as a nine-hole golf course. The infield plantings of juniper trees are remnants of the golf course, as is the rolling terrain. Also present in the infield was (and still is) an elliptical-shaped temple designed by Charles Cella as a memorial to his favorite dog, who is cast, life-size, in bronze. A portion of the infield was enclosed by a white board fence; this area was used as a pasture for the horses and

mules that pulled the harrows (wagons used to water the track); it was also grazed upon by a team of Clydesdale horses that pulled the starting gate into place before each race. (The animals are gone today, but the pasture is still there.) Cella also purchased an English gazebo that appears to be from the eighteenth century but is actually made of fiberglass.

Another feature of the infield is a little restaurant with a big, open barbecue pit for grilling huge, Texas-style hamburgers. A small crab-apple orchard and a fair number of dogwood trees make the infield a bucolic picnic spot in springtime. There are plenty of picnic tables,

Picnics in the infield are part of the tradition during the Apple Blossom Festival racing days.

but lots of people prefer to lie on blankets. The infield is open to fans on weekends and during the main racing week at the end of April (formerly known as "The Festival of the South," this last week of April has been renamed the "Apple Blossom Festival"). During the Apple Blossom Festival, when the big stakes races are run, fans take to the infield to enjoy the atmosphere, the camaraderie of other racing fans, and to get an up-close look at the horses. During the festival, the horses are saddled in the infield on a strip of grass edged by blossoming apple trees. Spectators gather around them to gauge their physical demeanor or simply to admire their beautiful physiques. This proximity to the magnificent animals adds much to the racing experience.

The grandstands at Oaklawn have been built slowly over the course of many years. These grandstands are noted, among other things, for being steam heated and enclosed by glass. The first grandstand, built in 1904, was made of glass and cement—it included an indoor paddock room with a mezzanine for viewing the horses. There have been several replacements for and expansions to the grandstand, all coming between 1957 and 1977.

The last portion of grandstand was added by Arthur Froelich & Associates—an architectural group famous for designing Thoroughbred horse tracks. Froelich used vertical mullions and glass on this project (similar in design to his work on the Fair Grounds in New Orleans).

Stadium seating (circa 1970s) was brought from Rice University (in Houston) so fans could enjoy the outside breezes instead of air conditioning. These seats, of course, are jammed on major race days and may be the best place to see the races.

The backstretch contains an unusual variety of barns and is like no other place in racing. The oldest barns are called "cottages," and include stalls for horses on the ground floor, a hay room, a tack room, and upstairs living quarters under the gable roof. Built in 1904, they are as old as the racetrack. The second type of barn is called a "shed row," which is a group of stalls under one long roof with the roof extending out over a walkway. Horses can be exercised by making several turns around these brick shed rows. But unlike most shed row barns, these have an area for hay storage upstairs and a two-story house on each end to provide living quarters for stable hands, hot walkers, and other horsemen.

Until fairly recently there was an entire section of barns nicknamed "Silver City" because each barn in the section was painted in silver aluminum paint. It was a fairly funky place even during the daytime; at night, it glowed in the moonlight and provided an oasis for drunk stable boys making their way home after a night out on the town. Silver City was demolished in the 1980s to make way for a parking lot. A new group of barns was erected in 1981, based on the fireproof masonry block barns at Keeneland. These barns were given names of horses instead of numbers (like the barns on the rest of the backstretch). Because Arkansas is a generally muddy place, the main streets of the stable area are paved; however, the entire area still maintains a country atmosphere.

The state is still interested in keeping spa racing. Oaklawn received a $3-million state tax break in 1989, as well as licenses for riverboat gambling and a casino, to meet competition with Texas and Louisiana tracks.

The infield at Oaklawn once held a nine-hole golf course.

Milestones

Oaklawn's grandstand in 1948.

1905, February 24—Oaklawn presents its first racing card. The mayor of Hot Springs declares it a half-holiday for the city; 3,000 attend the races.

1906—Oaklawn has a second racing season, but closes down in 1907.

1916, March 11—Racing resumes at Oaklawn under the auspices of the Business Men's League of Hot Springs. The track is now owned by Louis Cella.

1917, March 24—Pan Zareta, one of America's greatest mares, races against Old Rosebud, winner of the 1914 Kentucky Derby. Pan Zareta wins the race, Colonel Vennie is second, and Old Rosebud comes in third. They meet a second time on April 6. This time, Old Rosebud wins and Pan Zareta finishes third.

1918—Louis Cella, Oaklawn's owner, dies at the age of fifty-one.

1919—Exterminator, the great gelding and subsequent Hall of Famer, makes his first two starts at Oaklawn. Exterminator goes on to win 50 of 100 starts in a remarkable career.

1934, March 1—After several interruptions in which Oaklawn cancels meetings because of the political climate, Oaklawn Park reopens with a crowd of 5,000 attending.

1935—Oaklawn joins and races under the Thoroughbred Racing Commission for the first time.

1936—The Arkansas Derby is born; it offers a purse of $5,000.

1940—The Chicago-owned stable of Emil Denemark is the leading owner of the season at Oaklawn. In mid-March the stable wins the feature race four days in a row. On March 30 the stable's horses finish first and second in the Arkansas Derby.

1940, October 29—Charles Cella, sixty-five, president of Oaklawn, dies in St. Louis. He had been in racing for forty-eight years. His son, John G., and grandson, Charles J., would later head the track.

1991, March 1—Pat Day, thirty-seven, becomes the sixth rider in history to earn $100 million when he rides Wild Sierra to a second-place finish in the first race at Oaklawn Park.

1994—Pat Day wins an unprecedented 12th consecutive riding title at Oaklawn.

1995—Off-track wagering increases by 31.3 percent while on-track bets decrease by 6.5 percent, marking the first time in Oaklawn history that off-track surpasses on-track handle.

1998—Victory Gallop wins the 62nd running of the Arkansas Derby. (He later would place second behind Real Quiet in both the Kentucky Derby and Preakness Stakes, and then finally end Real Quiet's Triple Crown bid by a nose at the Belmont Stakes.)

Belmont Park

Elmont, Long Island, New York
(Established 1905)

Belmont Park is a truly remarkable racing facility. It offers the truest racing of all American tracks; it holds one of the most important races every year; and it is the site of possibly the grandest moment in American Thoroughbred racing history. It is also quite different from all other Thoroughbred racetracks in America—not just because of its storied history, but also because of its physical proportions. Racing at Belmont requires different skills of horse and jockey than at other American tracks—skills that harken back to the beginnings of Thoroughbred racing.

In England, the motherland of Thoroughbred racing, the racing courses are either straight or, since they follow the flow and curves of the land, irregular. In either case, the courses are basically linear as opposed to circular. The courses are vast, having first been run on the king's land in royal parks where there was ample room. In most of the colonies where the English set up racetracks—Africa, Australia, and India, for example—the courses are large and follow the English prototype.

Furthermore, throughout the rest of the world, except for a few places in South America, all Thoroughbred races are run on grass.

In America, things are different. Races are most often run on dirt and on relatively small oval tracks (most races measure about one mile). Legend has it that the early Americans created round and/or oval courses because America was covered in forests—which were difficult to clear—and instead of cutting large clearings in the thick woods, early race enthusiasts would simply find a small clearing and lay out a round or oval track on which to race their horses. As time went on, Americans continued to build fixed, oval tracks for racing.

The oval was revolutionary primarily because it introduced a new element—turns. The short distance from the starting gate to the first turn creates an immediate need for horse and jockey to strategize. (Should they use a great deal of energy to make it to the front by the first turn? Or, should they sit back and conserve energy for a late move to the outside?) The oval also allows racing fans to see the entire race (assuming that it is small enough).

Racing on dirt is also an American innovation, and one that almost every course in the country has adopted. A dirt track provides a harder surface that results in faster races. Also, dirt is durable enough to be used in all weather conditions and every day, whereas grass is fragile and

Top: **Belmont's 1½-mile dirt track is the largest in the United States.**

Bottom: **The open-air grandstand holds more than 60,000 people.**

must be run on selectively (grass may be dangerous in the rain; and it is impossible to hold nine or ten daily races on grass). While grass is better for the horses, dirt is better for the cash flow. Even in the eighteenth century the priority of revenue may have influenced racing.

Obviously, American racing has evolved into a sport that is dramatically removed from its counterparts in the rest of the world. Belmont, however, is a different story.

The History of Belmont Park

August Belmont (1816–1890) was a banker and financier. His son, August Belmont II—a devoted breeder of horses—formed the Westchester Racing Association in 1895. From 1903 to 1905 Belmont Park was constructed at Elmont, at a cost of $2.5 million. The original grandstand was a large, open-tiered structure with a lofty roof held up by many slender posts. At one end was a square clubhouse. At the other end, set at a slight angle, stood a small, separate "field" grandstand. (By 1950 the two grandstands had been joined together to form one giant, slightly curved grandstand.) The clubhouse stood quite apart from the grandstand. The paddock was a large, informal lawn. Instead of containing many trees, like at Saratoga, the paddock had one famous tree, the white pine that now is the focus of the walking circle. From the beginning, there was excellent racing and an impressive showing of the great American racing families (names like Guggenheim, Mellon, Vanderbilt, Whitney, and Phipps come to mind). Opening day was May 4, 1905, and forty thousand people attended.

August Belmont, president of the Belmont Park Association and namesake of the Belmont Stakes.

Many of the opening day attendees may have been surprised to find a track more similar to the straight European courses than to the short, oval courses to which Americans had become accustomed. Measuring 1½ miles around, Belmont is said to stage the "truest" races in the United States because the turns are wide and sweeping, and because there is ample distance for the horses to run before entering each turn. The truest races leave as little as possible to chance.

Another wonderful feature of Belmont is the presence of two big turf courses—in addition to the main

Top: **Backstretch at Belmont.**

Bottom: **The famous white pine inside Belmont's wonderful paddock.**

dirt track—which make it unique from all other American racetracks. While many other tracks have turf courses, they are much smaller than Belmont's and are usually contained inside the typically mile-long dirt oval (therefore offering a racing distance of less than 1 mile). Measuring $1\frac{3}{16}$ and $1\frac{1}{16}$ miles, and also featuring substantial width, Belmont's bigger-than-average turf ovals historically offer the kindest turf racing for horses. By moving the railings, or "dogs," three to six feet in or out—which can be done because of the exceptional width—there can be a reduction of wear and tear on any one section of the grass. This means that grass races can be run every day of the season by alternating the course and practicing good maintenance. Of course, the weather also plays a part in the turf courses' utilization. When it rains, races cause too much undetectable damage to the turf, such as holes hidden beneath the grass. This can be dangerous, and races are often canceled due to rainy weather.

The tracks at Belmont circle an infield that is cleanly landscaped and features centrally located lakes. The lakes (similar lakes are found in many tracks' infields) seem to be used primarily as a means to reduce grounds maintenance—reducing grass-cutting duties by many acres—though they also offer an aesthetic appeal. The infield is also a place where people can enjoy themselves between races. It is a spacious and pleasant area conducive to a stroll or a picnic.

Over the years, Belmont Park has inherited the great racing legacy of New York City. During the eighteenth and nineteenth centuries, there were tracks operating from Coney Island to Harlem. One of these tracks, the bobby-pin-shaped Jerome Park, was the site of the first Belmont Stakes in 1867. By 1890 the race was named for August Belmont I and was moved to Morris Park (located in the Bronx, just north of Harlem and below Westchester). The Belmont Stakes was run at Morris Park until the opening of Belmont Park in 1905. Eventually the tracks in New York City closed down, and racing fans turned their attention to Belmont. Belmont Park would prove to be worthy of the attention.

The Belmont Stakes and the Triple Crown

The Belmont Stakes is either the third- or fourth-oldest Thoroughbred race in North America. The Queen's Plate in Canada dates back to 1860, the Travers Stakes at Saratoga was first run in 1864, and the Phoenix Stakes at Lexington precedes these two races (it was first run in 1831, but was not held consistently).

"Classic races" are races set exclusively for 3-year-old horses—each with its own fixed distance—which are run on virtually the same day every year at one of the foremost tracks in America. The three most famous classic races in America are the Kentucky Derby (run on the first Saturday in May), the Preakness Stakes (run on the third Saturday in May), and finally, the Belmont Stakes (run in early June). Together, they comprise what is known as the "Triple Crown."

Secretariat's Triple Crown trophies on display at the Kentucky Derby Museum in 1998, to commemorate the 25th anniversary of his achievement.

Sir Barton, the first winner of the Triple Crown, in 1919.

The Belmont is definitely the oldest Triple Crown event, predating the Preakness Stakes (1873) by six years and the Kentucky Derby (1875) by eight. Of the three events, the Belmont is the longest (by distance), the latest (by season), and the truest (by size and shape of the course). The Belmont is also the most grueling race—it comes at the end of a long campaign and has always proven to be a decisive moment. Only a horse of considerable mental and physical stamina can win all three Triple Crown events. That's why the Triple Crown is considered to be one of the greatest accomplishments in all of sports.

The first horse to win all three of these races was Sir Barton, in 1919. The term "Triple Crown," however, did not gain widespread use until nearly two decades later. When bay colt Gallant Fox, with Earl Sande up, captured all three of the classics in 1930, *New York Times* reporter Bryan Field referred to the colt "completing his Triple Crown." It is believed to be one of the earliest references to the modern holy grail of Thoroughbred racing.

Other sources, however, claim that credit for coining the term should be given to *Daily Racing Form* reporter Charles Hatton. Early in the 1930s, he began to use the term mostly for reasons of word economy. As with many

Affirmed edges out his rival Alydar to win the 1978 Belmont Stakes and the Triple Crown. Affirmed v. Alydar becomes one of the greatest rivalries in the history of the sport.

newspaper writers who employed the hunt-and-peck method of typing, Hatton tired of having to write all three race names in all of his copy each spring, and so he began to refer to them collectively as the "triple crown races." In time, as the story goes, his fellow reporters picked up on the cue, and the phrase became so popular that more and more owners began to point their horses toward winning these races. By 1941, newspapers were hailing the feat with banner headlines, such as: "Triple Crown to Whirlaway; Easily Takes Belmont Stakes."

To date, only eleven colts have captured the Triple Crown. They are: Sir Barton (1919), Gallant Fox (1930), Omaha (1935), War Admiral (1937), Whirlaway (1941), Count Fleet (1943), Assault (1946), Citation (1948),

Secretariat (1973), Seattle Slew (1977), and Affirmed (1978).

While it is difficult to pinpoint any one of the three races as the main reason why Thoroughbreds do not win the Triple Crown more often, it is clear that the Belmont Stakes has been the most common downfall for would-be Triple Crown champions. (It is also the most dramatic way to lose a Triple Crown bid, since to be gunning for the Triple Crown at Belmont means that the other two races have already been won.)

Specifically, the Belmont has ruined fifteen horses' bids for the Triple Crown. These are Pensive ('44), Tim Tam ('58), Carry Back ('61), Northern Dancer ('64), Kauai King ('66), Forward Pass ('68), Majestic Prince

('69), Canonero II ('71), Spectacular Bid ('79), Pleasant Colony ('81), Alysheba ('87), Sunday Silence ('89), Silver Charm ('97), Real Quiet ('98), and Charismatic ('99). As for horses that won the Belmont Stakes plus one of the other two Triple Crown races, nine were beaten in the Derby and eleven lost in the Preakness.

The combination of the Derby, the Preakness, and the Belmont represents a torturous five weeks. At the Kentucky Derby, the horses run 1¼ miles, a distance that virtually none of them has ever run before (usually, they run shorter distances than this). At the Preakness, the distance moves down to 1 3/16 miles—a distance that requires more raw speed than stamina. Belmont, the final race, requires the young horses to maintain a high level of physical and psychological endurance for 1½ miles. This is a tremendous exercise for a 3-year-old horse, and the achievement of winning the Belmont Stakes is a truly grand experience for the horse and all the people who surround it.

Secretariat

The 105th running of the Belmont Stakes—on June 9, 1973—was the grandest. To many people, it is the greatest moment in Thoroughbred racing history. It had to be seen to be believed, and many of the attendant sportswriters' reports echoed that very sentiment. To wit: Secretariat won the race by thirty-one lengths. Thirty-one lengths!

What the crowd had seen before Secretariat crossed the finish line was a horse that was running too quickly at each quarter mile—they believed—to have enough strength to even finish the race without tiring in the homestretch. Yet the great champion never let up—in fact, he may have gained speed as he neared the finish, shattering several records along the way. Secretariat covered the Belmont Stakes' 1½-mile track in a record time of two minutes and twenty-four seconds (2:24), a world record for 1½-mile races that still stands today. He also broke and still holds the records for each quarter mile from the half-mile mark through to the finish. He ran the fastest first ½ mile (:46⅕ seconds); the fastest ¾ mile (1:09⅘); the fastest first mile (1:34⅕); and the fastest 1¼ mile (1:59). All of these records are still unbroken.

Practically numb with amazement, the sportswriters present at that most glorious of Belmonts set out to compose their stories. It may have been the most difficult story many of them ever had to write. They faced the task of explaining what they had just seen—but couldn't believe—in the context of racing as they had known it.

"He ran so far beyond known reference points, he left us with no measurable comparison," wrote the editor of the *Blood-Horse Magazine* a few days after the race. "We saw it, believed it; we are having trouble, however, comprehending the preternatural."

Secretariat (1970–1989) was affectionately known as "Big Red" and is widely considered, now that we approach the millennium, to be "the horse of the century." (An article in the *Blood-Horse Magazine* dated February 27, 1999, however, named Man o' War number 1 and Secretariat number 2.) The Kentucky-bred son of Bold Ruler and Somethingroyal, he became the first horse since 1948 to win the Triple Crown. He was big (16.2 hands tall), and his stride measured twenty-five feet, longer than that of most horses. Analyzed in slow-motion, his running was found to be a study in perfect equine locomotion. He was spectacular in coloring, with a red (bright chestnut) coat, white markings on his face, and three white stockings. He also had an enchanting personality, primping for the camera upon occasion and teasing the odd turf writer with a nip or some spit. His famous red coat and signature checkered hood graced the covers of *Sports Illustrated*, *Newsweek*, and *Time* magazines.

Secretariat was a running machine. His extraordinary, record-breaking victory at the Belmont Stakes perfectly complemented his victories at the Kentucky Derby and the Preakness, which were also achieved in record-breaking* times. The chestnut colt ran the 1¼-mile Kentucky Derby at Churchill Downs in 1:59⅖ minutes (the fastest record to this day), and the Preakness in what many people consider the best time.

Secretariat works out just before winning the most memorable Belmont Stakes in the history of the race.

* In the Preakness Stakes, track officials listed Secretariat's winning time as 1:55, but two separate *Daily Racing Form* clockers had him finishing the race in 1:53⅖. The great champion Nashua had held the Preakness record with a winning time of 1:54⅗ in 1955. Those who agree with the *Daily Racing Form* clockers believe that Secretariat owns the record times for each of the Triple Crown races.

Secretariat was bred at Christopher T. Chenery's Virginia farm, Meadow Stud, Inc. Chenery had bred and raced horses since 1936, including five champions and thirty-six stakes winners. By the 1960s Chenery had become ill, and the farm came under the management of his daughter, Penny Chenery. It was she who accompanied Secretariat to his glory, and she matched her glorious racehorse with her own stylish manner.

Secretariat won sixteen victories in twenty-one career starts, and earned $1,316,808 before being retired to stud after his 3-year-old season. He sired more than forty stakes winners. He was put down at Claiborne Farm in Paris, Kentucky, after suffering from laminitis—a painful, degenerative hoof disease. His obituary was noted on the front page of the *New York Times*. Very few people or animals are truly a legend in their own time—Secretariat was the exception.

The Phipps Family

Some of the wealthiest American families have spent decades patiently breeding Thoroughbred horses in hopes of winning even one of the great Triple Crown races. It is not easy.

Ogden Mills Phipps and the Phipps Stable's horse Easy Goer.

"I've always considered the Belmont Stakes one of the great American races," says Ogden Phipps, a well-known and accomplished champion of Thoroughbred racing. His horse, Easy Goer, took the Belmont in 1989 while clocking a time second only to Secretariat. "I had never won it and I was thrilled to have a great horse like Easy Goer."

Mr. Phipps's son, Ogden Mills Phipps, explains: "My grandmother was in racing since the 1930s. Out of her many champions and other stakes winners, Bold Ruler was the only horse she bred that went on to win one of the Triple Crown events. She was very proud." Bold Ruler won the Preakness in 1957. Bold Ruler was a great sire—the sire, in fact, of Secretariat.

"She got the entire family involved," he continues. "She got my father interested in racing. She got Mrs. Janney [Mrs. Stuart Janney, her daughter] involved, who owned Ruffian. She got me involved, and now her great grandchildren."

The Phipps family, whose stable is located at Belmont Park, has had many great moments during their involvement in racing. Personal Ensign's Breeders' Cup race—held at Churchill Downs on November 5, 1988—will go down in history as one of the great races of all time. She was the first undefeated champion race mare since the beginning of the century. Despite the metal screws in her ankles as a result of an injury in her youth, Personal Ensign simply would not quit. She ran in a season populated with wonderful female horses, including Winning Colors (who won the Derby), Goodbye Halo, and Epitome. The Phipps's prize Thoroughbred mare was a great among greats and was an important addition to the female breeding line.

Trainer Woody Stephens

In 1986, trainer Woody Stephens (1919–1998) saddled Danzig Connection to win his fifth consecutive Belmont Stakes. Stephens won the previous races with Conquistador Cielo in 1982, Caveat in 1983, Swale in 1984, and with Creme Fraiche in 1985. It was an amazing accomplishment, considering how difficult it is to win this particular race.

"Nobody's likely to break it," Stephens himself says of the record five consecutive Belmont victories. Before 1986, in fact, only one other trainer had won even two consecutive Belmonts, and since then only one trainer has posed a challenge to Stephens' record. (Lucien Laurin won the Belmonts with Riva Ridge in 1972 and Secretariat in 1973. In 1994, D. Wayne Lukas began a Belmont winning streak that ended after three years.) Stephens was so respected a figure in racing that he was elected into the racing Hall of Fame long before he won the five consecutive Belmonts.

A sharecropper's son, Stephens grew up in Kentucky and became involved in racing first by riding horses, then as a trainer—he had his first victory as a trainer at Keeneland in 1936. He trained ten national champions; two colts that won the Kentucky Derby—Cannonade in 1974 and Swale in 1984; Preakness winner Blue Man, in 1952; and the famous Belmont winners. His champions

Woody Stephens

were Bald Eagle, Conquistador Cielo, De La Rose, Devil's Bag, Forty Niner, Heavenly Cause, Never Bend, Sensational, Smart Angle, and Swale. (Every year, one horse from each division—colt, filly, 3 year old, mare, etc.—is elected into the gallery of national champions by a panel of horse industry officials.)

By all accounts, Stephens' heart was with the horse that got away, so to speak. "Swale was the best of all," he says. Swale collapsed and died two weeks after winning the Belmont Stakes in 1984—he had also won the Kentucky Derby that year, and ran seventh in the Preakness Stakes. An autopsy revealed no clues to the cause of death.

Stephens, a small, dignified man, spoke softly, had impeccable manners, and took care when he answered questions. He always wore a kind of trainer's uniform consisting of a soft hat, a cap with a brim, a windbreaker, and slacks. On racing days, he wore a suit or blue blazer. He was a familiar and friendly sight at Belmont Park; his legacy will remain for a long time.

D. Wayne Lukas works out Tabasco Cat before winning the 1994 Belmont Stakes.

Milestones

1867, June 19—The inaugural Belmont Stakes is run at Jerome Park in the Bronx and is won by a filly, Ruthless, who defeats a field of colts to earn $1,850. (Ruthless was one of a group of fillies known as the "Barbarous Battalion," all daughters of the mare Barbarity, owned by Francis Morris of New York. The other "battalion" members, all full sisters, were Remorseless, Relentless, Regardless, and Merciless.)

1895, August 14—The Westchester Racing Association is formed by a group headed by August Belmont II, after the demise of the New York Jockey Club.

1903–05—Belmont Park is constructed at a cost of $2.5 million.

1905, May 4—Belmont Park opens. Races are run clockwise before 40,000 fans. The featured race is the Metropolitan Handicap. It results in a dead heat between Sysonby and Race King.

1908—The Hart-Agnew Bill outlaws betting at racetracks. The sport continues, however, under the Director's Criminal Liability Act passed in 1910.

1910, October 30—The Wright Brothers supervise an international aerial tournament before a crowd of 150,000 at Belmont Park.

1911–12—No racing is permitted in New York State due to antibetting legislation.

1913, May 30—Belmont Park reopens without official betting. Initial purse money, except for nominations and entry fees, comes from the Westchester Racing Association shareholders, and is barely met by gate receipts.

1917, April 7—A series of fires causes an estimated $1 million in damage and nearly closes Belmont. The main grandstand, jockeys' quarters, and Long Island Railroad terminal are completely destroyed. However, the racing meet opens on schedule on Memorial Day.

1918—Belmont Park serves as the New York terminal of the first American air-mail service between New York and Washington, D.C.

1919, June 11—The first Triple Crown is won by Sir Barton after he completes the Belmont Stakes, then run at 1⅜ miles.

1920—The grandstand is completely rebuilt and seating capacity is increased to 17,500. Promenade and mezzanine levels are added.

1920, June 12—Man o' War wins the Belmont Stakes over 1⅜ miles, in 2:14⅕, shattering the existing world record by 3⅕ seconds and also setting the American dirt-course record for that distance. Only two horses ran in the race. Man o' War beat Donnacona by 20 lengths.

1921—Counterclockwise racing begins.

1924, December 10—August Belmont II dies. He is succeeded as president of the jockey club by Joseph E. Widener, who institutes the Widener Course, a seven-furlong straightaway turf course.

1926, June 12—The August Belmont family presents their permanent commemorative Tiffany trophy to the winner of the Belmont Stakes for the first time. (The silver trophy was created in 1869 in recognition of Fenian's win in the Belmont.)

1930, June 4—Gallant Fox becomes the second winner of the Triple Crown under jockey Earl Sande. (Gallant Fox subsequently sires another Triple Crown winner, Omaha.)

1933—Legislation, due to become effective in 1934, gives New York quasi-legal bookmaking for the first time.

1935, June 8—Omaha, son of Gallant Fox, becomes the third winner of the Triple Crown.

1936—A public address system is introduced to let fans know horses' running positions during the race. A photo-finish camera is also introduced.

1937, June 5—War Admiral wins the Belmont Stakes and becomes the fourth winner of the Triple Crown. Wrought-iron gates from Jerome Park in the Bronx, the scene of the inaugural Belmont Stakes, are presented to the track by Perry Belmont, son of August Belmont II.

1930—Bookmaking era at Belmont Park ends.

1940—Pari-mutuel betting becomes law.

1941, June 7—Whirlaway wins the 73rd running of the Belmont Stakes and becomes the fifth horse to win the Triple Crown.

1943, June 5—Count Fleet ends his racing career by winning the Belmont Stakes by twenty-five lengths. He becomes the sixth Triple Crown winner. Count Fleet is such a heavy favorite for the race, going off at odds of 1–20, that no place or show wagering is allowed.

1943, October 2—With World War II in full action, Belmont Park hosts "Back the Attack Day," with admission granted by purchase of War Bonds only. The total gate receipts are $30 million.

1946, June 1—Assault becomes the seventh horse to win the Triple Crown.

1947—Calumet Farm's Armed faces King Ranch's Assault in the first $100,000 winner-take-all match race ever at Belmont. A crowd of 51,573 sees Armed's six-length victory.

1948, June 12—After riding Citation to victory in the Belmont, jockey Eddie Arcaro becomes the only rider in history to have won two Triple Crowns. His previous Triple Crown was with Whirlaway, in 1941. In winning the Belmont, Citation becomes the eighth Triple Crown winner. Citation never lost a race at Belmont—in the fall of 1948 he wins the Sysonby Mile, Jockey Club Gold Cup, and Belmont Gold Cup in little more than two weeks.

1955, June 11—Eddie Arcaro ties James McLaughlin's record of six Belmont Stakes wins when he rides Nashua to victory.

1963, June 15—Five weeks prior to his 90th birthday, Hall of Fame trainer "Sunny" Jim Fitzsimmons retires. ("Mr. Fitz," as he is also known, trained such outstanding runners as Nashua, Bold Ruler, and Johnstown, and triple Crown winners Gallant Fox and Omaha.)

1963—After sixty years, Belmont closes to undergo new grandstand construction (it will reopen in 1968). The racing meeting is held at Aqueduct and Saratoga.

May 20, 1968—The new Belmont Park reopens after a $30.7 million renovation. The 100th running of the Belmont Stakes is won by Greentree Stables' Stage Door Johnny.

1973, June 9—Secretariat wins the Belmont Stakes by thirty-one lengths—the longest winning margin in the race's history—while setting a track record of 2:24, which has not been surpassed. Secretariat's victory makes him the ninth Triple Crown winner and first since Citation in 1948.

1973, June 11—Secretariat simultaneously makes the covers of *Time*, *Newsweek*, and *Sports Illustrated*.

1976, September 20—Two-year-old Seattle Slew makes his racing debut, winning a six-furlong maiden race by five lengths at Belmont Park. After only three starts (including the Champagne Stakes) in the space of twenty-seven days, Seattle Slew is voted champion 2-year-old colt for 1976.

1977, June 11—Upon winning the Belmont Stakes, Seattle Slew becomes the tenth Triple Crown winner, and the first Triple Crown winner to remain undefeated as a 3 year old, with a career record of nine-for-nine.

1978, June 19—Steve Cauthen, at age eighteen, becomes the youngest jockey ever to win the Triple Crown when his mount, Affirmed, wins the Belmont Stakes. Also on that day, Alydar becomes the only horse ever to finish second in all three Triple Crown races. Affirmed is the 11th Triple Crown winner.

1980, June 7—Genuine Risk becomes the first filly to compete in all three Triple Crown races. She wins the Kentucky Derby and finishes second in both the Preakness and Belmont Stakes.

1985, August 31—At Belmont Park, Angel Cordero Jr., forty-two, becomes the third jockey in history, behind Willie Shoemaker and Laffit Pincay Jr., to have his mounts earn $100 million.

1986, June 7—Trainer Woody Stephens saddles Danzig Connection to win his fifth consecutive Belmont Stakes. (James Rowe has saddled the most Belmont winners with eight, while Sam Hildreth had seven, and "Sunny" Jim Fitzsimmons six.)

Affirmed prepares for the 1978 Belmont Stakes.

1988, June 11—Risen Star, a son of Secretariat, wins the Belmont Stakes by fourteen lengths.

1991, September 16—Jockey Jose Santos wins his 2,000th career victory, aboard Sunny Sara at Belmont Park.

1993, June 5—Julie Krone becomes the first female rider to win a Triple Crown race when she wins the Belmont Stakes with Colonial Affair.

1994—Holy Bull wins Belmont's Metropolitan Handicap, Dwyer Stakes, and Woodward Stakes and is named Horse of the Year. Eclipse Award winner Sky Beauty wins the Shuvee, Hempstead, and Ruffian handicaps at Belmont.

1995, June 10—The Belmont is won by Thunder Gulch. This marks a record fifth straight Triple Crown race victory for trainer D. Wayne Lukas.

1995—The Breeders' Cup championship day is held for the third time at Belmont Park. Horse of the Year Cigar wins the Classic to cap off his undefeated ten-for-ten season.

1996—Cigar wins the Woodward but is defeated in the fall Jockey Club Gold Cup by 3-year-old champion Skip Away.

1998, June 6—The New York Yankees delay the start of the sixth inning of the Yankees-Marlins game at Yankee Stadium to show the entire 1998 Belmont Stakes on the DiamondVision screen (George Steinbrenner, Yankees owner, is a longtime Thoroughbred owner). The favorite and Kentucky Derby and Preakness winner, Real Quiet (trained by Bob Baffert), loses by a nose to Victory Gallop before a record crowd. Victory Gallop had come in second in both the Preakness and the Derby.

1999, June 5—Charismatic is the third horse in three years to make a run for the Triple Crown at the Belmont Stakes. Sadly, he stumbles at mid-stretch, finishes third, and completely breaks down just past the finish line with a shattered front left leg. Fortunately, his life is spared and he is retired to stud.

Trainer Bill Mott with the great Cigar.

Charismatic (left) breaks down in the stretch at the 1999 Belmont Stakes. He shows behind Lemon Drop Kid (#6) and Vision and Verse.

Arlington International Racecourse

Arlington Heights, Illinois
(Established 1927)

Erected in 1927, Arlington Park was the first great modern racing facility made of steel and glass. Located on the outskirts of Chicago, it was the inspiration of the legendary H. D. "Curley" Brown, a man who built, managed, and renovated racetracks. Arlington stood as his finest racetrack.

Part artist, part developer, and part hustler, Brown was always brimming with project ideas—but he simply did not have the money to bring his plans to life. What he did have, however, was keen vision and an ability to inspire others to help him develop racetracks across America. However, apparently he never solely owned any of the tracks he built. After he would put a project together and see it through to completion, the financial backers would take over daily operations of the tracks, and Brown would move on.

Brown's first project was a track called Clear Lodge, in Montana, which was built in 1890. After a period of inactivity, new Brown creations began to appear fairly regularly: City Park Race Course in New Orleans, Louisiana (1905); Moncreif Park in Jacksonville, Florida (1909); Laurel Park in Laurel, Maryland (1911); Washington Course in Charleston, South Carolina (1912); and, Oriental Park in Havana, Cuba (1915).

And then there was Arlington.

Brown's backers for the Arlington project were Laurance Armour of the great Chicago meatpackers, Armour & Company; John Hertz of Yellow Cab Co.; Weymouth Kirkland, a lawyer; Otto Lehman, a retailer; Major Frederick McLaughlin, owner of the Chicago Blackhawks (National Hockey League franchise); and John R. Thompson, owner of Thompson's Restaurant. While the largest racetracks of the day covered approximately 375 acres in area, the Brown group purchased 1,001 acres of productive crop land in the Illinois cornbelt for their project—and paid more than $1 million for it. On this vast expanse they constructed a track with grandstand seating for 18,000, a railway station to receive fans from downtown Chicago, and stables for up to 2,700 horses (more stables than any other track at the time). In keeping with the general extravagance, the track at Arlington had two racing ovals—an outer track made of dirt and an inner track made of turf. The seminal turf track would come to represent Arlington's future in the racing world.

Opposite: **The new Arlington grandstand is a beautiful and modern open-air facility.**

The group also developed tennis courts and a polo field, among other features, making this an early sports complex. The entire facility is estimated to have cost about $2 million, largely because of the pre-stock market crash price of the enormous acreage of productive farmland. In 1928, Brown was superseded by John Hertz as the leader of the track. A group of twenty Chicago businessmen purchased Arlington Park in 1929.

Chicago Racing

For more than half a century Arlington Park has been a highly respected and wonderfully appointed sporting facility, as well as an important component of Chicago's culture. In 1998, when Arlington was unable to effect changes to archaic racing laws, a dispute between the legislature and the current owner, Richard Duchossois, came to a head. Arlington did not seek racing dates, and Chicago racing moved to Hawthorne Park. Knowing the history of Hawthorne and other Chicago-area parks is important to understanding where Arlington fits into the world of Illinois racing.

The old Washington Park is one of the oldest racetracks in the country and the site of the American Derby—one of the big races of the season in the nineteenth century. Washington Park opened in 1884 and closed in 1904. In 1932, the park was resurrected and managed by Colonel Matt J. Winn, the man who popularized the Kentucky Derby in the 1920s. Winn revitalized Washington Park and popularized racing among residents of Chicago's South Side.

Chicago also had Thoroughbred races at parks located in its sprawling suburbs. These included Hawthorne, Lincoln Fields, Balmoral, Harlem, Sportsman's, and Exposition Park. Some have scandalous histories that involve notorious Chicago mobsters. Most illustrative of the racing environment in Chicago in the 1920s and '30s was the situation involving Sportsman's Park, in Cicero, which was started as a dog track by Al Capone. The inception of Sportsman's Park followed closely after the "St. Valentine's Day Massacre," a multiple-victim mob hit that the horrified public rightly linked to Capone. The legislature responded immediately by outlawing dog racing. Capone, in turn, simply converted the track to horse racing, and it was business as usual.

On opening day Edward J. O'Hare, president of the National Jockey Club for Sportsman's (and namesake of Chicago's main airport), was present. So was Emil Denemark—Capone's father-in-law—who owned a lucrative Chicago automobile dealership that sold Cadillacs and LaSalles (Capone was one of his best advertisements, riding around in an armor-plated $20,000 custom Cadillac). Denemark had the leading stable at Sportsman's.

In the context of Sportsman's and other Chicago tracks, Arlington Park—with its swimming pools and tennis courts, its inclusion of polo fields, and its overall allusion to high society—masked the toughness of horse racing and its satellites: gambling, bookies, and the mob.

In 1940 John P. Allen (vice president of Brinks & Co.) and Benjamin F. Lindheimer (director of Washington

Park) purchased Arlington Park. Lindheimer directed the two parks until his death in 1960, when his adopted daughter, Marje Lindheimer Everett, assumed control. In 1967 the two parks merged with Gulf & Western. In 1971 they were purchased by Madison Square Garden.

In the 1970s Joseph F. Joyce Jr., a New Yorker who had been the vice president at MSG, took over the management of Arlington (Joyce has been described as a "natural" at racetrack management). Joyce found that he enjoyed the business and believed that he could transform the park. And so with the authority to implement changes to the entire operation, Joyce set a goal to transform Arlington Park into a distinctive, popular, and feasible enterprise—he just needed a gimmick.

A few years earlier, the New York Jets (National Football League franchise) gave quarterback Joe Namath a contract worth $400,000 at a time when the average quarterback was paid $50,000. This highly publicized deal instantly rocketed Namath to stardom. The significance of this deal is that it helped Joyce to understand a crucial phenomenon: show business fills seats. Joyce decided to apply this theory to Thoroughbred racing.

In 1981 Joyce announced that Arlington Park would host a $1 million stakes race—with $600,000 going to the winner. The race would be run on Arlington's inner turf track, and would attract the best horses in the world. Some critics called this new race a case of "buying glory." In essence, that is exactly what it was. But it worked! Joyce and his associates had created Thoroughbred racing's richest race to date: the Arlington Million. It generated enormous attention from the start, and it remains one of the biggest race days of the year.

John Henry and the Arlington Million

It rained heavily in Chicago before the first Arlington Million—held on Sunday, August 31, 1981—and the turf was soft and soggy. The field of horses was set at twelve, with representatives from the United States, France, England, Canada, and Ireland. The race was being televised via satellite to North America, Europe, Hong Kong, and Australia. The international press called it the "ultimate race," and a groundswell of interest created the

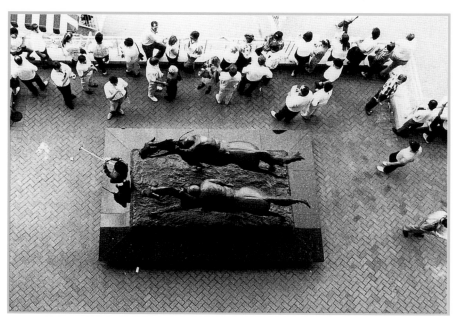

A statue at Arlington celebrates the intense rivalry between John Henry and The Bart.

distinct sensation that fans had been waiting forever for this very race. The favorite was 6-year-old John Henry, an American horse that, as his exercise rider affectionately boasted, "gallops like an old cow."

On Saturday at Arlington the sun finally shone, and the long grass dried out a bit. By Sunday the track was firmer. Although John Henry was the favorite, not everyone was optimistic about his chances to win. Paul Mellon's horse, Key to Content, was said to "love the wet." John Henry's jockey, Willie Shoemaker, warned that the wet grass favors the Europeans.

At the start of the race, Key to Content ran out in front along with The Bart, a "dark horse" from Kentucky whose odds were 40-to-1. John Henry came out of the gate in eighth place. Not until the horses came to the last bend (it was a 1¼-mile race) did John Henry start to

The great John Henry edges out rival The Bart in the first Arlington Million, 1981.

charge, first through an inside gap, and then to the outside. The Bart and John Henry ran head and head. They reached the wire simultaneously, and no one could tell which horse had taken the victory. Clive Gammon of *Sports Illustrated* wrote that the photo finish "showed there wasn't much more than one horse's hot breath in front." The race was won by John Henry. He later was voted Horse of the Year.

This victory, one of John Henry's greatest, was hardly his last. His racing career lasted well into his ninth year, and he lived well into his twenties. The glory John Henry achieved could hardly have been predicted early in his career. As a matter of fact, his first six owners sold the horse for a variety of reasons—mainly due to his "calf's knees" that bent backward, and his difficult temperament.

John Henry was notoriously ill-tempered, and he had what was gracefully described at the time as a "Napoleonic attitude." However, as every lucky truant meets up with an officer who knows how to play his game, John Henry had the great good luck to draw trainer Ron McAnally, a quiet Kentuckian who has a way with older horses.

John Henry's seventh and final owner, bicycle importer Sam Rubin, comprised the final side of the lucky triangle. He made the purchase at the suggestion of John Henry's previous agent/owner Hal Snowden, who was selling the horse for the bargain price of $25,000. Rubin had been interested in Thoroughbred racing and had told Snowden that he wanted to buy "the

Ron McAnally, John Henry's trainer.

right horse, at the right price." Quite serendipitously, Rubin bought John Henry sight unseen. He didn't even know the horse's name! But he, and the rest of America, was about to learn of John Henry.

What better place is there to boost the career of an "equine Napoleon" than Los Angeles, California? On the West Coast, McAnally entered John Henry in the 1980 Hollywood Invitational ($250,000), the 1980 and 1981 San Luis Rey Stakes ($150,000 each), the 1981 Santa Anita Handicap ($500,000), and the 1981 Oak Tree Invitational ($300,000). John Henry won all of these races. By the age of six (after winning the first Arlington Million in 1981), John Henry had amassed $1,864,510 in career earnings. Only two horses at that time, Spectacular Bid and Affirmed, had gone over the $2 million mark in career earnings.

The team of Rubin and McAnally kept John Henry running—usually over grass—for many years. He became the first horse to pass the $3 million mark in earnings. The formula for keeping John Henry competitive was simple: careful selection of races, plenty of rest, and also plenty of work. At the age of 9, the team added a new and compatible jockey, Chris McCarron, and made more money than ever. In 1984 John Henry again was voted Horse of the Year! He retired from racing in 1985, at the age of 10, tried a comeback in 1986, and retired for good later that year after tearing a ligament in his left foreleg. He went into show business as an educational Thoroughbred (as a gelded horse, he could not go to stud).

He went on to the Horse Park in Kentucky, making daily appearances for the horse museum audiences. People continued to love him, visit him, recount his races, or learn about them anew. He's a symbol of hope for late bloomers. He's an apology for bad tempers. In 1989, when Thoroughbred Racing Communications Inc. conducted a poll of the "Best of the Decade," John Henry received the top honors.

"There is no way to explain him," Hall of Fame trainer McAnally said. "People told us that he had been badly treated before the time we got him. [Someone] had taken the hose above the webbing across the stall and hit him with it. He is twenty-four now. He still tests you. . . . He bluffs." McAnally visited John Henry's stall while on a trip to Kentucky in 1998. He speaks clearly, quietly, seriously about his temperamental super horse. "He was able to take the hate he had and put it into racing."

Arlington Today

The present owner of Arlington Park, Richard Duchossois, met Joseph Joyce the day before the 1983 Kentucky Derby and reportedly said, "If Arlington is ever for sale, I'd be interested." True to his word, on August 18, 1983, Duchossois bought Arlington Park. Joyce retained some stock shares and maintained an interest in track operations. The new owner proved to be a true champion of horses in general—he himself bred Thoroughbred race horses; his son was involved with hunters and jumpers.

On July 31, 1985, a fire destroyed Arlington Park. The grandstand blazed and melted. The ruins were spec-

Arlington owner Richard Duchossois.

A tragic fire destroyed the grandstand in July of 1985. But by August, the debris was cleared, temporary bleachers were erected, and 35,000 fans watched "The Miracle Million."

tacular in their wreckage of twisted and melted metal girders. Duchossois immediately cleaned up the debris. On August 25 of that year more than 35,000 fans watched the Arlington Million from temporary bleachers. They called it the "Miracle Million." Arlington received an Eclipse Award for accomplishing the feat of rising from the ashes—it was the first ever Eclipse Award to be presented to a racetrack. Duchossois immediately ensured everyone that he intended to rebuild Arlington. In his determination, he emerged as the main character in Illinois racing. He bought out his partners and exerted his political power—as a track

owner and a wealthy man—to replace the track.

Duchossois exhibited personality traits closer in spirit to Curley Brown than to any of the other previous owners. He began to tell people of his personal vision of a racetrack in order to stir up interest. His wildest plan was to relocate the track north of Chicago, near the Wisconsin border. This business plan was meant to attract the sports fans from Milwaukee to his track, as well as Chicagoans. Members of the Milwaukee community were not thrilled with the prospect of having a racetrack, however, and made their opinions known. Meanwhile, the city of Arlington Heights had had time to contemplate

The new grandstand.

An actual and digital finish, 1989.

the possible loss of their prestigious racetrack. They responded by offering Duchossois a tax break—they were going to assess the taxation levels of the new park based on the pre-fire taxation levels. Eventually, Duchossois turned his sites back to the original Arlington land and initiated plans to rebuild a new grandstand there. Woodbine, the Canadian track in Toronto with an appreciation for grass racing, hosted the Arlington Million in 1988 (until the new grandstand at Arlington could be erected).

Once the new track was opened in June 1989, however, the local taxing bodies revoked their deal and determined taxes on the property at current levels instead of at the pre-fire levels, as promised. Neil Milbert, the *Chicago Tribune*'s turf writer, states that "[Duchossois] was double-crossed." He continued to operate the track, however.

The new grandstand and paddock at Arlington, which opened in 1989, surprised and delighted the rac-

ing world. Although the complex gives the impression of being large, it is actually modest in size. Racing no longer needs supertracks. Now, most people seem to prefer a television monitor. Arlington was one of the first venues to build a completely separate building away from the track to accommodate fans who want to sit at a table and handicap their horses—tip sheets and racing form spread out conveniently before them—and simply watch the monitor during the race itself.

The new grandstand is a traditional single-tier stand that is open to the weather. Like Woodbine (built before it), patrons are stacked up over the paddock and can

Chicago racing in style.

view the horses from balconies without stepping down to the paddock. Much of the grandstand is open to weather and unencumbered by glass. There are glass-enclosed restaurants set well back on the two upper tiers, and an apartment for private entertaining with a dance floor and a grand piano. And, like all recently constructed sports complexes, there is a row of corporate boxes located just under the roof along an open balcony.

The innovation of the track is clearly the sunken paddock. It is designed to be the center of all activity between the races, and it occupies the full length of the back of the grandstand building. It was inspired in part by Gulfstream Park's paddock, with a centrally located axis running from the saddling shed through the oval walking ring directly through the center of the building and out onto the track. But because the Arlington paddock is sunken, it is much more theatrical. The new Arlington is one of the most stylishly designed racetracks built in America in decades. But an excellent new grandstand hasn't solved all of Arlington's problems.

Since the reopening of Arlington on June 28, 1989, Duchossois has been seeking redemption for the unfortunate dealings he experienced with local taxing bodies. The battle is still in progress. By the 1998 season, Duchossois had shut Arlington's doors and the legislature had given Arlington's racing dates to Hawthorne Park. Arlington, however, will no doubt continue to thrive one way or another.

Left: **The perfect oval paddock at Arlington Park, waiting for the horses.**
Right: **Horse entering gap to paddock.**

Milestones

1926—Curley Brown and several Chicago investors form the American National Jockey Club.

1927, June 27—Ground is broken and construction begins on an 18,000-seat grandstand and clubhouse, and two racing strips— a 1¼-mile main track and a 1-mile inner track.

1929, January 5—Arlington Park is sold to twenty Chicago businessmen who incorporate as the Arlington Jockey Club.

1929—Arlington introduces four stakes races: the Arlington Classic, Arlington Handicap, Stars & Stripes, and Arlington Lassie.

1932, June 27—Calumet Farm records its first victory in a Thoroughbred race with 2-year-old Warren Jr., who wins by a nose at Arlington Park to earn $850.

1934—Illinois turf racing debuts at Arlington Park.

1940, April 16—Arlington Park is purchased by John D. Allen, vice president of Brinks & Co., and Benjamin F. Lindheimer, director of Washington Park (Chicago's south-side race track). Arlington Park and Washington Park combine racing schedules into a single, coordinated racing meeting.

1941—The Arlington Handicap shifts from dirt to turf.

1942—Arlington becomes the first track to bank the turns on the turf course.

1943–46—Arlington is closed due to World War II-era gasoline rationing, and races shift to Washington Park.

1952—The Arlington Classic becomes the world's richest race for 3 year olds with a $100,000-added purse.

1952, June 24—Jockey Eddie Arcaro rides his 3,000th career winner at Arlington Park. He is the first American rider to reach that mark.

1960, June 5—Owner Ben Lindheimer dies of a heart attack. His daughter, Marje Lindheimer Everett, assumes control of Arlington.

1961—Washington Park racing dates are shifted to Arlington Park for a schedule of sixty-seven days.

1964—Arlington receives all of Washington Park's Thoroughbred racing dates. Washington Park is used for harness racing only. Arlington has a 103-day schedule.

1967, October 8—Arlington and Washington Parks are merged with the Gulf & Western company.

1971—Arlington and Washington Parks (Chicago Thoroughbred Enterprises) is bought by Madison Square Garden.

1973, June 30—Three weeks after he won the Triple Crown, Secretariat scores a nine-length win in the specially created, $125,000 Arlington Invitational Stakes, where he is sent off at the shortest odds of his career (1–20). With no place or show wagering on the four-horse race, the track has a minus win-pool of $17,941. More than 40,000 spectators turn out for the event.

1981, August 31—Arlington introduces America's first $1 million Thoroughbred race with the inaugural running of the Arlington Million. John Henry, ridden by Willie Shoemaker, wins the race by a nose over longshot The Bart.

1982—Three of Arlington's top jockeys set records or receive awards. Randy Romero sets an Arlington season record with 181 wins; Pat Day wins the national riding title; and Earlie Fires wins his 3,000th career race and takes the Arlington money crown with $1.76 million in earnings.

1983, August 18—Arlington Park is purchased by former track president Joseph F. Joyce, Sheldon Robbins, Ralph Ross, and Richard L. Duchossois.

Track entrance.

1984, August 26—39,053 fans watch the legendary John Henry win his second Arlington Million. Wagering of $1,097,397 sets new state and track records.

1985, July 31—Arlington Park's grandstand is destroyed by fire.

1985—More than 35,000 fans watch the fifth running of the Arlington Million from temporary bleachers.

1985—Arlington receives an Eclipse Award, the first ever awarded to a racetrack, with an inscription that recognizes the track's "Indomitable Spirit."

1986—Richard L. Duchossois buys out Joyce, Robbins, and Ross, and assumes full control of Arlington Park.

1987—Using a temporary grandstand, Arlington celebrates its sixtieth anniversary with a ninety-one-day season. This is Arlington's first full meet since 1984.

1987, July 15—Trainer Jack Van Berg makes racing history at Arlington by becoming the first Thoroughbred trainer to win 5,000 races as jockey Pat Day rides Art's Chandelle to victory.

1987, September 7—Ground-breaking ceremonies are held in the Winner's Circle for the construction of the new Arlington.

1988—Arlington closes to allow for uninterrupted construction.

1988, August 20—The Arlington Million is transferred to Toronto's Woodbine Race Course, marking the first time a major American stakes race is moved to another country.

1988—Duchossois is named only the fifth recipient of the Special Sovereign Award from the Canadian Jockey Club, for unique achievement in the racing industry. He also becomes the fifth recipient of the prestigious Lord Derby Award in London from the Horse Racing Writers and Reporters Association of Great Britain.

1989, June 28—The new Arlington International Racecourse opens in Arlington Heights, Illinois.

1990—Arlington wins a third special Eclipse Award to acknowledge the extraordinary investment in the future of racing that the new track represents.

1990, August 19—Jockey Earlie Fires wins his 5,000th career race, riding Illinois Horse of the Year, Tex's Zing, in the ninth race at Arlington. He joins history-making jockeys Bill Shoemaker, Laffit Pincay Jr., Angel Cordero Jr., John Longden, Jorge Velasquez, Larry Snyder, Sandy Hawley, Dave Gall, Carl Gambardella, and Chris McCarron as jockeys who have achieved that mark.

1990, September 2—Golden Pheasant wins the Arlington Million enabling Charles Whittingham to become the first trainer to win the event three times.

1990—Arlington jockey Pat Day earns his fourth Eclipse Award as the nation's leading jockey and establishes a new record for stakes victories in a single season, with sixty.

1992—Arlington has the most successful season in the sixty-five-year history of the track, including records in attendance, handle, and group sales, despite a record-breaking cold and rainy summer.

1996—More than 34,000 people turn out to watch the great Cigar—two-time Horse of the Year—tie the modern record with sixteen consecutive wins, in the Arlington Citation Challenge.

1998—The racing season at Arlington is suspended due to a dispute with the state legislature, which refused to change old racing laws.

The clubhouse grandstand in the year the new facility opened, 1989.

Richard Duchossois's suite with grand piano at Arlington Park.

Hialeah Park

Hialeah, Florida
(Established 1932)

Despite all its past glory, Hialeah Park has become an endangered species among aficionados of Thoroughbred racing. Some are trying to rescue it, while others are more than ready to witness its destruction. For more than two decades the track has been involved in a local argument over winter racing dates, and because of this drawn-out conflict the great Hialeah Park is struggling to stay afloat.

However, there is no doubt about Hialeah Park's venerable place in racing history. During certain decades, particularly the 1930s through the 1970s, its prominence in the development of America's Thoroughbred champions was matched only by its distinction as a popular destination for high society. It is perhaps the loveliest racing facility in America. It is to racing what the Chicago Cubs' Wrigley Field is to baseball—a storied and beautiful venue whose obvious flaws have been embraced.

What an enormous pleasure to drive up the wide avenue of royal palm trees approaching the grandstand and clubhouse at Hialeah! It is the venue for weddings, jazz festivals, and, most importantly, Thoroughbred racing. Its distinct personality couldn't have developed anywhere but South Florida, with its lush flora, unique fauna, and delightful Cuban influences. The famous pink flamingoes flock around the infield lake. On racing days you can eat a *Cubano a la plancha* (a ham and cheese sandwich with pickle flattened by a hot iron) accompanied by a *cafe Cubano* (a little thimbleful of extremely strong coffee). The caterers and many of the racing fans come from Cuba. Like Habaneros (Havana natives), the patrons at Hialeah are extremely content to walk around in the tropical lushness of the grounds, take in the birds and the flowers, sip rum, drink strong coffee, play the horses, and appreciate the aging architecture. With any luck, the charming ambiance of Hialeah and its attendant excitement will linger for years to come, as well.

Hialeah in History

In the early parts of this century Thoroughbred racing existed in several parts of Florida, including Marion County, Tampa, Jacksonville, and Pensacola. By 1911, St. Augustine on the Gulf Coast was recognized as America's most popular winter resort, and Moncrief Park, a horse track situated north of St. Augustine, hoped to cash in on the area's economic success. But the Florida legislature passed a law against gambling in

Opposite: **The scenic entrance and grand architecture make Hialeah Park one of the most beautiful sporting facilities in the world.**

1911, and Moncrief closed. There was no racing in the state until the end of the decade.

Because Florida provided such a favorable climate for raising and racing horses, and because so many people were interested in the sport, horse racing regained momentum in the years after the gambling ban was lifted in 1916. In the 1920s, tobacco tycoon R. J. Reynolds owned a private track at Pompano, Florida, where he ran race meetings for friends and others. By the late '20s, there were three other tracks in the state: Tampa Downs, located on the Gulf Coast; Keeney Park, near St. Augustine; and Hialeah Race Track, located about ten miles north of downtown Miami.

Hialeah was an extraordinarily big land speculation deal of any kind for southern Florida, but it wasn't initially conceived of as a horse racing track. In 1917, businessmen James Bright and Glenn Hammond Curtiss formed a partnership which purchased all the land around what is now Hialeah, Miami Springs, and Opa-Locka, as well as a great deal of land around Lake Okeechobee. Bright used most land segments to graze beef and dairy cattle, but also sold land to two betting ventures: a dog track and a jai alai fronton. After seeing the quick monetary success of these betting ventures, Bright decided to start a horse track.

First he found a promoter, Joseph M. Smoot, to develop the project. (Smoot was a Buffalo, New York, promoter who was attracted to the Florida real estate boom.) Then he sold 160 acres of land to the city of Miami for a token $10 with the stipulation that it be

James H. Bright

used for a racetrack. Bright found backers among wealthy Miami businessmen—Frank B. Shutts of the Miami Herald, Ed Romfh of the First National Bank, and businessmen Luke Cassidy, Jack Cleary, John I. Day, Mars Cassidy, John B. Campbell, and William Urmey.

Next, Smoot provided a plan for organizing the Miami Jockey Club and building the track. The Hialeah Race Track opened on January 15, 1925. The grandstand was a little two-story pavilion roofed in Spanish tiles; the track, a 1-mile oval. On opening day, the spectator boxes were occupied by many famous people: John Philip Sousa, Gilda Grey, Joseph P. Kennedy, Gloria Swanson (in a blue foulard silk dress), a disgruntled Al Jolson (on his way back from Cuba where he had temporarily lost his voice), Mayor of New York Jimmy Walker (who was made honorary president of the club for opening day), Will Rogers, Bernard Gimbel, Albert Payson Terhune, and an unidentified Indian prince.

Although distinguished guests like Joe Kennedy and Gloria Swanson were in the clubhouse, the fact remained that Hialeah was set in a swamp in the wilderness. While there was plenty of room for horses (since the management had built stables to accommodate a thousand) there was no railroad spur to bring visitors and horses to the racetrack. One trainer, John Zoeller, tells of shipping his stable of racehorses from New York to Hialeah in the first years:

"They were dead tired . . . they could not stay on the railroad car another day. But there was a problem getting to the track. There was no unloading platform in the tiny town of Hialeah, so the horses had to be unloaded in downtown Miami and walked the ten miles to the track. The grooms carried baseball bats for protection against the snakes."

Betting was legal, but pari-mutuel wagering—a form of gambling in which the betting pool is divided among those who bet on the first three horses, minus a percentage for the management—was not, so various intriguing schemes were used to gamble. One popular method was selling postcards which depicted the horses in each race, and cashing in the winning cards. Another gambling quirk resulted when the Miami Jockey Club made a brief attempt to keep women from betting. The effort began and ended on opening day, when "flappers" charged the windows in such numbers that they could not be halted!

In 1929, the Great Depression hit Florida and the land boom ended abruptly. Smoot and his associates sold the track to J. H. Carstairs, who quickly resold it in late 1930 to Joseph E. Widener. James Bright, the original owner, remained on the board of directors until his death in 1959, and under Widener Hialeah became one of the leading tracks in the country.

When Widener, a Philadelphia philanthropist, art collector, and benefactor of the National Gallery of Art in Washington, D.C., purchased the small racetrack, he had a precise vision of transforming it into the most beautiful sports complex in America. He called it a "Park" from the outset, and he paid careful attention to the landscaping. He also imported exotic birds such as crowned cranes from Africa, peacocks from India, and parrots from Mexico. The most famous feathered acquisition of all was, of course, the flamingoes imported from Cuba.

Widener intended to reconstruct the facility soon after purchase, but the construction could not begin until a pari-mutuel bill was passed in the state legislature. A very confident man with much political clout, Widener lobbied against strong Cuban and Baptist competition—spending over $50,000 in the process—to push for legalized gambling. In 1931 a compromise was reached, and the legislature declared Hialeah Park the exclusive site of pari-mutuel gambling—while gambling in the rest of the state was banned. Of course, the deciding factors included money incentives for the government in general and for many politicians specifically in the form of jobs at the Park.

The Architecture

In 1931, Widener hired 28-year-old architect Lester Geisler to design an entirely new racetrack facility. Geisler, a New Yorker, was the protégé of Palm Beach society architect Adison Mizner. From the very beginning the young architect was able to communicate with Widener. He has said that theirs was a creative partnership of ideas. Though Widener had intended to direct the renovation toward a Spanish style, which was in vogue at the time, Geisler introduced the idea of building in the French style instead. Widener concurred and even sent Geisler to France to do architectural research.

Much of the genius of Hialeah's design is the landscaping. One of the most fascinating elements is the lattice that covers the back of the grandstand (made from the center hard wood from carefully selected cypress trees, sixty years later the lattice shows no effect of the usual tropical decay). In fact the entire backstretch area is particularly attractive. Rows of barns sit on white, sandy topsoil and everything seems clean, cushioned, and quiet.

The royal palms that line the avenues leading to the clubhouse and grandstand entrances are an exceptional sight, as is the bridle path, also lined with soft-needled Australian pines, which leads from the barns to the paddock.

Left: **Lester Geisler, Hialeah's architect**

Right: **The beautiful backstretch at Hialeah.**

The clubhouse end of the grandstand.

The paddock is where the horses are saddled, the owner has his last moment with the jockey, and the patrons are able to see the horses before placing a bet. At Hialeah, the layout makes it very easy to go from grandstand to paddock. There is nothing like it at any other track.

The infield, with its small lakes populated with flamingoes and rimmed with a lush grass turf course, is unforgettable. Widener is credited with conceiving the small lake and the flamingoes. They were imported from Cuba in 1931, flew away or died in the early years and, after getting their wings clipped, in four or five years established themselves and began breeding. (Today this refuge is monitored by the National Audubon Society.)

A Winter Place

Hialeah, north of Miami and about seventy-five miles south of West Palm Beach, depended on the Palm Beach racing fans for daily business. The railroad was the answer. A specific rail schedule was actually designed for race days. The engine alone would leave Palm Beach in the morning, and by the time it reached Hialeah it would be pulling ten to fifteen cars! Because of Mr. Widener's great drawing power, people flocked to his racetrack. Rows of attractive people sat in the boxes at Hialeah. The track itself offered an exquisite backdrop. Hialeah became the place to be in winter months. Society pages in New York were devoted to it. Better still, it was considered to be a healthy place for horses.

Jimmy Jones, the famous trainer for Calumet Farm (one of the nation's leading stables) has said that the track itself was very kind to a horse's legs. He would bring crippled horses to Hialeah to get them sound. He spent a lot of time at Hialeah putting his "babies" (2 year olds) in the starting gate, teaching them to get all four feet on the ground, getting them used to the ringing of the bell, making them feel at home, and getting to know them. Training horses, he says, is knowing your horses. Hialeah, with its kind track and beautiful weather, became his lucky place.

Hialeah (along with Keeneland) became the track where the prep races for the Kentucky Derby were run. The weather was a big factor, being much more attractive than the cold of the north for preparing horses for the arduous May-to-June Triple Crown campaign.

"To get to the Kentucky Derby properly, you had to bring horses to Florida," says Jones. "Otherwise, when you started training in January in South Carolina or Kentucky, you were running them in the cold and ice. You had to make your own competition among your own horses. We liked the Florida idea much better. You had a lot of foundation under your horse when you got through."

In 1937, in order to capitalize on northern trainers' need to bring their horses to Florida in the winter, Hialeah renamed the Florida Derby as the "Flamingo Stakes." (This race became one of the biggest national races of the winter season, attracting champions over the years like Citation [1948], Northern Dancer ['64], Seattle Slew ['77], and Spectacular Bid ['79].)

The Joneses

Ben Jones and his son, Jimmy, were the most successful and colorful trainers in the 1940s. Nineteen thirty-eight was a magic year for the Joneses, who came from Parnell, Missouri. You might say that 1938 was the year the Joneses were discovered. That year, Ben Jones had run Lawrin, a horse owned by a Kansas City department store owner, in the Flamingo Stakes at Hialeah. Lawrin went on to win the 1938 Kentucky Derby, becoming the first Kansas-bred horse to win the famous race. Bull Lea, Calumet Farm's leading horse, came in eighth. Calumet's owner, Warren Wright, hired Ben Jones to be his trainer that year. Wright said to Jones, "Your job is to win the Kentucky Derby."

"Calumet had won only nine races up to September that year [1938]," Jimmy Jones said. "The first race we ran for Wright, we got a second. Then we won seven in a row. . . . We had a dispute with Mr. Wright over taking the young horses to Florida to continue their education. He didn't want to bring in the babies, the young ones. It got a little expensive. Once you establish the pattern, you can get away with it; later, our older horses were picking up the tab and it was all right. But Mr. Wright was fussy about expenses. He looked over those statements every month. We had to win and make money. He had fired nine trainers before we got the job. If it hadn't been for Whirlaway, we might have been number ten."

Whirlaway certainly did pick up the tab. In 1940, though Jones didn't think the horse was ready, Whirlaway was entered into sixteen races as a 2 year old and won

Jimmy Jones, Eddie Arcaro, and Arcaro's wife.

seven. Perhaps this prepared him for his 3-year-old season, when he won the country's most prestigious classic races: The Kentucky Derby, the Preakness Stakes, and the Belmont Stakes—the Triple Crown.

"Whirlaway ran early at Hialeah but he didn't have it. So we took him out of training. Under duress. Wright wasn't happy about it. . . . Sometimes, handling an owner is about as important as handling a horse."

Jones adds, "The Old Man got so he was a good owner. He let us take our time. The average man . . . forgets that a horse is flesh and blood."

Citation

In 1948 Calumet Farm had another Triple Crown winner: Citation. As a 2 year old he won eight of nine races.

"I could see his ribs," said Jones. "I wanted to put weight on him at Hialeah."

Citation raced there and revealed just what a special horse he'd turn out to be, winning the Seminole Handicap, the Everglades, and the Flamingo Stakes. He won the Kentucky Derby by three-and-a-half lengths, the Preakness by five-and-a-half, and the Belmont by eight.

Citation's final racing years were a triumph marred

Hialeah salutes the great Citation with a brilliant fountain statue.

by tragedy. Warren Wright wanted Citation to become the first horse ever to win a million dollars. But the horse developed an inflammation of the ankle and the 1948 Horse of the Year spent the season in the barn and the pasture. Wright died, but apparently the Joneses were still burdened by the obsession of the Old Man. Mrs. Wright wanted the horse to go on record with a million. They ran Citation in race after race.

"The horses that beat Citation . . . it was terrible, really terrible," Jones said. "It wasn't really his fault . . . I'll take the fault. But it's a running game and you got to run some. We did what we thought was right at the time; Mr. Wright had wanted Citation to make that million-dollar mark. As I look back now, it was a mistake. If Citation had stopped after his 3-year-old season, he would have gone down parallel to Man o' War, and I don't think he quite reached that. He was like a crippled

old fighter trying to finish. It was the right thing to do at the time but now I regret it. You look backward a lot better than you do forward."

The career of Citation was analyzed by the *Daily Racing Form* and the *Morning Telegraph* when he finally crossed the wire and won his million. First they analyzed his accomplishments, viewing him as an athlete. The horse had run over every type of track, from heavy and muddy to dry and fast; he had covered both short and long distances early in his career; and he had accommodated various jockeys. In the end, of course—although the turf writer did not write this—Citation also adapted to a greedy owner.

From the beginning the horse thrilled those closest to him, before he was ever tried. A reporter from the *Daily Racing Form* reported: "One morning, after the tremendous amount of work carried out daily at Calumet was through, that Ben and Jimmy invited [me] for a tour of the stable, mainly to look over the youngsters. . . . When they came to Citation's stall, they both agreed, and quite emphatically, that 'if this one doesn't turn out well, then we don't know anything about horses.'"

During the first two racing years, Citation won $861,150 in purses. But he had to travel a rocky road in the next three years, beset by some heart breaking defeats and injuries, before he got the $134,850 he needed to make turf history. When the horse became injured in 1950 as a 4 year old, the next logical step would have been retirement with top stud fees, but the late Warren Wright's influence remained, demanding that his favorite horse be given every opportunity to become the first Thoroughbred millionaire. After

The great Citation works out at Hialeah in 1948, his Triple Crown year.

Wright's death, Mrs. Wright respected her husband's wishes and gave orders to ready Citation for another try at the million-dollar mark.

Citation then went through a succession of defeats as a 5 year old, losing by a nose several times. On June 3, 1950, Citation ran the Golden Gate Mile in 1:33⅗ (a world record), and became the world's leading money winner. He could have stopped then, but his owners and trainers wanted a million! Sent out to race again and again, he won only two more races despite breaking the million-dollar mark and setting the world record for a mile.

The *Racing Form* looks at all the reasons. Certainly one thing was clear: in handicap races, he carried the top weights, but he didn't let his opponents off easily. Race after race the turf writers had to describe the agonizing losses, adding telling descriptions like "[he] tasted the whip in the heat." In five races Citation finished second. But—and here is another bittersweet statistic—in total he was only beaten by three lengths in those five races. Finally, on July 16, 1951, he won the Hollywood Gold Cup and became a millionaire.

In retrospect, it is an agonizing story and one that most people don't think about. In 1976 Hialeah Park commissioned a bronze statue of Citation. It was erected in 1979 to celebrate the great horse who wintered with them as a youngster.

Jockeys' quarters at Hialeah.

Milestones

1925—Hialeah Race Track opens under the Miami Jockey Club.

1927—Florida Supreme Court reinforces ban on betting.

1929—Racing resumes.

1930—Joseph Widener buys Hialeah.

1932—The new Hialeah Park opens. Widener installs an Australian totalizer machine for betting.

1933—Racing on the grass begins for the first time in the United States.

1937—The Florida Derby is renamed the "Flamingo Stakes."

1938—War Admiral wins the Widener Handicap. Lawrin becomes first Florida-trained horse to win the Kentucky Derby.

1947—The "Hialeah Bill" passes state legislature, giving the track a midwinter racing-date monopoly that will last until 1972.

1948—Citation wins the Flamingo Stakes on his way to winning the Triple Crown.

1954—Eugene Mori buys Hialeah.

1964—Northern Dancer wins the Flamingo Stakes, then goes on to win the Kentucky Derby and the Preakness; he takes third at Belmont.

1966, March 3—Ogden Phipps's Buckpasser wins the Flamingo Stakes by a nose, under the guidance of Willie Shoemaker. The colt was such a prohibitive favorite among the field of nine that the race was declared a non-wagering contest and was dubbed "The Chicken Flamingo."

1971—The "Hialeah Bill" is ruled unconstitutional.

1972—Hialeah loses the prime winter dates for the first time. John Galbreath and associates buy the track.

1977, March 9—Seattle Slew makes his 3-year-old debut at Hialeah winning the 7-furlong race in 1:20⅗ (breaking the track record). He wins the Flamingo on March 26th, and goes on to win the Triple Crown.

1977—John Brunetti buys Hialeah.

1979—Hialeah has its first $3 million day. Spectacular Bid wins the Flamingo by a record 12 lengths. He also takes the Kentucky Derby and Preakness, and finishes third at Belmont.

View from the betting terrace.

1982, February 27—Florida apprentice Mary Russ becomes the first female jockey to win a Grade I stakes in North America when she captures the Widener Handicap aboard Lord Darnley.

1984—Hialeah has its first $4-million day. The meeting handle of $95 million is the best in the history of the track.

1987—Hialeah runs early dates for the first time.

1998—Pat Day wins his third straight Widener Handicap aboard Frisk Me Now (Tejano Run in 1997; Mecke in 1996). Each win earned $120,000. Frisk Me Now becomes the first horse since Nashua in 1955–56 to win both the Flamingo Stakes (1997, E.L. King Jr. up) and the Widener Handicap in back-to-back seasons.

The luxurious betting area.

Santa Anita Park

Arcadia, California
(Established 1934)

Santa Anita Park has one of the most majestic views of any racetrack in America. With the San Gabriel Mountains looming in the distance, spectators can enjoy thrilling Thoroughbred races below an invigorating backdrop. The first of California's three major tracks to be built, Santa Anita opened soon after the statewide ban on racing was lifted in 1933. With a great location; fantastic weather; and a resourceful, energetic, and determined group of people behind it, Santa Anita Park seemed like a sure bet right from the start.

The idea to build a new racetrack in southern California came from the famous Hollywood producer and director, Hal Roach, in 1933. (Roach was perhaps most famous for his television series, *Our Gang*.) That year, Roach began to assemble a group of friends and associates in Hollywood who were also interested in creating a racetrack. At the suggestion of one member of the group, Roach brought in Gwynn Wilson to develop and manage the project. Wilson had just completed his role as Associate General Manager of the 10th Olympic Games, held in Los Angeles in 1932, and was widely respected in California at that moment due to the Games' success.

The next step in creating the racetrack was raising a million dollars—this was the figure established by the State of California as the amount necessary to qualify for a license. Roach and Wilson were able to raise $500,000, mostly from people in the motion picture business, but were unable to secure the full amount. They approached every person they knew in Los Angeles.

"By the end of November," Wilson recalls, "people would no longer talk to me when they saw me coming down [the] street."

Wilson heard about a man in San Francisco—Dr. Charles Strub—who was trying to build a racetrack of his own but was having difficulty getting the city's approval to build it at his preferred location. Wilson visited Strub—a dentist and one of three owners of a minor league baseball team, the San Francisco Seals—in San Francisco. Strub decided to abandon his plan to build a track in the Bay Area and to join Hal Roach's group in Southern California. After that, everything fell into place.

"Dr. Strub was the dominant person . . . in terms of the direction," Wilson said. "He brought in the top money. We had $500,000 in cash, and that's all. He came in and brought in the rest. He was the spark."

Opposite: **The glorious entrance to Santa Anita Park.**

Gwynn Wilson, 1958.

Strub brought $350,000 from San Francisco investors and put up $150,000 himself, for which he was reimbursed in stock the following year. Strub, already successful in the professional sports business, took over the racing end of the project. In fact, Strub's decision to leave San Francisco and relocate in Los Angeles was contingent upon his taking that position.

In January, 1934, the Los Angeles Turf Club was incorporated, with Hal Roach as the first president, Charles Strub as the executive vice president, and Gwynn Wilson as the assistant general manager. Wilson claimed that only two people kept offices at the racetrack: himself and Charles Strub. They were the heart of its administration for the next twenty-five years.

On the Road

Neither Wilson nor Gordon B. Kaufmann, the architect selected to design Santa Anita, had visited race-tracks on a regular basis, so they decided to take a trip across the country to visit a number of tracks. The trip turned out to be quite an odyssey.

"We traveled on a plane," Wilson said. "[It was] like a barn with wings that shook and had lots of ventilation." They went first to Abilene, Texas, then continued by train to a few western tracks which Wilson describes as "rough, and not our conception of a racetrack at all." They reached New Orleans—during Mardi Gras—to go to the Fair Grounds. They found that track to be too rowdy. They were tired and disappointed and, according to Wilson, didn't learn anything.

From Louisiana, they traveled east to Hialeah Park, in Florida, and immediately realized that this was what they wanted: a resort-like track, intended to be more for recreation than for strictly gambling. They studied the buildings and the track—Kaufmann made notes and sketches while Wilson took measurements. They continued north to Maryland and New York to explore the old tracks at Pimlico and Belmont, and then went to Arlington Park outside Chicago. At Arlington, they found a track that interested them in its modernity.

After having traveled across the country and halfway back, visiting numerous facilities and discussing race-tracks twenty-four hours a day for the three week trip, Wilson and Kaufmann knew what they wanted.

"Arlington and Hialeah are the basis from which we started," Wilson said. After seeing Arlington, they took an airplane from Chicago, which was grounded in Kansas City due to high winds and snow; a train from

Kansas City to Phoenix; and, finally, another airplane from Phoenix to Los Angeles. Wilson was thirty-seven years old; Kaufmann was forty-five. Wilson remembers the trip affectionately, saying, "Nobody knew Gordon better than I did after that."

Santa Anita, like Hialeah, was built in a small amount of time—about seven months. To expedite the process, they employed twenty-eight different general contracting firms to construct the buildings, tracks, and everything else.

A Magnificent Setting

Kaufmann knew that he had a magnificent setting. The site of the racetrack is the former Rancho Santa Anita, at the foot of the San Gabriel Mountains. These handsome, bare, sometimes snow-capped mountains rise up just beyond the backstretch. As the light changes throughout the day, the mountains appear to change color.

An earlier racetrack had been built on Rancho Santa Anita. Its owner, Elias Jackson "Lucky" Baldwin, pioneered the breeding of Thoroughbreds in California in

The San Gabriel Mountains provide a majestic view to Santa Anita's racetrackers.

The development of highway access and large parking areas stoked attendance at Santa Anita.

The Turf Club located in the clubhouse at Santa Anita.

the 1880s. His track closed in 1909 due to the California ban on racing. This fine, empty, remote land lay there virtually unused until 1934, when legal racing finally resumed in California. It is most appropriate that California racing resumed at this particular locale, since it had been such an important location for western racing in the recent past. It is also interesting to consider that the new track—which represented California racing's future—would be built with society's future in mind. It was the 1930s, and Kaufmann understood the importance of the emerging automobile culture.

Kaufmann drew into his plans something new at the time: a large parking lot. He intended fans to come to Arcadia in their cars, via the highways. There was Pasadena to the north and west, Los Angeles to the south, and San Bernardino to the west. The most glamorous way to drive to Santa Anita was along a long, palm-lined drive leading from Huntington Avenue in Pasadena directly to the modern Georgian clubhouse

where they offered valet parking. The patrons who chose not to use the valet service could easily find a spot in the brand-new, ample parking lot—which held 10,000 cars—that lay directly behind the paddock and the main entrance. This setting made fans feel as though they were arriving at a great film spectacular, with a grand marquee at the gate to welcome all. In 1934, the daily average attendance was 9,000 racing fans. This number doubled by 1937.

A short time later another parking lot was built on the north side of the racetrack, which allows patrons to easily reach the infield via a tunnel. Once on the infield, patrons can follow a wide walkway from the infield to a tunnel that leads to the grandstand and the paddock.

Kaufmann believed that circulation was the essence of good racetrack design, allowing great numbers of people to congregate on a relatively small area of the homestretch but also move quickly to restaurants, refreshment stands, betting areas, service areas, the infield, the paddock, and the parking lots as well. Kaufmann was smart. This is a beautiful and efficient racetrack.

The cost of building the racetrack was $850,000; the land cost $200,000; and, Wilson recalls, Kaufmann's design fee was $5,000 in secured stock. And it is a wonderful design.

Santa Anita has a clubhouse with lounges, restaurants, and a betting room, and a Turf Club composed entirely of private rooms. The most dramatic room is the Director's Room, with its brass bamboo trees and mag-

nificent chandelier. The Brazilian Room is a dining area decorated with early nineteenth-century wallpaper that depicts Spaniards battling with Indians.

One of the images that best symbolizes Santa Anita is the stylized version of a Thoroughbred race found on decorative panels on the front of the grandstand. The entire piece is made of punched-out sheet steel—window glass, now painted over, backs each panel.

The paddock and infield are the work of landscape architect Tommy Tomson. The paddock is based on a formal garden, with the oval walking ring at center. It can be approached from as many as eight walkways, which

The Santa Anita surroundings create a relaxing atmosphere for racetrackers.

are trimmed with boxwood hedges, topiary, and highly decorative Brazilian pepper trees. Low wooden fences that roll on casters separate the spectators from the horses, but are quickly rolled back after the horses proceed to the track, leaving the entire area free for pedestrian crossing. Statuary urns and a column in the center of the walking circle were brought from England in the 1950s by Dr. Strub. The building housing the jockey's quarters and the saddling shed was built in 1950. Santa Anita honors Seabiscuit with a statue of the famous horse on the premises.

Seabiscuit (1933–1947) was purchased in 1936 for $7,500 and has been described as an ill-tempered, half-crippled horse that, in spite of such a negative outlook, went on to become the leading money-winner of his time. A come-from-behind winner, his victories were often decided by a nose. He was ridden primarily by the oft-injured jockey Johnny Pollard, and also by the legendary George Woolf. Seabiscuit twice lost the Santa Anita Handicap by inches but, in 1940, in the final race of his career, he won it. The prize money enabled him to become the greatest money-winner of the time.

The great Seabiscuit, who lost this Santa Anita Handicap to Stagehand, eventually won the race in 1940.

Left: **Racetrackers in search of a winner.**
Right: **The bugler calls the horses to the post.**

Relaxing Entertainment

Santa Anita is the only racetrack that uses its infield every day. Track officials consider this vibrant area a great resource for the fans, and one that should be developed and maintained with their comfort and aesthetic sensibility in mind. In the early days, the flower design changed annually. It is overall a very comely, vibrant, and relaxing setting.

Wilson sums up: "My contribution was the recreation. . . . We knew that racetrackers will come, but if you include recreation, more people will come, relax. You've got to have beauty and you've got to have comfort. Olympic Stadium was the heart and soul of the whole thing [referring to the stadium designed by John Parkinson for the 1932 Olympics held in Los Angeles and used again in the 1984 Olympic Games for the main

events]. . . . You have to provide a facility to show the elegance of the sport. . . ."

Currently the infield is composed of a variety of playgrounds, refreshment stands, pavilions, and fountains and is landscaped with palm trees placed in islands of English ivy. Mariachi bands stroll the main walkway and play music before the races. The infield provides space for people to relax, play with their children, and get away from the noise of the crowd in the grandstand. Even on the biggest racing days, a fairly quiet place in the infield is usually available.

Santa Anita's patrol judges—who go to towers placed at strategic intervals around the track to monitor any interference during the race—ride to their positions in hackneys drawn by teams of two or four standardbred horses. The drivers wear tall black silk hats and coats with tails.

Morning workouts, which take place between 5:00 a.m. and 7:00 a.m., are especially colorful at Santa Anita because the ponies (the word "ponies" refers to all horses other than Thoroughbreds) are frequently Western-bred spotted horses, which provide a striking visual contrast to the sleek, solidly hued Thoroughbreds. Furthermore,

Morning workouts are open to the public and are quite a spectacle.

unlike Thoroughbred jockeys, the ponies' riders wear jeans, leather chaps, and big Western hats. It is quite a sight for general equine enthusiasts.

All these things combine to make Santa Anita a world-class facility; the professionals who operate at the track—trainers and jockeys in particular—add even more renown.

"Recreation, creature comforts, and you've got to have confidence in racing," Wilson explains. "I think that Willie Shoemaker contributed as much to racing as anyone. Everyone has confidence in Willie because he has character. . . . Willie and [Charles] Whittingham, the two of them together have created a sort of relationship between the public and the participants in racing that is a little closer than it usually is." Wilson refers to William Shoemaker, a jockey from 1949–1989, and now a trainer; and Charles Whittingham, a trainer at Santa Anita from 1934 until the present. Both established significant national records and are Hall of Famers.

Charles Whittingham, "Mr. California"

Whittingham has trained horses at Santa Anita since 1934. His office is in Barn No. 4 at the entrance of the stable area. No trainer has won as many nationwide stakes races as Charles Whittingham. On August 29, 1987, he became the first trainer to win five hundred stakes races when Ferdinand won the Cabrillo Stakes at Del Mar. One year earlier, Whittingham became the oldest trainer, at age seventy-three, to win the Kentucky

Charles Whittingham

Derby, also with Ferdinand. His jockey, Willie Shoemaker, was also the oldest jockey (he was 54) to win the classic race. Three years later, in 1989, Whittingham captured his second Kentucky Derby with Sunday Silence. The following year the Hall of Fame trainer set a new record with his 600th stakes victory (May 31, 1991, at Hollywood Park). More than two hundred of his stakes winners were ridden by Hall of Fame jockey Shoemaker. They were a great pair—Whittingham and Shoemaker—and were great winners.

In modern terms, Whittingham could be referred to as a mega-trainer. In Santa Anita's Media Guide, winning horses are listed along with the achievements of the trainer. Normally, each winning horse is listed, but heavy editing must be done each time such a biography is prepared for Whittingham: Santa Anita simply lists his top stakes wins because they couldn't fit all of his victories into the program.

When it comes to Whittingham's races in California, the information given in the Santa Anita Media Guide isn't even that specific. For instance, Whittingham's horses have won the San Juan Capistrano at Santa Anita fourteen times (most recently with Nasr El Arab in 1989), and so the Media Guide simply notes that he "won the 'Big Cap' in five different decades." He has won the Santa Anita Handicap a record ten times, the

Hollywood Gold Cup eight times, and the Oak Tree Invitational seven times, pretty much dominating California racing until trainer D. Wayne Lukas came along. (Lukas's victories are still at the stage of full listing in the Media Guide. He has not yet won enough to demand a general summary.)

Whittingham has been a leading trainer at different times at all the tracks in Southern California, earning the nickname "Mr. California." The schedule for racing in California is such that trainers can conveniently run their horses at all the Southern Californian tracks. When Hollywood Park closes at the end of July, racing continues at Del Mar until September. On Christmas Day, Santa Anita opens.

For more than twenty-five years in a row, between 1966 and 1991, Whittingham finished in the top ten money-earners for trainers nationwide. He led the list seven times: in 1970–73, 1975, 1981, and 1982. He set the single-season earnings record as a trainer in 1982, when his horses won $4,588,897. On June 19, 1992, he became only the second trainer in history to train horses that earned more than $100 million in purses. He has trained more than twenty horses with career earnings above $1 million.

Whittingham's personality could also be described as "Mr. California." Charming, fun-loving, and sociable, there are tales of his lively participation in the after-race dances held in the opening years of Del Mar. He was not only a good trainer and a good horseman, but also a very generous spirit. He taught younger men, was encourag-

ing to many, and helped others become trainers. It has been said that a great deal of the success of Santa Anita is owed to "Charlie."

Sadly, Charles Whittingham passed away on April 20, 1999—just one week after his eighty-sixth birthday.

Santa Anita's Stakes Races

During the first year of the racetrack, Roach and Strub introduced the concept of having a stakes race with $100,000 added, thereby creating the richest race in history at the time—the Santa Anita Handicap. This figure was all the more astonishing since it was set during the Great Depression. But the minds behind the new and unknown racetrack were from show business and sports entertainment—they knew they needed something big to attract attention.

One hundred thousand added was not only good advertising; it was an enticement. This rich purse lured the prominent eastern racing families to ship their horses to California for the race. With the first $100,000 Santa Anita Handicap on February 23, 1935, the importance of the Santa Anita Park was established immediately. (In 1986 the Santa Anita Handicap became the world's first stakes race with $1 million added.)

Azucar, ridden by jockey George Woolf and trained by James Rushton, won the first $100,000 (1935). Greinton, trained by Charles Whittingham and with jockey Laffit Pincay Jr. up, was the one million dollar winner in 1986. The Santa Anita Handicap has developed into one of the biggest and most important preliminary races to the Kentucky Derby. A major race in its own right, the race locally goes by the name "Big Cap."

Santa Anita's other main stakes race is the San Juan Capistrano Handicap, which is run on the park's wonderful turf course. Strub introduced the turf course in 1953. Beautiful in its conception, the course starts on a hillside northwest of the track oval and proceeds southward and downhill for about ¾-mile, with the Botanical Gardens as a backdrop. It swoops into a curve near the barns, proceeding across the dirt track and onto the turf course proper, which runs inside the dirt track oval. The race is 1¾ miles with a 6-furlong start. This course is often described as a European-style course, because the horses are out of sight for part of the race, and also because the course is irregular. This extremely handsome course is called the Camino Real (pronounced "ca-MEE-no ree-AL"). The $100,000 San Juan Capistrano Handicap was introduced during the first season of the turf track's existence. First run on March 6, 1954, the San Juan Capistrano Handicap was the first stakes race of such magnitude run on grass in the entire United States. It remains a very valuable prize.

The turf course (background) was added in 1954.

Wartime at Santa Anita

In 1941, an arbitrary and totally heartbreaking situation interrupted this world of big money, grand entertainment, and exciting racing. As soon as the United States entered World War II, Santa Anita Park was commandeered by the U.S. government.

Wilson recalls the time with sadness: "Everything was ready. The horses were in the barns, the flowers were in their beds, all we had to do was just ring the bell. Then came December seventh and all was shot down. Within a week they came and took it over and made an internment camp there. . . . The horses had to go back to the farms. The government told the horsemen to get out. We were ready to go and the rest of the racetracks were dead at that time. They could have picked Hollywood Park."

From December 1941 until October 1942 the racetrack was the site of one of the most tragic policies in American history: the internment of Japanese Americans in detention camps during World War II. Santa Anita was used as an assembly camp where Japanese Americans were housed until they were sent to camps in Wyoming, Montana, and several other states. More than 19,000 Asian people were held at Santa Anita. Barracks were erected in the parking lots and the infield; the barns were used for living spaces; and the grandstand was used as a classroom area. Wilson and Strub managed to arrange for the paddock and the Turf Club to be kept off-limits. The rest of the facility was used heavily.

When the government relocated the camp on October 27, 1942, they gave the Los Angeles Turf Club $1 million to restore the facility. Wilson says, "They went in rough shod and did a pretty good job of tearing it down. It was hard . . . but there was no damage done that couldn't be put back together." Racing resumed in 1945.

D. Wayne Lukas: Mega-trainer

With the sad departure of Charlie Whittingham, racing seems to have entered a new period of successful Western trainers. The foremost among them is D. (Darrell) Wayne Lukas. To date, Lukas has won a total of ten classic races—an impressive record. He has won the Kentucky Derby three times: with Thunder Gulch in 1995, Grindstone in 1996, and the filly Winning Colors in 1988. He has won the Preakness Stakes four times: with Codex in 1980, Tank's Prospect in 1985, Tabasco Cat in 1994, and Timber Country in 1995. He's won the difficult Belmont Stakes three straight times: with Tabasco Cat in 1994, Thunder Gulch in 1995, and Editor's Note in 1996.

For about a decade, starting in the 1980s, Lukas seemed invincible. His success left the racing world both proud of him and disconcerted by him. Lukas, however, was not an overnight success. Before training Thoroughbreds (he started in 1978), he was the leading trainer in quarter horse racing, with twenty-three world champions. As a Thoroughbred trainer, he has won the Eclipse Award four times, in 1985, 1986, 1987, and 1994. In 1986 he trained Lady's Secret, daughter of

Secretariat, to ten stakes race victories (eight of these were Grade I stakes).

Lukas's career has not been all wine and roses, however. It is the nature of sports to experience major letdowns and upsets. Starting with Tabasco Cat's victory in the 1994 Preakness, D. Wayne Lukas-trained horses won six straight Triple Crown races. This stupendous winning streak ended when a horse named Louis Quatorze—trained by Lukas's rival, Nick Zito—won the Preakness in 1996. Though the Preakness loss may have dampened its sweetness a bit, 1996 was still one of Lukas's greatest years, having won two of the three Triple Crown races. They were his third Kentucky

D. Wayne Lukas

Derby (with Grindstone) and his third straight Belmont Stakes (with Editor's Note).

Now past sixty, the trainer of twenty national champion horses is still a dashing figure in the world of Thoroughbred racing. Often considered cold in nature, he is labeled corporate. This would appear to be inevitable since the ante is high. In 1988, Lukas surpassed Charlie Whittingham as the all-time leading money-earning trainer. He holds the record for earnings for a single season, $17,842,358, in 1988. With the exception of 1993, Lukas has led the nation in earnings every year since 1983. In 1997, he led the nation with horses that won over $10,000,000 in purses. This is an important figure since he earns a percentage of many of his horses' winnings. One aspect of his job, in fact, is to act as the purchasing agent for owners wishing to buy unproved yearlings—la creme de la creme with good pedigrees and good bodies—for $500,000 or $1,000,000. His expertise in determining the right horses to buy is virtually unmatched, and he earns a handsome sum for the effort.

Regarding his barns, Lukas is what you'd call "house proud." His are the most immaculate stables on any backstretch. It does not matter if they are temporary (those used for a few weeks before the Breeders' Cup or at the Kentucky Derby, for example), Lukas still transplants strips of grass, brings in potted hedges, hangs flower boxes, adds an iron jockey—whatever it takes—to make the rattiest barns irreproachable. His flagship barns are located at Santa Anita and are, of course, perfect.

Milestones

1934, December 25—Santa Anita Park celebrates its Opening Day.

1934—Photo-finish cameras are put into operation for the first time at any Thoroughbred track, just in time for the 1934–35 meeting.

1935—Gillie, owned by Mrs. Henry Payne Whitney's Greentree Stable and ridden by Silvio Coucci, wins the inaugural Santa Anita Derby, which offers a purse of $26,650.

1937—Seven horses literally start from outside the stall gate as twenty-one starters went to post; it is the largest Santa Anita Derby field ever. Fairy Hill is the upset winner.

1938—Stagehand captures the Santa Anita Derby and the Santa Anita Handicap. He is the only horse ever to win both races in the same season.

1939—Ciencia becomes the first filly to win the Santa Anita Derby, doing so by a five-length victory.

1940, March 2—Beaten by a nose in both the 1937 and 1938 Santa Anita Handicaps, Seabiscuit finally wins the "Big Cap" (Santa Anita Handicap) in his final race. He retired as the then-leading money-winning horse in the world.

1945—Santa Anita reopens, three years after the government commandeered the track for use as an internment camp during World War II.

1946—Legendary jockey George Woolf is killed in a racing accident at Santa Anita.

1950—The George Woolf Memorial Jockey Award is established to honor a jockey whose career and character reflect credit on the sport. Gordon Glisson is the first winner.

1952—Hill Gail (Calumet Farm) wins the Santa Anita Derby, and then carries its owners' devil's red and blue colors to victory in the Kentucky Derby, becoming the first horse to win both races.

1954—Determine completes the Santa Anita Derby/Kentucky Derby sweep.

1954, March 6—Santa Anita Park presents the first $100,000 stakes race on the grass when the San Juan Capistrano Handicap is run. By Zeus, ridden by Ray York and trained by W. J. "Buddy" Hirsch, is the winner.

1955—For the third time in four years, the Santa Anita Derby winner goes on to win the Kentucky Derby, as well. This time it is the great Swaps.

1957, February 28—Johnny Longden becomes the first jockey in history to reach 5,000 victories.

1959—Silver Spoon becomes the second filly to win the Santa Anita Derby.

1966, March 12—In the last race of his forty-year career, Johnny Longden wins the San Juan Capistrano Handicap at Santa Anita Park, aboard George Royal. He retires with a record number of victories, 6,032.

1969, March 1—Tuesdee Testa, twenty-seven, becomes the first female jockey to win a race at a major American Thoroughbred track when she wins the third race at Santa Anita Park aboard Buz On.

1970—Jockey Laffit Pincay Jr. is awarded the Woolf Award.

1971, January 28—Hazel Longden, wife of jockey Johnny Longden, becomes the first woman to train a Santa Anita stakes race winner when Diplomatic Agent wins the San Vicente Stakes.

1972—Jockey Angel Cordero Jr. is awarded the Woolf Award.

1975—Avatar is the first Santa Anita Derby winner to capture the Belmont Stakes. He is second in the Kentucky Derby and fifth in the Preakness.

1976, March 14—Willie Shoemaker wins his 7,000th career victory, aboard Charlie Whittingham-trained Royal Derby II, in the fifth race at Santa Anita Park.

1978—The great Affirmed wins the Santa Anita Derby, then goes on to win the Triple Crown! (The Santa Anita Derby has produced the winners of twenty-six Triple Crown races.)

1980—In his third season training Thoroughbreds, D. Wayne Lukas wins the first of his record four Santa Anita Derby runnings with Codex. Pat Valenzuela, at seventeen, becomes the youngest jockey to win the race.

1984, July 29–August 12—The equestrian sports of the Los Angeles-hosted Olympic Games are presented at Santa Anita. Crowds averaging nearly twenty-six thousand per day attend the nine-day event.

1985, March 3—Willie Shoemaker becomes the first jockey in history to win $100 million in purses after he wins the Santa Anita Handicap aboard Lord at War.

1985, March 8—Jockey Chris McCarron rides his 4,000th career winner, Hawkley (Great Britain), in the fifth race at Santa Anita Park.

1985, March 30—Laffit Pincay Jr. becomes the second jockey in history to surpass Johnny Longden's record of 6,032 victories, riding Sovereignty to victory in the sixth race at Santa Anita.

1986, November 1—Santa Anita hosts the third Breeders' Cup. The event draws 69,155 fans.

1987—Jockey Willie Shoemaker, fifty-seven, wins a record eighth Santa Anita Derby with Temperate Sil, trained by Charlie Whittingham. It is Whittingham's first Santa Anita Derby win.

1988—Winning Colors becomes the third filly to win the Santa Anita Derby. She goes on to become the third filly to win the Kentucky Derby.

1989—Sunday Silence—trained by Charlie Whittingham—wins the Santa Anita Derby by eleven lengths. Then, against heavily favored Easy Goer, he captures the Kentucky Derby and the Preakness (although Easy Goer wins the Belmont). Sunday Silence becomes the Horse of the Year and wins the Breeders' Cup Classic.

1990, February 3—Willie Shoemaker rides the final race of his illustrious forty-one-year career as a jockey in the $100,000-added Legend's Last Ride turf race. The largest crowd of the season turns out for "the Shoe's" retirement; 64,573 fans come to the track.

1992—A. P. Indy wins the Santa Anita Derby and is the seventh Derby horse to be honored as Horse of the Year.

1993, March 10—At age forty-one, jockey Eddie Delahoussaye has his 5,000th career winner, aboard Ackler in the fifth race at Santa Anita Park. He is the fourteenth rider in North American Thoroughbred racing to reach that plateau.

1993, November 6—The tenth Breeders' Cup is held at Santa Anita Park. The day of races attracts 87,674 people to Santa Anita.

1997, February 17—Alex Solis is honored with the Woolf Award as the most consistent winner on Southern California's riding circuit during 1996. In that year he rides 39–1 longshot Dare and Go to a stunning upset over the great Cigar in the $1 million Pacific Classic at Del Mar.

1999, April 20—Charles Whittingham, "Mr. California," passes away. He was eighty-six.

Keeneland Race Course

Lexington, Kentucky
(Established 1936)

In many ways, Keeneland is the closest to God of all the American racetracks. It runs two racing meetings per year (totaling thirty-one days), in April and November, to showcase its fine Kentucky horses.

Everything is a little different at Keeneland, and some would argue, a little better. Take the layout of the facilities, for example. The clubhouse is at the head of the homestretch rather than in the direction of the first turn—as it is at most other American racetracks—and the grandstand faces west instead of east. Keeneland benefits from both of these deviations since getting a good view of your horse as it moves down the stretch toward the finish is paramount; and facing into the sun during the late afternoon on a chilly spring or autumn day is more of a pleasure than a hardship.

Until recently, Keeneland didn't have a public address system because it was generally accepted that the citizens of this part of Kentucky knew what was going on. In the past at Keeneland, you could hear the horses hooves as they raced over the track—and, occasionally, a bird song. Now, since 1997, an announcer calls the races over a loudspeaker system. Thankfully, the loudspeaker remains silent between races.

One would never consider Keeneland a rural racetrack, even though it is located in rolling bluegrass country and surrounded on three sides by horse farms. The front of Keeneland, where all visitors come and go, is adjacent to the airport. Personal planes grounded in view across from the racetrack convey the wealth of the people in attendance, especially during July's annual selected yearling sales. One regular notable attendee is Mohammed bin Rashid al Maktoum, of Dubai, whose

Opposite: **Keeneland's grandstand faces west, an unusual but intentional position.**

Top: **Keeneland lies in the middle of horse country.**

personal Boeing 727 with "United Arab Emirates" painted on the body announces his presence.

Keeneland Race Course is a highly regarded corporation that, among other things, conducts five significant Thoroughbred auctions each year that are attended by owners and breeders from the United States, Japan, Australia, the Middle East, and Europe. Regular attendees include millionaires Kazuo Nakamura, Fusao Sekiguchi, Morio Sakurai, Zenya Yoshida, M. V. O'Brien, Savros Niarchos, and Robert Sangster. Keeneland, in fact, is one of the most illustrious Thoroughbred markets in the entire world.

Gatepost from the old Kentucky Association track, moved to the driveway at Keeneland.

John Oliver Keene's Racetrack

The entrance of Keeneland Race Course is straddled by the old gateposts of the Kentucky Association track constructed in Lexington in 1826 (which itself was a replacement of racetracks dating from 1787). A long driveway leads from the highway up a gradual slope to the race course. Fieldstone buildings, relatively small for a racetrack but still imposing in scale, give one a sense that one is approaching a country house. Although the present track was organized under its current name in 1936, it is in fact a continuation of a private racetrack built by John Oliver "Jack" Keene in 1916.

At the core of the modern racetrack are Keene's old buildings, constructed of limestone with flat roofs and ironwork ornamentation. The main track and the paddock's walking ring are direct remnants of Keene's private racetrack complex, as well. (Expansions in 1936, 1953, 1963, 1984, l986, 1990, and 1994 are quotations of that early straightforward architecture.)

A native of Lexington, Keene was an international-

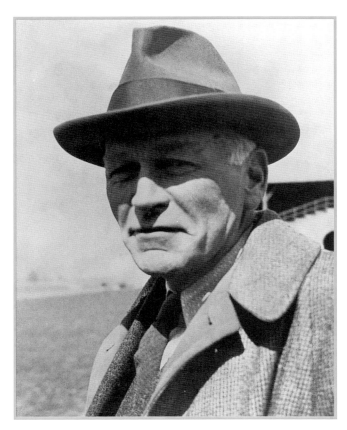

John Oliver "Jack" Keene

ly celebrated horse trainer. He trained horses in Russia in 1902–03 in the stables of Henri Block and Michael Lazeroff. Lazeroff's Keene-trained horse, Irish Lad, won an important series of races in Warsaw, Moscow, and St. Petersburg. Keene also trained and raced horses in California and Japan, where he won seventeen races with American Thoroughbreds.

He returned to Kentucky in 1909 and trained horses at the Kentucky Association track located on 5th Street in Lexington. At the same time, he was planning his dream track. He began construction in 1916. He was not a rich man, nor did he want to develop his private track for commercial purposes. Keene planned to build a track that would celebrate great Thoroughbred racing, for its own sake.

Keene's first track manager, W. T. Bishop, recalled in a 1983 interview that Keene was "a man who wished to have a private racetrack where he could invite his friends; where they could bring their horses and race against each other even if racing were outlawed on all the racetracks in the nation or if racing was declared to be illegal or illicit or otherwise. His thing was that he would have some kind of place where he could continue to operate and that he could continue to own horses, breed horses, produce horses, race horses, train horses—do all those kinds of things."

Much of Keene's original creation is still there today, including his big fieldstone stallion barn. But it didn't come easily. After nearly twenty years and a $400,000 investment, Keene ran out of money. By 1933, when the Kentucky Association track closed after falling into general disrepair, Keene's racetrack was still unfinished. Lexington horsemen in need of a racetrack set about making a deal with Keene. Their priorities were simple: they wanted to see good horses race, in their own particular part of Kentucky, furnished with bluegrass and God's sunshine. Although Thoroughbred racing was experiencing an economic boom in California, Illinois, Arkansas, and Florida—mostly thanks to the wagering that sustained them economically—neither Keene nor the people of Lexington wanted to depend on gambling. This created a dilemma. These were Depression years and it was not particularly easy to raise money for a horse track.

However, many of Lexington's city fathers favored reviving racing in the city. They felt the loss of racing in the heart of Thoroughbred country was unconscionable. Major Louie A. Beard, Jack Young, Hal Price Headley, and James Bassett Jr. were leading figures in the preservation of the sport. They envisioned a new kind of track, to be operated by a nonprofit association, with racing conducted for the benefit of those most concerned—the horsemen—and with the profits to be invested into the track and into the community. Keene's private racing complex was chosen as the site of the new venture. Recognizing a "kinship of ideas" between himself and the character of the proposed venture, Keene sold the property to the newly formed Keeneland Association at a bargain price. The terms of the sale were 147½ acres and the buildings for $130,000 in cash and $10,000 in preferred stock plus a conceptual understanding and agreement.

The corporation was formed in April 1935. By June, the drive to raise $350,000 for the racetrack's start-up costs had begun. Preferred capital stock was offered for $100 per share, with payment to be made in four installments. (By October 15, 1936, $305,000 had been collected from the sales of preferred stock.)

In May 1936, as part of the capital building drive, memberships to the Keeneland Club were offered by invitation only. Lifetime memberships cost $500; associate memberships were sold for $50 per year. By October 1936, an additional $55,000 was collected by the initial sale of memberships. (More than fifty years later, the membership process reflects practices that are routinely called "elitist" in America. Lifetime memberships are closed, but associate memberships are still offered to a select few.) Lifetime membership required

Hal Price Headley

no further dues, entitled the member to access the clubhouse and any part of the grounds, and ensured two seats on the "Club Balcony." Associate memberships allowed admittance to the clubhouse.

A list of members printed in the *Lexington Herald* (October 15, 1936) consists primarily of life members from Lexington and New York. Some owners of other racetracks throughout the country, like Dr. Robert Strub and Hal Roach of Santa Anita Park, and Joseph Widener of Hialeah Park, subscribed out of good will. The list of associate members was almost entirely composed of people from Lexington, Kentucky and Cincinnati, Ohio.

Once the money was raised, Keeneland's founders set out to create a wonderful place for Thoroughbred racing. After reviewing submissions by three local architects, the Keeneland Association hired Robert W. McMeekin to develop a design for making adaptations to the clubhouse, creating new jockey's quarters, and building a new grandstand. The architect modified Keene's buildings slightly to make a clubroom, then designed a grandstand of limestone and wood which seated 2,500 people—the gable end being comprised of a series of arches later repeated throughout the racetrack buildings.

Alice Chandler, daughter of Hal Price Headley (president of Keeneland from 1935 to 1951), was eight years old when Keeneland Race Course was started. She recalls spending a lot of time there with her father. "If I wasn't under his heel, I was running straight behind."

The magnificent Keeneland Library.

Chandler stressed the effect that the Depression had on Keeneland. She remembers that all the equipment used at the track in the early days came from Beaumont Farm, which her father owned. Beaumont Farm—one of the largest in Lexington—covered more than a thousand acres. (Beaumont is still the site of a large farm, but much of it has been sold off and now includes several shopping centers.) The horseman's kitchen served soft boiled eggs in drinking glasses because the track could not afford to buy plates or flatware. The first race meet was held in the fall of 1936. The track made a $20 profit on this inaugural meet, but the simple fact that a profit was turned was an important issue.

Chandler likes to describe the development of the racetrack as a community effort. She talks about the "spirit of Keeneland," a racetrack formed by Thoroughbred owners and for Thoroughbred owners, and which remains largely an owners' track.

For the first thirty years, none of the officers were paid a salary. (To this day, directors serve without salaried remuneration, and stockholders never have and never can receive stock dividends. Instead, profits are returned in the form of stakes purses and are used in capital improvements. And, because all the usual profits are supplemented by the sale of wonderful Kentucky Thoroughbreds, Keeneland is a very rich racetrack.)

Appropriately, since Keeneland is a bit like a country house, there is a library. It opened in 1939 with the gift of 2,300 volumes from William Arnold Hanger, a trustee and the director of Keeneland at the time. It is a wonderful place to visit or to work. Everything there is done the old-fashioned way—the librarians are helpful and the volumes are leather bound. The account of the first Kentucky Derby in the *Spirit of the Times* is there, bound in leather. There are overstuffed couches and armchairs for taking a break. The current collection holds six thousand volumes and contains stud books, rare volumes, early racing periodicals, and a major photography archive, including the archive of early track photographer Charles Cooke. Racing aficionados from all over the world consult this photography collection. But, of course, most people go to Keeneland for the racing.

Racing at Keeneland

In 1938, Preeminent—a horse owned by Hal Price Headley—won the Phoenix Stakes, the oldest stakes race in the United States. It dates back to 1831 when it was run at the Kentucky Association track in Lexington. The race has been known as the Brennan, the Chiles, the Phoenix Association, the Phoenix Hotel Stakes, and the Phoenix Handicap. Last run at the Association track in 1930, the Phoenix was revived at Keeneland in the spring of 1937 and was named for the old Phoenix Hotel in Lexington.

In 1943–45, the Phoenix was renewed as part of the dual wartime meeting of Keeneland and Churchill Downs (both tracks couldn't operate at the same time during World War II). Keeneland actually leased Churchill Downs during those years, and the Phoenix had been run at Churchill around then. After the war, the Phoenix became an important spring race for 3 year olds. (Today, the race is held in the fall season at Keeneland and is called the Phoenix Breeders' Cup—it's an important prep race for the national Breeders' Cup.)

The most famous stakes race at Keeneland is the Blue Grass Stakes. Its major attraction is the fact that it is held each spring prior to the Kentucky Derby. Through the years, eighteen horses have run in the Blue Grass Stakes and gone on to win the Derby, including Unbridled in 1990, Strike the Gold in 1991, Sea Hero in 1993, and Thunder Gulch in 1995.

During one period of its history, the Blue Grass Stakes produced nine Derby winners in a fourteen-year span, starting with Tomy Lee (1959), and followed by Decidedly ('62), Chateaugay ('63), Northern Dancer ('64), Lucky Debonair ('65), Proud Clarion ('67), Forward Pass ('68), Dust Commander ('70), and Riva Ridge ('72).

The first Blue Grass Stakes race was run in 1937. It was won by a horse named Fencing, ridden by jockey Earl Sande. (Billionaire and Brooklyn came in second and third.) The second Blue Grass Stakes, held in 1938, was won by Bull Lea, a colt owned by Calumet Farm. He beat

Opposite top: **Preeminent, winner of the 1937 Phoenix Stakes.**
Opposite bottom: **Crossing the finish line, last race day of the season, October 29, 1988.**

Menow, a horse owned by racetrack president Hal Price Headley's Beaumont Farm. Alice Chandler says she had not thought it possible that Menow could be beaten. "I was twelve years old, and cried and cried."

The Farm Next Door: Calumet

Calumet Farm is located next door to Keeneland Race Course. It is a huge farm with barns that are painted white with red trim, and there are miles of white fences surrounding. In the Kentucky landscape, where fences and tobacco barns are covered in black creosote which blend in and hug the landscape, Calumet catches the eye like a flash of light with its unique colors. Many

of the farm's horses caught the attention of the entire world in its best years, and many of them cut their teeth at Keeneland.

The story of Calumet Farm is one of the most glamourous chapters in Thoroughbred racing history. Warren Wright, son of William Monroe Wright (owner of the Calumet Baking Powder Company), inherited Calumet Farm in 1931. From 1931 to 1936 he transformed it from a farm with standardbred horses to Thoroughbred breeding and racing horses. He was influenced by Chicago's John D. Hertz, Yellow Cab tycoon, then-director of Arlington Park in Chicago. Warren Wright, a financial genius, had increased the holdings of his father's

1941 Triple Crown winner Whirlaway with owner Warren Wright.

company, Calumet Baking Powder, and then sold the company to General Foods, Inc. for $40 million. In the context of the period, the 1930s, Wright had ample money for his Thoroughbred venture.

It is generally agreed that Warren Wright made three profound moves that led to Calumet's success. First, Wright bought one-quarter interest in Kentucky breeder A. B. Hancock's imported stallion, Blenhiem II. (A. B. Hancock was the first breeder to import stallions.) Second, he purchased Bull Lea at the Saratoga yearling sale. These two stallions became the foundation for much of Calumet's success (from them came two Triple Crown winners—Whirlaway and Citation—and many other great Thoroughbreds followed). And finally, Calumet acquired the services of Ben Allyn Jones as its trainer. By 1939, Calumet had set the stage for the legendary decade to follow.

In 1940, Whirlaway, a 2-year-old colt (sired by Blenheim II out of the mare Dustwhirl), won seven out of sixteen starts. Among these were two important fall races, the Saratoga Special and the Hopeful Stakes, earning $77,275. This young colt vaulted Calumet to third place on the list of leading money-winning owners.

Ben Jones stepped in and added the magic touch of an exceptional trainer. When Whirlaway began his 1941 campaign with the tendency to bolt toward the outside rail, Jones corrected this flaw before Derby Day by modifying Whirlaway's blinkers. These blinkers (now on display at the Kentucky Horse Park near Lexington) consisted of a hood with ears and a face mask that cov-

ered the right eye. The young colt won the Derby by an 8-length margin in 2:01⅖. He went on to win the Preakness and the Belmont Stakes, becoming the fifth Triple Crown winner and the 1941 Horse of the Year. The money he earned made Calumet the leading money-winning owner with $475,091. Whirlaway won thirteen times after starting twenty races in 1941.

Whirlaway became Horse of the Year once again in 1942, winning twelve of twenty-two starts, and by July he had become the world's leading money winner with $560,911.50 in purses. He was the first horse to pass the $500,000 mark in wins. He was America's favorite horse. At 5 years old, in 1943, Whirlaway made two starts and was retired. He had a lifetime racing record of thirty-two wins out of sixty races. He was later leased to Marcel Boussac to breed, in France, where he died in 1953. He bred seventeen stakes winners.

Calumet had other champion horses. The farm began shipping them to compete in races all over the country. Some of Calumet's notable winners include Some Chance, Sun Again, and Mar-Kell (a filly). Their names are engraved on the hundreds of silver and gold trophies, plates, and cups that were won by Calumet Farm during its fabulous racing decade of the 1940s. Other winning fillies bred at Calumet include Twilight Tear, Miss Keeneland, and Nellie.

At the time, Calumet was a farm like no other. A normal Kentucky-based farm with a good racing division would send a few choice horses to an occasional race on the eastern seaboard. Calumet started racing horses everywhere: from Lexington, Kentucky to New York, California, Chicago, and Florida—wherever they needed to go to run in the greatest stakes races.

Furthermore, the farm bred 98 percent of the horses they raced—another large and exacting operation. The trophies amassed by Calumet Farm are overwhelming evidence of this great feat and of their success.

Calumet's owner, Warren Wright Sr. died on December 28, 1950. In nineteen years he had built a turf giant. His widow, Lucille Parker Wright, successfully held onto Calumet's position for quite a few years.

In 1978, Lucille Wright, who had remarried and was now Mrs. Gene Markey, was still the owner of Calumet. She and her husband, also an octogenarian, turned up to see Calumet's 3-year-old colt, Alydar, run in the Blue Grass Stakes at Keeneland. The couple sat in a station wagon parked on the clubhouse lawn. Then they struggled out of the station wagon to the rail to catch a glimpse of their horse.

"As the horses came to the head of the stretch," said ABC-TV's Jim McKay, "the couple seemed to forget their arthritis and wheelchair status. The thrill of victory was so visible. Mrs. Markey, winner of eight Kentucky Derbies, looked like a young owner winning her first race."

The track historians report that she raised her right hand and shook it as Alydar raced by on his way to an overpowering 13¼-length victory, and that she never attended another race. Nor did Alydar win so easily again. He raced all year, losing at times by fractions to Affirmed, a kind of metaphor for the end of Calumet Farm.

In March, 1992, Calumet Farm was sold to Henryk de Kwiatkowski for $17 million. He renamed the entity Kennelot Stables Ltd. Calumet Farm.

Keeneland Sales

From the very beginning, Keeneland Race Course seemed destined to become a leading venue for sales of Thoroughbred yearlings. By the 1960s buyers came from all over the world to purchase Thoroughbreds at the auctions. The consignment of horses for auction, primarily from the farms nearby, is the major business conducted at Keeneland and is commonly referred to as "The Sales." It all started a half-century ago.

**Eddie Arcaro and Mrs. Gene Markey
in paddock, April 12th, 1952.**

During World War II, due to travel restrictions, it became impossible to ship horses to Saratoga for the annual August sales. That year, horses were sold at Keeneland, in the paddock under a tent, by the Breeders' Sales Company (which was absorbed by the Keeneland Association in 1962). The inaugural sale at Keeneland, in the summer of 1943, lasted three days (August 9–11), with two sessions daily, at 3:30 p.m. and 8:30 p.m. The sale commanded front-page news each day in the *Lexington Herald,* which referred to the auction as "the transplanted" Saratoga yearling sale. (The 1945 Kentucky Derby winner—Hoop, Jr.—was sold for $10,200 at that very first yearling sale. To date, fourteen Kentucky Derby winners have been sold at Keeneland.)

Some of these auctions have been conducted with record-breaking results, and with more drama than some runnings of the Kentucky Derby! In the early 1980s, Northern Dancer's offspring were greatly coveted. The Irish in attendance were particularly keen to acquire progeny from the "fire line" produced by Northern Dancer's genes. A team of buyers—Robert Sangster, Vincent O'Brien, and John Magnier—began purchasing the yearlings (these were young, untried horses) for around a million dollars each. Suddenly they encountered a competitor, Sheik Mohammed bin Rashid al Maktoum, who was equally interested in increasing the speed of his racing stable. The bidding started to climb from $1 million to $2 million to $3 million per horse! Sheik Mohammed walked away, and Sangster, who owns betting establishments in England, left with the horse he wanted but paid double his usual amount. The following year Sangster and his colleagues once again got what they were bidding for, but at a price of $4.2 million.

Left: **"The Sales" at Keeneland is an important annual event.**

Right: **Sheik Mohammed bin Rashid al Maktoum (center) with Charles Spiller at the 1989 Yearling Sale.**

In 1983, the sales arrived with general hysteria in the air. The bidding opened at $1 million and continued upward to a new high, $4.5 million. Everyone else who was in on the bidding stopped at $5.2 million. Now it was a duel. Up and up it climbed, then evened out at $9.5 million. Sheik Maktoum raised to $9.6 million. Sangster then sang out $10 million! Everyone was shocked. Maktoum must have realized that the Sangster group had come a bit unwired. They had reached their absolute financial and emotional limit: $10.2 million. The horse went to Sheik Maktoum.

The Strongest Pedigrees

The importance of this small area of Kentucky to the worldwide Thoroughbred community is that it is the home of the fastest and strongest pedigreed horses in the world. In the farms lying around Keeneland is a concentration of premier stallions and eight thousand broodmares. If you want fast horses, you must consider a trip to Kentucky. That was the reason for Queen Elizabeth II's trip to America in 1984. She was visiting her broodmares at Lane's End Farm where she had been advised to breed her mares in order to increase the speed in the progeny. (More than fifteen years later, the last of the queen's broodmares are housed at Mill Ridge Farm, with Alice Chandler.)

Chandler's career as a breeder has functioned completely in stride with Keeneland. It is here that she raced her best horses, and here that she firmed up her reputation as a world-class Thoroughbred breeder.

"We've topped the September sales at Keeneland several times," Chandler says. "I always say that I'd rather be a boutique than a department store. And all of our clients are friends."

And, it appears, she counts England's monarch as a friend, as well. "She has a great sense of humor. I am very comfortable with her because she is very knowledgeable about horses. . . . She is a woman who likes horses," Chandler says.

Each year Chandler is invited to Ascot—England's most prestigious racing event. "We have tea. It is our chance to visit. . . . She is not my queen. She is an extremely intelligent person who is concerned about her horses. I've never talked to her about anything else."

In 1984, Elizabeth II attended the races at Keeneland when the race course inaugurated a 1⅛-mile turf race for fillies. The race was called the Queen Elizabeth II Challenge Cup, and is now commonly referred to as the QE2. For Elizabeth II's visit, Keeneland built a half-oval winner's circle in order that she might present the challenge cup in comfort. It is a small area carved out of the apron floor of the grandstand, enclosed by a low iron fence set in rustic field stone and floored in crushed brick. This replaced the usual winner's circle—a circle drawn in the dirt by the chalkman who, with a muslin bag of chalk and flour on a string with a peg, created a fresh one after each race. Most tracks had graduated to permanent winner's circles years earlier, but Keeneland considered it unnecessary until the royal visit.

For really big events (after stakes races, for example) Keeneland normally holds the presentation awards in the infield so that everybody in the stands can easily see all the principals—the horse, jockey, trainer, owners, and the gold or silver cup, plate, or bowl that is carried out and placed on a table covered in black and orange felt cloth (the colors of Princeton University, Keene's alma mater). A series of skiffs are placed across the dirt track, carried there by the grounds crew, which provide a walking bridge to the grass on the other side. This precise simplicity, the best of racetrack ritual, is unmatched even at Saratoga.

Keeneland Today

On April 24, 1998, Keeneland added a steeplechase race to its roster. Called "The Royal Chase for the Sport of Kings," the event was inaugurated by England's Princess Anne. More commonly called "The Royal Chase," this race is run on a course of 2¼ miles over twelve fences. In sanctioning such a race, Keeneland is endorsing the skill and stamina of older horses, encouraging European competition, and promoting running on the grass.

The racetrack now seems to be gearing up for bigger events. Recently Keeneland Race Course has become a much larger complex—larger and more visually sophisticated. The grandstand has been extended and a row of corporate boxes added. Oddly enough, it only makes the racetrack more intimate. The new extension brings the end of the grandstand quite near to the barns that fan out in a small valley that lies below. The barn area at Keeneland is unlike most, if not all, in America. Where other tracks require credentials for people to enter the barn area, Keeneland's backside is open. Anybody can walk into the stable area. How is this possible?

Kentuckian Keene Daingerfield, a noted racing official, observes that "almost everybody in that community has seen some races; almost everybody knows somebody that owns a horse or a part of a horse or owns a mare. The entire community is so horse-oriented that I think you've got a very educated crowd."

Queen Elizabeth meets the jockeys, 1984.

Backstretch at Keeneland.

Milestones

1936, October 11—More than 15,000 people attend open house at the racetrack.

1936, October 15–24—Keeneland holds its first nine-day fall meeting. Paid attendance totals 25,337 spectators.

1937—Preeminent wins the Phoenix Stakes—the oldest stakes race in the United States, which dates back to 1831 at the Kentucky Association track in Lexington.

1938, April 2—Future Triple Crown winner Whirlaway is foaled at Calumet Farm in Lexington, Kentucky.

1938, April 25—The first auction of Thoroughbreds is held in the Keeneland paddock. A total of thirty-one lots brings $24,885—an average of $802.74 per horse.

1938—Bull Lea wins the Blue Grass Stakes (which was first run at the Association track in 1911), an important prep race for the Kentucky Derby.

1940—Whirlaway wins the Breeders' Futurity (a race inaugurated at the Kentucky Association track in Lexington in 1910). He comes in second in the Blue Grass Stakes, then goes on to win the Triple Crown.

1943, August 9–11—The first yearling sale at Keeneland is conducted under a tent in the paddock. The auction runs for three days.

1948—Citation wins the Blue Grass Stakes and goes on to win the Triple Crown.

1956, October 18—Nashua, the 1955 Horse of the Year, gallops at Keeneland in his final public appearance prior to going to stud at Spendthrift Farm.

1956, October 19—Keeneland holds the inaugural running of the Spinster Stakes.

1962, April 3—At the age of forty-six, jockey Eddie Arcaro announces his retirement. He retires with 4,779 victories including two Triple Crowns, won with Whirlaway and Citation.

1965—Kelso, five-time Horse of the Year (1960–1964), appears at Keeneland the day before the Blue Grass Stakes as part of his tour of American tracks. Proceeds from his appearances go for equine research.

1965—Foreign purchases at all of Keeneland's sales go over the million-dollar mark ($1,019,725) for the first time in history.

Paddock and saddling shed.

1971—The Blue Grass Stakes marks the first million-dollar day of wagering in Keeneland's history ($1,052,866). Riva Ridge, from Meadow Stable, finishes first in the Blue Grass and goes on to win the Kentucky Derby.

1979—Spectacular Bid, from Hawksworth Farm, finishes first in the Blue Grass and first in the Kentucky Derby.

1984—The first phase of a $3-million construction project is completed before the spring meeting.

1984, October 11—Queen Elizabeth II attends the races at Keeneland.

1985—Keeneland, in the fall meeting, becomes the first organized track in Kentucky to hold grass racing.

1991—Strike the Gold, trained by Nicholas P. Zito, wins the Blue Grass and also takes first in the Kentucky Derby.

1992, March 26—Henryk de Kwiatkowski purchases Calumet Farm for $17 million at auction, paying an additional $210,000 for the Calumet name.

1993—Keeneland holds its inaugural "April Two-Year-Olds-in-Training Sale." A total of 108 horses sell for $6,817,500, averaging $63,215, the highest average of any 2-year-old sale in North America in 1993.

1993—For the first time in Keeneland history, the in-the-money finishers in the Kentucky Derby (Sea Hero, Prairie Bayou, and Wild Gale) and the Preakness Stakes (Prairie Bayou, Cherokee Run and El Bakan) had all first raced at Keeneland's spring meeting.

1997—Ending a longtime tradition of having no public address system, Keeneland introduces an announcer to call the races over the loudspeaker.

Winner's circle at Keeneland.

1997—D. Wayne Lukas receives the Kentucky Thoroughbred Media's 1997 Trainer of the Year award, after winning seventy-three races on the state's circuit. He was the leading trainer in winning purses at Keeneland thirteen times, and at Churchill Downs ten times. He has saddled the winners of a record thirty-three stakes winners at Keeneland. He has been the nation's leading trainer with an amazing number of wins—fourteen—winning thirteen Breeders' Cup races, three Kentucky Derbies, four runnings of the Preakness, and three Belmonts.

1998, April 24—The first running of the Royal Chase for the Sport of Kings steeplechase for 4 year olds and older is held. The event is inaugurated by Princess Anne of England.

Del Mar
Fairgrounds and
Thoroughbred Club

Del Mar, California
(Established 1937)

The Del Mar Fairgrounds and Thoroughbred Club, located twenty miles north of San Diego and one hundred miles south of Los Angeles, was commissioned and built in 1937 by the State of California for the 22nd District Agricultural Association. Actors Bing Crosby and Pat O'Brien were

the founders of the club. Crosby, an extremely well known singer and movie actor, was president, and O'Brien was board president. Bill Quigley (a former professional football player) initiated the idea of the combining the fairgrounds and Turf Club, and was its first vice president.

Before the Fairgrounds and Thoroughbred Club were built, the town of Del Mar was little more than bluffs on the sea, a pier, a stop on the highway between Los Angeles and San Diego. A golf course covered the area that was to become the Fairgrounds. When the golf course was hit by a Pacific storm in 1926 it became sea-logged and largely unusable, and then was finally closed in 1930.

In 1933, California's 22nd District was searching for a permanent location for its agricultural fairgrounds. The agricultural fair was not held at all in the early 1930s because of the Depression, but when pari-mutuel wagering was legalized in California in 1933, the project of combining the fairgrounds and racetrack was conceived. But the process of bringing this idea to life was a difficult one, since gambling and tax money didn't mix well with the public. Crosby—who owned Thoroughbreds and lived in nearby Rancho Santa Fe—was brought in on the project. He contributed a very substantial portion of the initial investment for the horse track (along with O'Brien and Quigley), and also put a good face on the project sim-

Opposite: **Del Mar lies on the coast of the Pacific Ocean.**
Left: **Bing Crosby greets patrons on opening day.**

ply by being Bing Crosby. The state of California, in turn, paid for the Fairgrounds.

Crosby was the president of the racetrack for its first nine years. His personal touch was everywhere. He co-wrote and recorded a theme song for Del Mar called "Where the Turf Meets the Surf," which he often sang on race days. On opening day, he personally greeted the racing fans at the entrance gates. His presence and the presence of his friends made Del Mar work right from the start. The seaside setting was a pretty good draw, too.

The racetrack is located near the beach of a small inlet where the San Dieguito River Basin joins the Pacific Ocean. Trainers would take their horses to the ocean for conditioning. Here, they swam in the therapeutic saltwater, rolled in the sand, and ran along the waters' edge on the beach. It is not at all difficult to imagine how pleasant it must have been. Meanwhile, everyone at the Thoroughbred Club was relaxed as well. The creators of Del Mar always made it a priority to establish a comfortable atmosphere at the track. This spirit has prevailed over the club ever since.

The Del Mar Scene

The design concept behind the Fairgrounds was to replicate the main plaza of a pueblo from a bygone era. The buildings, in fact, were re-creations of major architectural and tourist landmarks of the Spanish Colonial Southwest. This architectural concept helped create an affable spirit that was unique to Del Mar. Instead of being a scene of desperation and lost money (like many

racetracks), the atmosphere at Del Mar has always promoted a sense of entertainment. Before museums and theme parks routinely created replicas of historic villages, there was Del Mar.

Two exhibit buildings stood at the western edge of the Fairgrounds. The horticultural hall, called the East Exhibit Building, was based on San Francisco's Mission Dolores (founded in 1776 by Father Palou). The West Exhibit Building, where agricultural products and handicrafts were displayed, was directly across the square; its entrance was a copy of the San Gabriel Mission in Los Angeles (a bell tower was added). The interior space of the plaza served as the paddock. At the back of the plaza stood the continuous wall of the grandstand, which was based on the great buttressed walls of the San Gabriel Mission.

A second plaza stood at the eastern end of the grandstand. Here was the clubhouse—a copy of the entrance and tower of the Mission San Jose de Aguayo near San Antonio, Texas (built in 1767–1768). The cantina, a wonderfully simple edifice, was positioned on the plaza outside the clubhouse. Across the plaza stood the most romantic saddling shed one could imagine. It had a dirt floor, adobe walls, and square posts supporting a roof sheathed in bark-stripped logs and covered in Spanish tiles (which, by the time of its demolition in 1991, had become overrun by a thick patch of ivy, trimmed so perfectly that it looked like a thatch). There were other plazas on the Fairgrounds that were surrounded by exhibition halls since the fairgrounds were

The Agricultural Building

The Old Exhibition Hall

The ivy-covered saddling shed

designed to be used by the people of San Diego County for agricultural and horticultural exhibits. The buildings all had the look and feel of the wild Southwest; you could almost say it looked like a movie set!

Del Mar was a success right from the start. And part of the success was due to the horses and the horse people that were attracted to the club. On August 12, 1938, Del Mar hosted the famous "Seabiscuit versus Ligaroti" match race. Just one year earlier, Seabiscuit had been involved in what is known as the "Race of the Century," another matched race that pitted him against War Admiral. (Both of these horses were in the lineage of perhaps the greatest Thoroughbred of all time: Man o' War.) Seabiscuit won the matched race against War Admiral, held at Pimlico Race Course, by a length-and-a-half. At Del Mar, he defeated Ligaroti by just a nose. Seabiscuit would go on to earn the honor of Horse of the Year in 1938. In 1939, trainer Charlie Whittingham moved his training operation to the backstretch at Del Mar. With horses like Seabiscuit and trainers like future Hall-of-Famer Whittingham present, Del Mar's reputation grew quickly.

The newspapers began to call Del Mar "Movieland's Own Track." Bing Crosby's friends came to the races and stayed for the parties he hosted at the end of most racing days. Barbara Stanwyck, Robert Taylor, Bette Davis, Donald

O'Connor, Ava Gardiner, and Dorothy Lamour were usually among the crowd in the late-'30s. Del Mar became one of the hottest spots for celebrities to unwind and enjoy themselves, along with thousands of locals and Thoroughbred fans from around the country. The club was a success right from the start.

By 1942, however, the United States Army commandeered the Fairgrounds and Thoroughbred Club for the war effort. Initially, the grounds were used for training by the Marines, and then as a manufacturing site to make parts for B-17 bombers. All in all, the track was closed to racing for the better part of the war. The army released the Fairgrounds from its national duty in 1942, and the Thoroughbred Club reopened, after some necessary renovation, on August 15, 1945.

Ava Gardner (right, with her mother, Beatrice) was one of many celebrities who frequented Del Mar.

The main entrance to the gap and the grandstand.

In 1947, the Santa Fe Railroad inaugurated the "Racetrack Special"—a commuter train that brought Thoroughbred fans down to Del Mar from L.A. This further bolstered the track's popularity and importance. Besides bringing more people (and more revenue) to the track from the Los Angeles area, the Racetrack Special also served to transport racehorses from more northern reaches of the state. The interstate competition that ensued also furthered the track's burgeoning success. Things continued to grow steadily at Del Mar through the next few decades. Eventually, it would become the most successful track in the nation.

The New Del Mar

While Del Mar has always been a wonderful place to relax, watch the horses, and watch the movie stars, its incredible success eventually necessitated growth. This included an expansion of the facilities, as well as the development of a major stakes race.

In 1992 and '93, all the original buildings from the '30s were demolished and replaced by the "new" Del Mar. The scale of the buildings was increased dramatically. The new grandstand is five stories high and has private sky boxes. Gone are the cantina and Mission Dolores. One huge building for agriculture and horticultural exhibits has replaced the four earlier exhibition buildings. Adobe has been replaced by cement all around, but the roofing is still mission tile. The Turf Club entrance is still inspired by the Mission of San Jose de Aguayo, but it now has two towers instead of one, and it

As soon as it reopened, the stars reappeared. Jimmy Durante was the first star to buy a home in Del Mar and move there for the entire season. (Today the track is located on Jimmy Durante Boulevard.) Many movie stars made Del Mar a frequent social stop, and many more actually bought property nearby to make visiting Del Mar a regular convenience. Eventually, television's most famous couple—Lucille Ball and Desi Arnaz—bought a beach home near the track. They owned Thoroughbred horses and visited the track frequently.

has been moved further up the grandstand. On the whole, however, the plan of the old track and the design references to the Spanish Revival Style remain.

Alas, the region outgrew the little old racetrack and fairgrounds; the primary reason being the expansion of San Diego County. You only have to look at the statistics to understand why Del Mar needed to grow—it has been the most successful racetrack in the nation since 1989, when it recorded a daily average handle of $7,320,623. When California legalized intertrack wagering, L.A. horseplayers only had to go to the television monitors at Hollywood Park or Santa Anita to bet on races at Del Mar, which added to its growth.

One of the keys to Del Mar's success has been its casual attitude. From the very beginning, the track's brain trust wanted to convey a lack of desperation. One of Del Mar's most famous publicity slogan's says it best: Del Mar is a place where "nobody's in a hurry but the horses." At Del Mar, you are supposed to be happy. The infield is open for sunbathers and picnickers, and dances are held in the plaza (called the Plaza de Mexico) after the races. Del Mar still follows Bing Crosby's old pattern of hospitality: a party after the races to thank his friends for coming down to Del Mar. It is a great idea—or perhaps illusion—that nobody goes home broke, sad, or lonely.

But no matter what kind of luck spectators have at

The infield crowd awaits the 1996 Pacific Classic.

the betting windows, a day at the races, particularly at Del Mar, is always at least entertaining. That's why so many people continue to go to where the turf meets the surf.

The Pacific Classic

With all this success, it was only natural that Del Mar should create a sizable stakes race. In 1991, Del Mar Fairgrounds and Thoroughbred Club created the $1 million Pacific Classic. It was for 3 year olds and up, and the distance was set at 1¼ miles. The first Pacific Classic was won by Best Pal, a hometown horse and the only 3 year old running that day (all the other entrants were strong older horses). It was the richest race ever run at Del Mar.

Best Pal's owners, Mr. and Mrs. John Mabee, own Golden Eagle Farm, one of California's leading breeding and racing operations. Mabee is the Chairman of the Board of the Del Mar Thoroughbred Club and has been the man responsible for much of Del Mar's new image. Founder of the successful supermarket chain, Big Bear, Mabee put the same successful combination of large scale, good taste, and polish on the racetrack.

The Pacific Classic is the final race of the three-race series known as the Classic Crown, which also includes the Santa Anita Handicap and the Hollywood Gold Cup. The Pacific Classic is the measure of success in West Coast racing. And, since it is a race for older horses, it is a measure of the horses' soundness of body and of the trainers' conditioning programs. Like all great race courses, it has seen at least one dramatic upset in its short career—in 1996 the unbeatable Cigar lost to Dare And Go (trained

Free House, winner of the 1998 Pacific Classic.

by Richard Mandella). A record 44,181 people came to the Pacific Classic to see Cigar break Citation's record of sixteen consecutive wins. The roar of the crowd turned to quiet disbelief as Dare and Go upset Cigar, then the highest money-earning horse in the nation.

Other races at Del Mar prove to be prep races or showcases for horses who go on to greater things. On the closing day of the 1996 season, a young colt named Silver Charm won the Del Mar Futurity race. It was the beginning of a great career, and it started at Del Mar.

Robert and Beverly Lewis

In 1997, the Lewises were awarded the Eclipse Award of Merit for being "joyous winners and gracious losers" during Silver Charm's nearly successful Triple

Crown bid. Their colt lost the Belmont Stakes, the final leg of the Triple Crown, after having won both the Preakness Stakes and the Kentucky Derby. Not since Mrs. Penny Chenery (Secretariat's owner) acted on behalf of her famous Thoroughbred had owners been such good ambassadors for racing. Their life story touches people.

The Lewises are normal, hard working people. They were college sweethearts who got married and have been together ever since. They have always shared a love for Thoroughbreds, and even spent part of their 1947 honeymoon at the racetrack. Their greatest moment to date, perhaps, was Silver Charm's run for the Triple Crown. The horse finished the 1996 season as a 2 year old by winning the Del Mar Futurity. After that race, the horse gained some recognition and created some buzz. Then, in 1997, he stepped up and won the Preakness Stakes and the Kentucky Derby! However, in the Belmont Stakes, he lost the race by half a length. The Lewises took the silver in the Belmont, not the gold, but they were very gracious about losing such an incredible opportunity. Wasn't it Bing Crosby who sang, "Every cloud must have a silver lining. Wait until the sun shines through."? The silver lining in the loss at Belmont is the fact that they still have a great horse that won both the Preakness and the Kentucky Derby—not much to complain about!

Penny Chenery, Bev and Bob Lewis.

Trainer Bob Baffert

Silver Charm's trainer, Bob Baffert, in 1997 was the leading trainer at Del Mar and second in the nation. With offices at Del Mar and Santa Anita, he is one of a very prominent and successful group of California-based trainers.

Baffert is a man of many contradictions. Boyish-looking but with silver hair, hardworking but also obviously lucky, Baffert has the educational background of a Thoroughbred industry professional but also possesses the self-styled personality of someone in the entertainment business. Aloof but gregarious (he travels with a small pack of friends and relatives), Baffert's deadly seriousness is often hidden by his playful antics.

Baffert once said, "I am different from the other trainers. I have fun." Did he mean that he has fun putting trophies on his head in the winners' circle, as he often does? Or, perhaps he meant that he has fun with money—other people's money in particular? He certainly must have enjoyed spending $17,000 for a horse—Real Quiet—that won $1.5 million fairly quickly! Since many of his clients don't have as much money as some trainers demand—in a world of $1 million horses—he will buy a $17,000 horse and groom it into a champion. Although he does have some big-money clients (the Lewises and Mabees have recently sought Baffert's services), it seems fairly obvious that Baffert's small clients aren't just secondary interests for him. His smaller clients are there, and will always be there, because they are his friends. He is ambitious, but loyal.

The first Thoroughbred Baffert ever owned was a 1 year old he purchased at auction named Thirty Slews. The horse cost $30,000 at the Keeneland September Yearling Sale in 1988, but went on to win the $1 million Breeders' Cup Sprint in 1992. Baffert genuinely knows horses. Metaphorically speaking, he turns sow's ears into silver purses.

Baffert's keys to success are hard work and innovation. He uses a two-way radio to communicate with his workout riders, clocking his horses as they go. He makes the decisions, moment to moment, about how fast or slow to exercise the horses, instead of leaving this up to the rider. This kind of intimate, active, and decisive training process is Baffert's way of getting the most out of his horses. It is also instrumental in his getting to know his horses. Ask Baffert about one of the great horses he's trained and you'll get an interesting reaction:

Bob Baffert

he'll normally smile, think for a moment, and then talk about the horse as if it were a colleague. He understands a horse's "personality," which is an important element in gaining its trust and commitment.

Baffert grew up on a cattle and chicken ranch in Nogales, Arizona. By the age of twelve, he was grooming and galloping quarter horses owned and trained by his father. He rode some of those horses for a brief period, acquiring enough experience as a jockey to develop a knack for communicating with them. In 1974, he graduated from the University of Arizona's Race Track Industry Program (RTIP) with a major in Animal Science and a minor in the industry curriculum. For the next decade he trained quarter horses. A decade after entering the world of Thoroughbreds, he is the nation's leading money trainer.

Milestones

1937, July 3—Bing Crosby greets the first fan through the gate as Del Mar opens.

1938, August 12—The famous Seabiscuit–Ligaroti match race is held. Seabiscuit wins by a nose.

1939—Trainer Charlie Whittingham makes the backstretch at Del Mar his home base of operations.

1940—Dorothy Lamour, W. C. Fields, Paulette Goddard, Edgar Bergen, June Haver, Ann Miller, Don Ameche, Ava Gardner, Red Skelton, and others regularly attend the races, helping to increase the track's popularity.

1942–44—Del Mar closes during World War II. Initially, the grounds are used for training by the Marines, then as a manufacturing site for parts to B-17 bombers.

1945, August 15—The track reopens.

1947—The Santa Fe Railroad brings both racehorses and fans from Los Angeles to Del Mar on the "Racetrack Special."

1948—A new crop of Hollywood personalities begins to frequent Del Mar, including Lucille Ball, Desi Arnaz, Betty Grable, George Jessel, Mickey Rooney, and Jimmy Durante.

1949—A young rider out of Texas, William Shoemaker, sets a Del Mar record of 52 wins and becomes the first apprentice to claim the track's riding title.

1950—Shoemaker and Johnny Longden go head-and-head all summer competing for the riding title. In the end they tie with 60 wins each. It's the "Kid" versus the "Vet."

1956, September 3—Johnny Longden becomes the world's winningest rider with 4,871 victories, passing Sir Gordon Richards on Arrogate in the Del Mar Handicap.

1958—Mr. and Mrs. Fred Turner Jr.'s Tomy Lee wins the Del Mar Futurity under Shoemaker and goes on to win the Kentucky Derby.

1960—Del Mar unveils its new $\frac{7}{8}$-mile turf course with a diagonal chute that allows for $1\frac{1}{16}$- and $1\frac{1}{8}$-mile starts.

1965—The leading rider for the season at Del Mar is William Hartack, winner of five Kentucky Derbies.

Del Mar circa 1974.

Breaking from the gate at Del Mar.

1970, September 7—Willie Shoemaker becomes winningest rider of all time (6,033 victories) on Dares J at Del Mar.

1981—Gato Del Sol under rider Eddie Delahoussaye wins the Del Mar Futurity and goes on to win the Kentucky Derby.

1984—Racing commentator Trevor Denman—whose style of calling races includes comments about strategy and calling the position of all the horses—takes command as announcer at Del Mar.

1987—Jockey Willie Shoemaker and trainer Charlie Whittingham team up for the third time to win the Del Mar Handicap on Swink. Shoemaker retires after his ninety-third stakes victory at Del Mar.

1989—Del Mar becomes the leading track in the country with a daily average handle of $7,320,623.

1990—Del Mar retains its hold as the nation's leading track with a daily average handle of $7,510,867. The track also announces plans for its richest race ever: the $1,000,000 Pacific Classic for the 1991 season.

1991—John and Betty Mabee's Best Pal wins the Pacific Classic. Del Mar retains its top position among tracks nationwide with a daily handle of $7,806.430, and moves into first place in average daily attendance: 37,072. Construction begins on a new grandstand.

1993—The "new" Del Mar is dedicated by Governor Pete Wilson. The construction cost is $80 million. Bertrando wins the Pacific Classic. Laffitt Pincay Jr. wins his 8,000th race. The track still leads the nation with an $8,122,609 average handle and 34,415 daily attendance.

1994—Del Mar leads in handle and attendance for the fourth straight year. Trainer Bobby Frankel wins his third Pacific Classic with Juddmonte Farms' Tinners Way.

1995—Del Mar's average daily handle has jumped to $11,263,896. Frankel with Tinners Way wins the Pacific Classic once again. Chris McCarron wins his fifth riding title at Del Mar.

1996—A record attendance of 44,181 people attend the Pacific Classic to watch Cigar attempt to break Citation's 16-consecutive wins streak. But Dare and Go, trained by Richard Mandella, wins instead. On closing day, a young colt named Silver Charm wins the Del Mar Futurity (and goes on to win the Kentucky Derby and the Preakness Stakes races in 1997).

1997—Argentinean horse Gentleman, trained by Richard Mandella, wins the Pacific Classic. The track is still first in daily average handle, $12,115,024.

1998—Free House wins the Pacific Classic, Gentlemen finishes second.

Hollywood Park

Los Angeles, California
(Established 1938)

I t rained on opening day at Hollywood Park on June 10, 1938. The *Los Angeles Times* reported that actress Claudette Colbert had expected to wear a polka-dot silk net dress with a straw hat, but wore instead a deep gray tailored skirt, light gray box jacket,

deep gray pumps, and a two-tone sailor hat with gloves and a bag of olive green suede. She was pronounced the epitome of racing day chic. Mrs. Walter G. McCarty, wife of the president of both Hollywood Park and the Beverly Wilshire Hotel, had meant to wear powder blue, but due to the rain, wore, instead, a black dress and a silver cape. The ladies looked right at home in and around the grandstand and clubhouse which stretched, curved, and wrapped around the landscape in smooth plaster pierced by aluminum. It was one of the best pieces of the new streamlined Moderne architecture in California.

The Hollywood Turf Club was formed under the chairmanship of Jack L. Warner of Warner Brothers, an extremely successful motion-picture corporation. Most of the six hundred original shareholders came from the film industry. Al Jolson and Raoul Walsh were on the board of directors; Joan Blondell, Ronald Coleman, Walt Disney, Bing Crosby, Samuel Goldwyn, Darryl Zanuck, George Jessel, Ralph Bellamy, and Irene Dunne were stockholders. Mervyn LeRoy, the director of grand epics such as *I Am a Fugitive from a Chain Gang*, *Quo Vadis*, and *No Time for Sergeants*, was the racetrack's chief executive officer. LeRoy headed Hollywood Park from 1941 until his death in 1986.

From the beginning there was a lot of hype. The publicity department sent out press releases saying that

Left: **The stylish clubhouse entrance.**
Right: **The infield at Hollywood Park with a topiary horse and rider.**

Hollywood Park—swept by ocean breezes—was fifteen degrees cooler in the summer than nearby Los Angeles. The new park was located in Inglewood, fifteen miles south of Hollywood, and so it needed extravagant promotion.

This was the glamorous 1930s. Did Hollywood Park have a huge revolving cocktail bar? No, but the architect had designed a revolving paddock. (A pity it was never built!) But still, the racetrack exuded the essence of modernity. Architectural historian David Gebhard wrote that Los Angeles had "discarded its earlier historic garments and fully embraced the Moderne."

A Third Racetrack in California

The California Horse Racing Board (CHRB) was apprehensive of opening a third racetrack in Southern California. Santa Anita had opened at the end of 1934, and then Bing Crosby and Pat O'Brien's Del Mar was granted a license in 1936. The board wanted both of these tracks to do well, and had to wonder whether a third track would cause intertrack squabbling or oversaturation of racing. Also, the state's 1909 ban on bookmaking and the public's negative feelings toward gambling were still fresh in the board's memory. Nationwide, due to public sentiment, the number of racetracks in America had dropped from 314 to 25 by 1909.

Still and all, in 1937 the CHRB issued a temporary license to the Hollywood Turf Club. The club immediately began construction on the racetrack. After a few months, and after the club had spent $300,000, the license was rescinded because the racing board wasn't convinced that Los Angeles could support two tracks. But Hollywood's board of directors decided to keep building, and they began a strenuous lobbying campaign, too. In January 1938, they won their battle with the racing commission, and the CHRB granted the Hollywood Turf Club a thirty-three day summer meeting.

Santa Anita, meanwhile, had offered winter racing to the big eastern racing stables, and it was an attractive proposition. The Whitneys, Vanderbilts, and Calumet Farm shipped their horses to California for winter racing, but once spring came to New York, Maryland, and Kentucky, these stables moved their horses back East. Del Mar had only just opened and had yet to establish itself as the star-studded track by the sea.

To survive, Hollywood eventually had to attract eastern Thoroughbreds while immediately cultivating California owners and breeders. For the 1939 season, Hollywood Park instituted awards to breeders of California-bred winners. Also, since summer racing was hard to sell, Hollywood's publicity campaign appealed to handicappers by promising a rainless season with no "off" (weather-impaired) tracks. They assured the betting public that Hollywood Park would be a "handicapper's paradise."

Hollywood Park continued to look for other innovations. They promised motion pictures from start to finish—covering every race, every day. Patrol-judge stands were built on the inside rail of the track—rather than the outside rail—and the motion pictures were

Leaving the paddock on route to the track at Hollywood Park.

taken from those stands. This provided a brand new perspective in horse racing: from the inside rail with horses coming around the turns. In 1941, Hollywood cameraman Lorenzo del Riccio adapted a hand-held camera to attach to a pair of binoculars. It was called a "vibrationless camera." Each of the eight patrol judges around the track used one of these devices. Each filmed their ⅛-mile of track as the horses came into view. The film was developed overnight at a nearby studio and made available to the racing officials the next day. Spliced together, it formed a movie of the race. These pictures showed everything—the horses' performance at various stages of the race, as well as any jockey shenanigans that occurred on the far side of the track. Hollywood Park had reached a milestone, and it had established itself as a viable operation.

Hollywood Goes To War

Just as things were getting good, Hollywood Park was forced to close after the Japanese attack on Pearl Harbor in 1941. (Racing, in fact, came to a halt at many tracks across the nation.) The Park served as a storage facility for the defense industry until 1944, when the Fourth Army Command awarded it a racing meeting to raise money for War Relief. There was one provision: they could not hire anyone who might better serve in war work, so they hired women. Women became grooms, hot walkers, and exercise riders; they also ran the pari-mutuel betting windows. All in all, these women ran a successful race meeting. In November 1944, when the thirty-four-day meeting began, southern California's defense plants were booming. The average daily handle of the meeting was more than $1 million! (Meanwhile, Hollywood Park's director, Mervyn LeRoy, made the movie *Thirty Seconds Over Tokyo*.)

In 1945, after World War II ended, racing started up again across America. Always innovative with the cameras, Hollywood Park adapted war technologies (the army had mounted movie cameras on airplanes to record aerial combat) to the racetrack—at least, that was how they described it. Cameras mounted high up on trackside towers provided 16-mm film of the races, and new developing techniques—which they described as a "secret method"—made the film available in minutes. For the first time in the history of horse racing, judges could wait for an instant photo finish. Continuing to set the photographic pace, in 1947 Hollywood Park became the first track to make color movies of each race.

After Santa Anita reopened in 1945, it maintained a small but definite edge over Hollywood Park in attendance and handle. Always competitive, though, Hollywood planned and spent $1.6 million in 1949 to expand the grandstand and clubhouse. Eleven days before reopening day, however, tragedy struck. . . .

Grandstand in Flames

Shortly before midnight on May 5, 1949, a night watchman discovered a small fire in the elevator motor room in the grandstand. By the time he got to a phone, the flames were shooting out of the elevator shaft on top of the grandstand. A motorist, bus driver, and airline pilot all saw this and called in alarms. Fire departments arrived

from Inglewood, Hermosa Beach, and Los Angeles, but, because the water pressure was low in Inglewood, firemen found it extremely difficult to contain the blaze. They were able to draw water from the infield lakes, however, which helped considerably. Fortunately, the wind was low and didn't carry the blaze across the track to the barns. None of the Thoroughbreds were endangered. The next day, Gwynn Wilson, Santa Anita's general manager, offered their full facilities to the Hollywood Turf Club. Hollywood could operate their meeting at Santa Anita, and they could open on time. It was an invitation they gratefully accepted.

After seeking project submissions from various architects, the Hollywood Turf Club chose architect Arthur Froelich's firm to design their new grandstand. Forever after, it appears, racetrack design would be a gold mine for that architectural firm. They created designs for grandstands from Canada to South America, and from the Middle East to South Africa. (The latest ones in America, by Froelich's associate Morio Kow, are at Del Mar and the Fair Grounds.)

In 1951, Hollywood was back in business with their new grandstand and clubhouse. The glamour, too, was fully restored. Cary Grant and Jimmy Stewart became regulars. In 1954, Hollywood Park achieved a position of dominance over Santa Anita and other racetracks across the country. They led in average daily attendance, handle, and purses. The reasons for these achievements are thought to include a greater population in an expanding Los Angeles and a general increase in the prosperity of the community. Finally, Hollywood Park had good management and, not to be underestimated, an attractive new facility.

From the beginning, Hollywood Park was called the "Track of the Lakes and Flowers." There are four infield lakes stocked with waterfowl and, in the old days, a swan boat pedaled by a young woman called the "Goose Girl." Recently the lakes and infield have been restored and the "Goose Girl" was revived for a brief period. (But she has since been given a pink slip.)

The Hollywood Gold Cup

From the very beginning, Hollywood Park featured a valuable stakes race. The first Hollywood Gold Cup in 1938 offered a purse of $50,000. The Santa Anita Handicap, meanwhile, offered $100,000 at the time.

Nonetheless, the inaugural race meeting was a success and Hollywood Park turned a profit. That profit went toward the construction of new barns and a training track. Also, thanks to the initial success, minimum purses at daily races were increased to $1,000.

The first Hollywood Gold Cup was won by Seabiscuit, the Horse of the Year for 1938. The second year, it was won by Kayak II, from Argentina. Since that time, the Cup has become famous, to many people's surprise, as an international race with winning horses over the years representing England, Ireland, Canada, South Africa, Australia, New Zealand, Brazil, and Argentina. (Europe had very few lucrative races for older horses.) The Gold Cup, open to 3-year-olds and up, attracted the good horses with its big purse. Hollywood Park was also a pioneer in recruiting South

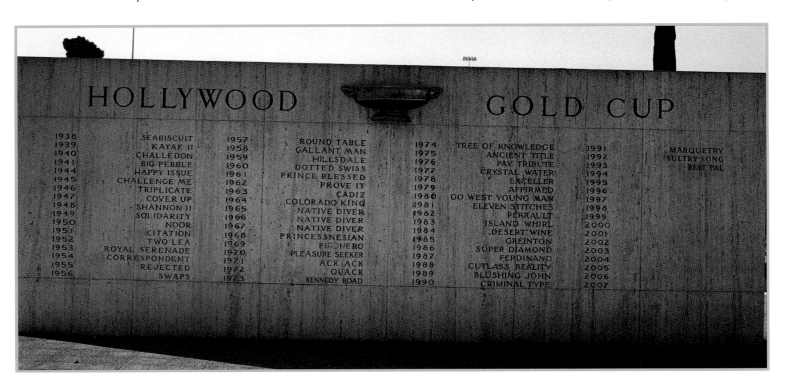

Hollywood Gold Cup winners.

American horses, thanks to two West Coast trainers (Charles Whittingham and Ron McAnally) who scouted that continent and an owner (Clement Hirsch) who purchased horses there. The South American connection remains strong to this day.

The Hollywood Gold Cup is a classic race for 3-year-old horses. It is the second leg of the West Coast's triple crown—known as the "Classic Crown"—a series created in 1990. It opens with the Santa Anita Derby in early March, followed by the Gold Cup in late June, and finishes with Del Mar's Pacific Classic in early August.

The Gold Cup has become one of the West Coast's most coveted races to win, and it has always been stylish. Eastern horses were even shipped to Hollywood to compete in the Gold Cup, since a race like this offered a chance to increase their coffers. The famous Citation ended his career by winning the 1951 Gold Cup and becoming the first horse to earn $1 million. Affirmed won it in 1972 and became the first horse to win $2 million.

Native Sons

The legendary Swaps, a favorite son of Hollywood Park, is immortalized by a bronze statue at the clubhouse entrance. He was one of the most popular horses in California racing history. During a three-year racing career that began with a maiden (first-race) victory at Hollywood Park on May 20, 1954, the California bred son of Khaled set five world records and equaled another while winning nineteen of twenty-five starts for owner Rex C. Ellsworth.

Top: **Swaps with Willie Shoemaker up and trainer M.A. Tenney.**
Bottom: **An Iron tribute to the great Swaps, winner of the 1956 Hollywood Gold Cup.**

After his maiden victory in California at Hollywood Park, he went on to stun Nashua, the favorite, in the 1955 Kentucky Derby. West Coast fans followed him during a nine-race winning streak that spanned eight months and included the Santa Anita Derby, the Will Rogers and the Californian at Hollywood Park, and the American Derby at Chicago's Washington Park. His most famous race may have been the one he lost: the historic Washington Park Match Race with Nashua on August 31, 1955. It was a rematch of the Kentucky Derby from a few months earlier, and Nashua redeemed himself. Injured in this match race, Swaps later recovered and won eight of his ten races to be named Horse of the Year in 1956.

Top: **Trainer Buster Millerick works out three-time Hollywood Gold Cup winner Native Diver.**
Bottom: **Native Diver beats the field in the 1996 Hollywood Gold Cup.**

But the horse that Hollywood Park calls its own is Native Diver. He still holds the record for the most wins of the Hollywood Gold Cup and is its oldest winner. Called "The Black Horse" by the track announcer, Native Diver captured the fancy of racing fans during the 1960s with his speed and personality. The Black Horse assumed the name "Mr. Gold Cup" after winning Hollywood Park's most prestigious stakes race a still-unparalleled three successive years in 1965, 1966, and 1967. He was also California's first $1 million earner.

Owned by Mr. and Mrs. L. K. Shapiro, Native Diver was trained by Buster Millerick and ridden by Jerry Lambert in all three Gold Cup triumphs. His third Cup win caused excitement in southern California to rise to a feverish pitch, only to have it drop suddenly into sadness and mourning with the Thoroughbred's untimely death in September of that same year.

Native Diver's burial place is Hollywood Park's paddock. A ceramic tile monument depicts his Gold Cup triumphs. The monument was erected soon after the Thoroughbred's death and was dedicated on April 11, 1969.

Richard Mandella, Mr. Diplomat

"You have to have some idea what a horse is thinking before you can help it in its training," said Richard Mandella in a *Thoroughbred Times* interview in 1993.

The late Jim Murray of the *Los Angeles Times*, one of only four sports writers to win a Pulitzer Prize, provided a perfunctory biography of Mandella: "Dick Mandella

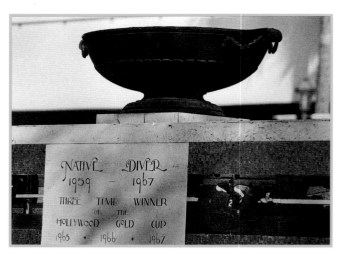

A commemorative cup honors the great Native Diver at Hollywood Park.

came by his horse sense legitimately enough. He grew up in a paddock. [His] dad was a blacksmith who used to plate horses for the Three Rings Ranch in Beaumont [California]. Young Dick was around horses when his classmates were around hot rods. He got to know more about horses than a Pony Express rider.

"If horses could talk, they'd say, 'Get me Mandella!'" Murray concludes.

Mandella recalls his early years around horses: "My dad, Gene, owned a ranch in Cherry Valley and was a horseshoer. We took quarter horses, Thoroughbreds, appaloosas, and stock horses. We bred and broke every type of horse. My father was a very good horseman and gave me a good foundation.

"I went to galloping horses before my sophomore year in high school. I was put in charge of forty or fifty horses." Born in 1950, and still relatively young, he leaves no doubt about his capability. "That's where I learned to accept the responsibility of the business."

Mandella, who keeps his stable office at Hollywood Park, learned the business of winning through experience. And with his experience he has come to develop deadly competitive tactics. He sets up the race like a boxer might, using whatever skill and strategy it takes to achieve a knockout. In the 1996 Pacific Classic at Del Mar, for example, he ran two horses—Siphon and Dare and Go—against Cigar, the decorated Horse of the Year. Cigar came into the race having won sixteen races in a row, tying Citation's record. The fans at Del Mar expected to see Cigar win. But Mandella's twosome wreaked havoc on Cigar's bid for the record. Siphon led in the midstretch, tiring Cigar, and Dare and Go passed Cigar to win. Mandella modestly says about this shocking defeat of Cigar, "In all honesty, I thought we might get second and third."

"Mandella is respected by his peers," says James E. Bassett III, former president of the Breeders' Cup. He has nerve, which wins him respect from other trainers. Mandella entered three horses in the $1 million 1997 Santa Anita Handicap and they all finished "in the money." Siphon, Sandpit, and Gentlemen finished first, second, and third, respectively. It was the first time any trainer had gone 1-2-3—a master's stroke!

Mandella is also renowned for keeping horses around for long careers. Turf writer Steve Schuelein in 1991 likened Mandella's stable to a revitalized senior citizens' center with 7-, 8-, and 9-year-old horses still racing and winning. Writer Jay Privman summed up his achievements: "If they have four legs, Mandella will get the best out of them."

And, he makes money. In earnings, Mandella was the second highest in the country in 1997. He won the $1 million Pacific Classic in 1997 with Gentlemen. He won the Santa Anita Handicap once again in 1998, entering a favorite, Gentlemen, but winning with another horse named Malek. The one-two punch is becoming a Mandella blueprint, and all these million-dollar races add up.

He trains for a strong group of owners—owners who are often also breeders of horses. His clients include Golden Eagle Farm (owned by Mrs. and Mrs. John Mabee), La Presle Farm, Burt Bacharach, Kentucky breeders Claiborne and Jonabel Farms, Daniel Wildenstein, Herman Sarkowsky, and the owner of Hollywood Park, R. D. Hubbard (in syndicate with South American breeders).

Richard Mandella

Milestones

1938, June 10—Hollywood Park opens with much fanfare; many movie stars are present for opening day festivities.

1938—The Hollywood Gold Cup stakes race is born (with an initial purse of $50,000). The first Gold Cup is won by the legendary Seabiscuit, 1938's Horse of the Year.

1941—The U.S. Army commandeers Hollywood Park for use as a storage facility.

1945—Hollywood Park develops the first photo finish camera.

1947—Hollywood Park scores another innovation by making complete color motion pictures of every race.

1949, May 5—The grandstand goes down in flames.

1951, July 14—In his last race, Calumet Farm's legendary 6 year old, Citation, wins the Hollywood Gold Cup by four lengths and becomes racing's first millionaire horse.

1952, May 15—Jockey Johnny Longden wins his 4,000th victory, riding at Hollywood Park.

1961, May 19—Jockey Willie Shoemaker notches his 4,000 career win aboard Guaranteeya at Hollywood Park.

1954, May 20—At odds of 13–1, Rex Ellsworth's 2-year-old Swaps wins his maiden race by three lengths at Hollywood Park.

1973, June 24—Charlie Whittingham sweeps the top three spots in the Hollywood Gold Cup Invitational Handicap when his trainees Kennedy Road, Quack, and Cougar II finish first, second, and third, respectively.

1975, July 17—Jockey Laffit Pincay Jr. notches his 3,000 career victory, aboard Lexington Lark, at Hollywood Park.

1976, July 4—Charlie Whittingham sweeps the top three spots in the American Handicap at Hollywood Park with his trainees King Pellinore, Riot in Paris, and Caucasus. On July 26, he repeats the feat in the Sunset Handicap, with Caucasus first, King Pellinore second, and Riot in Paris third.

1978, July 4—Trainer D. Wayne Lukas wins his first $100,000 stakes race—over turf—taking the American Handicap with Effervescing, ridden by Laffit Pincay Jr., at Hollywood Park.

1979, June 24—Affirmed, ridden by Laffit Pincay Jr., becomes the first horse to top $2 million in earnings after he wins the Hollywood Gold Cup.

1982, July 3—D. Wayne Lukas-trained Landaluce, ridden by Laffit Pincay Jr., wins the first of her five consecutive victories at Hollywood Park. The daughter of Seattle Slew, owned by Barry Beal and Lloyd French, dies of a viral infection in November of that year, but is posthumously voted champion 2-year-old filly of 1982.

Paddock at Hollywood Park.

1985, June 23—With a victory aboard Greinton in the Hollywood Gold Cup, Laffit Pincay Jr. becomes the second jockey in history to surpass $100 million in purse earnings.

1990, June 20—Retired jockey Willie Shoemaker wins his first race as a trainer, sending 2-year-old filly Tempest Cloud to her maiden victory at Hollywood Park.

1991, June 30—One year after his first victory as a trainer, Willie Shoemaker records his first Grade I win, with Alcando in the Beverly Hills Handicap at Hollywood Park.

1992, May 21—Jockey Gary Stevens gets his 3,000th win in the fifth race at Hollywood Park, aboard Sharp Event.

1992, June 19—Charlie Whittingham becomes the second trainer in history, behind D. Wayne Lukas, to top $100 million in purse earnings when he sends Little by Little to a second-place finish in the sixth race at Hollywood Park.

1993, July 18—Jockey Gary Stevens tops $100 million in purse earnings after winning the seventh race at Hollywood Park aboard Don't Presume (from Great Britain).

1994, June 26—Jockey Chris McCarron rides his 6,000th career winner, Andestine, in the Milady Handicap at Hollywood Park. He is the 11th rider to reach 6,000 and the third youngest, behind Willie Shoemaker and Laffit Pincay Jr.

1995—Cigar, winner of the Hollywood Gold Cup, is named Horse of the Year.

1998—Skip Away became the eighth horse to win the Hollywood Gold Cup and be named Horse of the Year in the same year.

Gulfstream Park

Hallandale, Florida
(Established 1944)

In the late 1930s it was difficult to imagine why anyone would attempt to compete with Hialeah Park for a share of the Thoroughbred racing interest in southern Florida. Hialeah, established in 1932 northwest of Miami Beach, had become a major destination for some of the East Coast's finest Thoroughbreds, as well as the place to go for the wealthiest and most avid racing enthusiasts. And with a setting that was unmatched by any other racetrack, Hialeah seemed to hold a monopoly on the sport in that region.

Yet in 1937 the newly established Hollywood Jockey Club proposed a new track in Broward County. The track was planned and organized by the legendary Joseph Smoot. In August 1937 the county voted its approval, and construction began. The Florida State Racing Commission, however, refused to grant the racing dates Smoot had wanted. Smoot appealed the matter. The State Supreme Court ordered the commission to grant the dates of February 3rd through March 16 of the following year for racing at the new track. On December 9, however, Smoot was forced to announce that construction had been ceased on the new track, and the planned meet that he had fought so hard to get appeared to be doomed. Upon hearing this announcement, the racing commission then officially revoked the assigned dates. But, not wanting to give up so easily, Smoot sued the commission and won; the dates were restored the following season.

John C. Horning, a local contractor who built many homes in Hallandale, resumed construction of the track. He was only twenty-eight years old, but had emerged as the chief stockholder of the Gulfstream project (with 62 percent of stock) because of the amount of construction money—$1.5 million—he had already put into it. Smoot, at this point, simply dropped out of the picture.

In 1939, with construction not quite completed, the track had a fairly successful opening day under the management of Horning and his mother. Unfortunately, they were forced to close the track almost immediately (it opened on February 1 and closed February 5) because the public clearly preferred Hialeah. But that wasn't the only reason for the track's initial failure. The track was located a little too far north from Miami Beach. Also, people complained that it was no more than an alligator swampland.

Ultimately, it was clear that the biggest factor in Gulfstream's initial failure was Hialeah's success—espe-

Opposite: **The paddock at Gulfstream.**

cially since races at Hialeah were running concurrently with Gulfstream's. Since Hialeah had become such a well-established society track, it was natural that its crowd would not choose to suddenly defect to an unestablished venue in Hallandale. Also, Hialeah had better horses. But the concept (and eventually, necessity) of expanded prime midwinter racing dates in southern Florida had been born.

On February 7, 1939, Horning, still committed to the project, sought more capital to continue construction of the park. To his dismay, he was not allowed to issue stock because the Florida Securities Commission determined that it was an unsound venture. On February 11, he declared bankruptcy. The track may or may not have had to close for the war effort, but, in any case, it was closed from 1940 through most of 1944 for financial reasons. All it needed was a champion.

James Donn and
the Rebirth of Gulfstream

James Donn, a well-known Miami florist, would soon come into the picture. Donn was the son of a blacksmith, and so he knew something about horses. He grew up in Scotland and emigrated to New York in 1909. He quickly became a successful florist with a shop on Fifth Avenue in New York City, and counted some of the wealthiest socialites as his clients: the Rockefellers, Goulds, and Carnegies. In 1915, for medical reasons, he was advised to move to a warmer climate. He moved to Florida.

Donn loved Florida from the very first, with its abundant tropical flora and agreeable climate. He opened a nursery on Fifteenth Avenue in Miami and called it Exotic Gardens. It became famous. He was no longer just a florist—in Florida, he developed the ability to manipulate landscapes, and his reputation grew.

In 1941 Donn was hired to rejuvenate a closed-down racetrack—Tropical Park. (Also located in the Miami area, Tropical Park is now a football and soccer field.) When the work was completed, his clients and all the track's patrons agreed that he had turned it into "a paradise." Tropical Park reopened, but the operators were unable to pay for Donn's services. His bill may have been extremely high, but the quality of the work was undeniable, and the two sides entered into an amicable compromise: Donn received mortgage bonds that would mature in ten years. Now that he had a fairly big stake in the track, Donn entered into the management of Tropical Park and learned about the business of horse racing.

Before Donn's mortgage bonds were to mature, Tropical Park had come under new management. At that point, he turned his eye to Gulfstream Park. In May 1944, Donn bought Gulfstream for $100,000—plus assuming $750,000 in liabilities. (A group of investors and other stockholders added another $1 million combined.) Donn said that the sad circumstances of Horning and his mother giving Gulfstream everything they had appealed to his sense of sentimentality. He would have to raise money to pay Horning and at the same time raise even more money to revive the racetrack. He admired what Horning had accomplished. He liked the grandstand, the track, and the infield lake. Upon reviewing the popular criticism against the track, and the reasons for its closing, he must have thought, "If they called this an alligator swampland, I'll give them alligators."

Of course, he had big plans for Gulfstream's landscape from the start. But first he had to get the racing commission to permit the operation of three tracks—Hialeah, Tropical Park, and Gulfstream—in the Miami area during the winter season. Then he would set his energies on creating an incredible atmosphere for horse racing.

Donn was well-connected. His personal mandate was a matter of convincing the politicians to add another forty racing days to the beginning of the racing season.

The scenic paddock always draws a crowd.

The prime season was January through March, and Donn wanted to add November through January. He had to convince the politicians that the income from the handle of those racing days would result in additional income for the state in the form of tax dollars.

On another front, Donn had to negotiate Gulfstream's bankruptcy so that he could buy the property. So he put together a team that consisted of Stefan H. Zachar (a Miami Beach architect and Thoroughbred breeder); William E. Leach (a breeder in Ocala—a bluegrass-rich area in central Florida); and businessmen George W. Langford, James Mack, and Harold I. Clark. Together, they bought Gulfstream.

Donn, meanwhile, got to work. He planted geraniums, hibiscus, and, more laboriously, transplanted royal palm trees all around the track, knowing that they were the best feature of Hialeah and should be a major feature at Gulfstream, as well. For the first ten years of the racetrack's operation Donn devoted a great deal of effort to landscaping.

"It is in the landscaping and beautification of the track that the real changes have been made," Donn told *Turf & Sports Digest* in February 1955. "During our first year there wasn't a tree or shrub to relieve the barren waste. Today more than eight hundred royal palms have been planted, tropical plants, and shrubbery."

Left: **Ogden Mills Phipps (center) and James E. Bassett III stand in the paddock, 1990.**

Right: **The terrace is a choice location for spectators.**

By the 1950s the fine collection of royal palms had been established. The trees had been imported from Davie, Florida, where they were planted in the 1920s and '30s. (Today, the track has 350 of these trees, significant for their number, beauty, and age, especially since Florida experienced a palm disease which reduced their number enormously throughout the state.)

Coconut palms and hundreds of varieties of plants were carefully placed. Another signature was the small circular flower beds that were planted annually and which dotted the infield in the 1950s (they have since been moved to the paddock area).

(Today, the infield lake has a miniature Mississippi riverboat, the Swanee Queen, as well as brightly colored sailing boats and a fair amount of alligators. There has been at least one account of an alligator sighting on the track as a race is run. This is an exotic rarity. Perhaps it is a guest appearance in honor of the old man's memory.)

By 1955 the racetrack had built a new clubhouse and grandstand. The track has continued to enlarge and improve facilities. A restaurant was added on the clubhouse turn, and included several terraces. The ground level of the clubhouse is covered with a spectacular tensile roofing made of polyester fabric covered in Teflon. The upper terraces have a series of individual tents with center support poles which are covered in Teflon-coated striped canvas. This exotic oasis that resembles a Bedouin tent is now a signature of the grandstand at this racetrack.

Racing Days

In 1947, the state legislature passed a law that divided the winter racing season into three meets of forty days, with each track receiving one of these time slots (two tracks could not operate when the other one was operating). The prime dates were always the middle ones, from January to March. According to the new law, the track with the best revenue during the previous season was awarded the middle dates. This was known as the "Hialeah Law." Hialeah had the best dates—those which fell just after Christmas holidays at the beginning of the Florida tourist season. Hialeah made the most revenue and kept the middle dates year after year.

Meanwhile, Gulfstream decided that it needed to establish a stakes race to compete with Hialeah's Flamingo Stakes—but in order to truly compete with the venerable Hialeah, Gulfstream had to make their stakes race richer. The Florida Derby was established at Gulfstream in 1951, and by 1952—its second running—the purse was increased to $100,000. With a purse of $100,000, the Florida Derby became the richest race in Florida, and the first in Florida with a six-figure value. The Gulfstream Park Handicap, first run in 1946, also attracted good horses, such as Coaltown in 1949, with a purse of $50,000. (The Handicap is worth $500,000 today.) The Florida Derby, however, truly put Gulfstream on the map.

The Florida Derby began attracting most of the good horses, who would sometimes also run later in the Flamingo. But in general, it attracted the owners and breeders to Florida earlier, and was a good prep race for the Kentucky Derby in May. In fact, the Florida Derby proved to be a significant preview for the famous Triple Crown. Many of its starters and winners went on to fare very well in Triple Crown races. For example, in 1955 Nashua won the Florida Derby, came in second in the Kentucky Derby, and won the Preakness and the Belmont. The following year Needles won all but the Preakness where it came in second. In 1958, Tim Tam won all but the Belmont, in which he came in second. In 1959, Sword Dancer was second in all but the Belmont, which he won. In 1961, Carry Back won in Florida, Kentucky, and Baltimore, but not in New York. In 1964, the great Canadian horse Northern Dancer won all except the Belmont. The same pattern was repeated by Spectacular Bid in 1979.

In 1971 the Hialeah Law was repealed. In 1972, Gulfstream was awarded the choice middle dates for the first time in the history of the track. They responded by increasing the Florida Derby stakes to $125,000 and raised it again in 1974 to $150,000. (By the 1980s, the Florida Derby became one of the nation's richest Thoroughbred classic races, with a purse of $500,000.)

In the 1970s, four tracks were engaged in a desperate struggle to get the good racing dates back. The issue was reviewed and discussed by the state legislature during the late 1970s and nearly all of the 1980s. (By 1988, after offering solutions that were never deemed acceptable by everyone, the legislature washed its hands of the affair and authorized deregulation.)

Horses approaching the clubhouse turn, Breeders' Cup Distaff, November 4, 1988.

In 1979, Gulfstream set a record handle of $94,568,590 for forty-four days, and $3.6 million of this was generated on Derby day. The track, by this time, was owned by the third generation of the Donn family. In the 1980s, the track became more successful each year, and in 1989, it hosted the Breeders' Cup for the first time. (Gulfstream was chosen once again to host the Breeder races in 1992, and again in 1999.)

Best Man: Fred Hooper

Fred Hooper (b. 1897) is one of racing's national treasures. At 102 years old, Hooper is an accomplished owner and breeder of American Thoroughbreds, a savvy importer of foreign riding talent (jockeys), a builder of racetracks, and a respected leader of national racing organizations. In short, he has been a champion of Thoroughbred racing for the greater part of the twentieth century. When you read about Hooper's fifty years or so in Thoroughbred racing, you notice that his actions often resulted in triumphs for others. It was said by Joe Hirsch of the *Daily Racing Form* that Hooper was "as current as tomorrow in his thinking."

As a contractor (he started out in road construction, building one of Florida's early highways—a twenty-mile section from Daytona to St. Augustine) he built airport runways in Orlando, canals in Miami, bridges, dams, and many highways. In the 1960s, James Donn Sr. asked Hooper to construct a turf course at Gulfstream. Hooper took on the task. In some places his equipment had to dig down twenty-six feet to prepare a proper foundation. His engineering and construction efforts were excellent, and another of his many careers was born. He went on to work in tracks at Washington Park in Chicago and Hollywood Park in Los Angeles. Essentially a Florida man and a friend of Donn, he ran his horses at Gulfstream. He has been honored by almost every organization in Thoroughbred racing.

In the late 1950s, Hooper sponsored Braulio Baeza, a young jockey from Panama, by bringing him to the United States to ride. Later he did the same for Jorge Velasquez and Laffit Pincay Jr. They all became Hall of Fame jockeys.

Hooper was also one of the first trainers to fly horses across the country to race in other geographic areas. In 1949, he chartered a DC-4 from Eastern Air Lines to transport his horses to California. Before the trip, he had his construction crew build horse stalls and install oxygen tanks in the cargo holds of the airplane. The horses traveled beautifully, without any problems. His horse, Olympia, won the San Felipe Handicap at Hollywood Park, and then returned to Florida to win the Flamingo Stakes at Hialeah. This was a triumph for Hollywood Park, as well, since that park was eager to attract East Coast stables to the West. Hooper was inducted into the racing Halls of Fame in Georgia, California, and Florida, and the National Museum of Racing's Hall of Fame in Saratoga, New York. He received the 1991 Eclipse Award of Merit.

Fred Hooper

Milestones

1939, February 1—Gulfstream opens and runs for four days.

1940—Gulfstream closes for the unforseeable future.

1944—Gulfstream reopens and runs a twenty-day meeting in December with James Donn as president of the track.

1945—Gulfstream runs its first regular meeting, which lasts for forty days.

1948—A 6-year-old mare, Rampart, defeats the favored Armed in the Gulfstream Park Handicap.

1949—Coaltown, owned by Calumet Farms, sets a track record of 1:59⅘ in winning the Gulfstream Park Handicap.

1952—A clubhouse is erected along with a new addition to the grandstand. The Florida Derby is run for the first time.

1953—The Florida Derby becomes first stakes race in Florida with a six-figure purse ($100,000).

1955—Nashua wins the Florida Derby, is second in the Kentucky Derby, and wins the Preakness and Belmont Stakes. He becomes the Horse of the Year.

1956—Needles wins the Florida Derby, the Flamingo Stakes, the Kentucky Derby, and the Belmont Stakes; he is second in the Preakness Stakes and becomes the Horse of the Year.

1957—Gen. Duke sets a track record of 1:46⅘ in defeating Bold Ruler in the Florida Derby. Bold Ruler, however, wins the Preakness and becomes Horse of the Year.

1958—Tim Tam wins the Florida Derby, the Kentucky Derby, and the Preakness. He finishes second in the Belmont Stakes.

1959—Gulfstream Park opens its turf course.

1961—James Donn Jr. becomes president of Gulfstream. The world's largest tote board is erected in the infield. Carry Back wins the Florida Derby, the Flamingo Stakes, the Kentucky Derby, and the Preakness.

1964—Northern Dancer wins the Florida Derby, the Flamingo Stakes, the Kentucky Derby, the Preakness, and the Queen's Plate. He finishes third in the Belmont. He is Canada's Horse of the Year.

1968—Forward Pass wins the Florida Derby, the Kentucky Derby, and the Preakness; he is second in the Belmont.

1972—Gulfstream is awarded the choice middle dates (January 17–March 2) of the Florida racing season for the first time. Florida Derby becomes the state's richest race when raised to $125,000-added.

1974—The Florida Derby is raised to $150,000-added, making it one of the richest races in the country.

1978—Douglas Donn is elected Gulfstream president following the death of his father, James Donn Jr.

1979—Gulfstream sets a record for handle, with $94,568,590, for forty-four days. Spectacular Bid wins the Florida Derby, the Flamingo Stakes, the Kentucky Derby, and the Preakness; he is third in the Belmont.

1980—Angel Cordero Jr. sets a meeting record by jockeying sixty winners.

1981—A state-record handle is set with $103,531,722 for the fifty-day meeting.

1984—Swale wins the Florida Derby, the Kentucky Derby, and the Belmont Stakes.

1989, November 5—Gulfstream stages the $10 million Breeders' Cup. The handle is a whopping $12,323,213; the attendance is 51,342.

1990—Bertram and Diana Firestone, owners of the Calder Race Track and Tropical Park, purchase Gulfstream.

1990—Unbridled wins the Florida Derby and the Kentucky Derby. He goes on to win the Breeders' Cup Classic.

1991—The Gulfstream Park Racing Association is acquired by Catoctin, a subsidiary of the Orient Corporation (USA).

1992—Gulfstream again hosts the Breeders' Cup.

1992—Julie Krone becomes the first woman to win the meeting riding title at Gulfstream, with seventy-two victories.

1993—The handle for the sixty-eight-day meeting is $248,661,887, the largest in Florida history.

1994—The Orient Corporation, one-hundred-percent owner of Gulfstream Park, transfers fifty-percent of ownership to Higashi Nihon House of Japan.

1995—Cigar wins the Donn Handicap and the Gulfstream Park Handicap, and goes undefeated for the remainder of the year to become Horse of the Year. Thunder Gulch wins the Fountain Of Youth and Florida Derby before winning both the Kentucky Derby and the Belmont Stakes.

1996—Gulfstream posts a new high handle of $663,228,714-wagered during the sixty-four-day racing meet.

1997, February 2—A life-size statue of Cigar is unveiled in the Garden of Champions, a garden of eighty-three commemorative monuments.

Clubhouse turn at Gulfstream.

Monmouth Park

Oceanport, New Jersey
(Established 1946)

There have been three Monmouth Park racetracks. The first one, built in 1870, was the largest racetrack in the country at the time, with an iron grandstand measuring 1,100 feet long, a paddock with ninety-six stalls, and a track measuring 1¾ miles around—all located on 660 acres. The second track, built in 1890, was even larger.

Between 1891 and 1941, antiracing legislation in New Jersey largely eliminated the sport. After wagering was legalized in 1941, Thoroughbred enthusiasts in Cherry Hill and Atlantic City were the first to build new tracks. Although the racing commission approved a track at Monmouth at that time, it took five years to sell the stock shares to raise the $3.5 million needed to construct the new racetrack. It finally opened in June 1946. The only connection between the first two Monmouth Park and the one built in the 1940s was the fact that they were all located in an area called "Monmouth."

The new Monmouth Park was developed largely by Amory Haskell and a group of men interested in horse sports—hunting, jumping, showing, and racing. A New York native and Princeton graduate, Haskell began organizing the track while working for General Motors. He left GM to form his own company—the Triplex Safety Glass Company—during the years he helped establish Monmouth. Shortly before World War II began, Haskell intensely lobbied the New Jersey State legislature to create a constitutional amendment to the New Jersey constitution that would approve legalized pari-mutuel wagering for Thoroughbred and standardbred horse racing. The first president and chairman of the Monmouth Park Jockey Club, Haskell's name is still significant to modern-day New Jersey racing. (His name, in fact, is honored each year as the name of one of Monmouth's biggest races, the Haskell Invitational Handicap.)

Philip Iselin, one of Monmouth Park's founders, joined the group by chance. Iselin became concerned about the park because it bordered his property. Legend has it that Amory Haskell paid Iselin a visit to ask if he minded having a racetrack as a neighbor. Iselin is said to have replied, "Not at all, and I wouldn't mind joining you."

Iselin owned a successful company which produced women's apparel, but he also knew sports. (He was one of the original investors in the New York Jets professional football team, and in 1968 was president of the

Top: **Haskell Day, 1997.**
Middle: **Horses approach the famous parterre boxes.**
Bottom: **Touch Gold winning the 1997 Haskell Invitational.**

Amory Haskell

Philip Iselin

Jets.) Haskell and his group of investors were happy to include Iselin in the project. Iselin was appointed treasurer of the newly formed Monmouth Park.

"Amory was from an aristocratic family," said Betty Iselin (Philip's wife). "My husband came from nowhere. Yet, they got along fabulously together. Amory lived in a different world. He thought, for example, that racing should start around 3:00 p.m. He thought he had to play golf, go swimming, and could go to the track around two o'clock. Phil explained that it had to be run differently. Phil really worked at it."

Philip Iselin, though he joined the organizing group by somewhat of a chance, became one of its most important members. He developed a daily routine that

was meant to foster quality control, and he did so out of a love for the sport and for Monmouth Park.

"[Philip] could walk over to the racetrack from our house. He had breakfast at the track kitchen. But first, he and the track supervisor drove everywhere. They looked at every flower box, checked to see if a blade of grass was out of place. Then he had breakfast. After breakfast, sitting at a big round table in the track kitchen, all the trainers told him their problems. You know, 'the track's too hard or too soft.' After the races, the heads of all the departments came to his office. They talked about what had happened during the day."

In the 1940s, Monmouth Park became a popular resort racetrack for people who traveled to the New

Jersey shore in July and August. Many people packed trunks and traveled via a ferry boat from New York City to Sandy Hook, New Jersey, and then proceeded south to their summer houses. Once there, they did not want to travel to the tracks at Belmont and Saratoga. From the beginning, one of the ways to reach Monmouth was by ferryboat. You can still do so. "They would drink their way down," laughs Mrs. Iselin.

The Charity Ball

The Iselins have had much success in their involvement with Monmouth Park. Besides financial success, they also enjoyed the rewarding experience of being active members of the community.

"The greatest pleasure is the Charity Ball. My husband knew that it was very important to give back to the community," said Mrs. Iselin. "A racetrack is never well received. From the beginning, we didn't want it to be a society charity ball. In the early years it was called a 'Charity Ball and Carnival.' We had a midway, raffles, and a live auction after dinner. It was a community event. Everybody could come in for twenty dollars. You didn't have to go to the dinner beforehand. In 1947, there were two thousand people [in attendance]."

The Charity Ball gave all its earnings back to the community in 1947 and continues to do so each year. (The 1998 ball raised $175,000, which the committee decided to give to fifty-three different charities. The Charity Fund has distributed $7.4 million in its first fifty years [1947–1997], all locally.)

Taking the Ferry

Just like in the old days, the ferry from Manhattan is an exciting way for many summer vacationers to get to Monmouth Park. At 11:00 a.m. on Thursdays, Saturdays, and Sundays—from May through mid-September—the ferry leaves from Pier 11 at the end of Wall Street in Manhattan on its way south. It is definitely the scenic way to go to Monmouth Park.

The ferry is fat, modern, and low in the water. As the boat passes the tall buildings in the financial district, ferry riders can see tall masts waving gently from the clipper ships docked along the piers of the South Street Seaport, just north of Wall Street. The ferry then skims directly across the East River and follows the curve of Brooklyn. The Statue of Liberty and the Staten Island ferries, normal landmarks in this part of the city, are visible from the ferry.

The ferry stops at the Brooklyn Army Terminal where other racetrackers come aboard. After leaving the Brooklyn pier, the ferry joins a kind of shipping lane and enters a crossroads of ocean liners, container ships, freighters, tug boats, garbage boats, and pleasure craft. With Brooklyn on the left and Staten Island on the right, the ferry enters a part of the water called The Narrows—a shipping lane that goes under the Verrazano Bridge and out into the Atlantic Ocean. The last part of New York City that you see, up close, is Coney Island. Manhattan Island becomes a mirage of towers teetering on a narrow strip of land.

The boat enters the wide mouth of the harbor

where the shipping traffic starts to spread out, and then follows a channel straight south to the New Jersey coast. In this part of the harbor more sailing boats join the waters. After forty-five minutes the boat reaches Sandy Hook, New Jersey, and passes a little colony of nineteenth-century military buildings lined up in rows (the abandoned Fort Hancock). The lighthouse there is a national landmark. Sandy Hook curves like a scorpion's tail, and the boat basically follows this coastline before it pulls into the dock at The Highlands, an hour after leaving Wall Street. From there a bus takes passengers to Monmouth Park. In that hour of fresh sea air, new landmarks, exuberant passengers, and, yes, early morning cocktails, your perspective on life will change.

At the Racetrack

The first thing you'll probably notice, once inside the racetrack, are rows of aluminum umbrellas for picnickers. On big race days, these are inevitably filled with people. A formal garden with carefully shaped trees in its center is located behind the grandstand—this is where the walking ring is located.

To one side of the walking ring are a couple of administration buildings. Behind the walking ring is the saddling shed. On the far side of the walking ring, behind a fence, is an Olympic-sized swimming pool reserved for the jockeys' use. The jockey's quarters are behind the swimming pool.

The S.S. Peter Stuyvesant takes racetrackers from Manhattan to Monmouth Park in the 1950's.

The relaxing picnic area.

The jockeys' pool.

Monmouth's beautiful
saddling ring and paddock.

The pride of the racetrack is the small walking ring where spectators can see the horses being exercised before the race. It is smaller than the walking rings at many other tracks, but it is one of the most charming. There is an oval, oak-paneled saddling enclosure in which horses parade over woodchips. The jockeys, owners, and trainers stand in a formal area of grass in the center of the ring, shaded by four beech trees (the light green European fern leaf and dark plum colored American purple leaf beech). The tiny oval in which the horses walk is edged with a white fence similar to a gooseneck railing. This fence, a copy of the one at Ascot (in England), is the reason why the walking ring at Monmouth is always referred to as an "English" walking ring. Directly in front of the walking ring stands the clubhouse.

The most surprising aspect of Monmouth is the degree to which the interiors of the clubhouse are decorated and maintained in the style of the 1940s. There are black-and-white tiled floors, large gilded bird cages, rattan furniture with chintz slipcovers, '40s-style wallpaper, and beautiful paintings adorning the walls. Perhaps it is the decor that puts your spirit at ease and prepares you for a relaxing yet somewhat sophisticated afternoon.

The clubhouse is stacked five stories high. When it was first built, Monmouth Park's press material described the clubhouse as "the most amazing structure on American turf." Perhaps its most impressive feature are the two tiers of parterre boxes, considered at the time to be one of the most successful innovations of any

Parterre boxes.

racetrack in the country. (In 1990, in fact, when Keeneland Race Course decided to add corporate boxes, they eschewed the designs being built for baseball stadiums in order to copy the parterre boxes designed forty-five years earlier at Monmouth.) The parterre boxes are essentially opera boxes, each with six chairs overlooking the course and a private dining area for six people at the back of the box. These boxes were originally based on the design from a Hong Kong racetrack of the 1930s, where each box owner had a personal cook to prepare the meal.

There were seven outdoor dining terraces in the clubhouse when the Park opened in 1946; several remain today, although they are enclosed in glass partitions which are rarely opened. Besides these enclosed terraces, the main characteristic of the Monmouth buildings is openness, mostly because the buildings were designed before air conditioning was widely available. The spectators at Monmouth were drawn there because of the seashore location—part of the attraction was fresh, salty air. That was what summer was all about. One of the souvenirs was salt-water taffy. There are still sections of wall dividing the betting and receiving areas which are made entirely of wire mesh—this design provided pleasant breezes for patrons who were waiting for friends or standing in betting lines.

Balconies overlooking the paddock area were completely open when the clubhouse and grandstand were built. Later, they were fixed with sliding glass windows to keep out extreme weather. At the core of the clubhouse is a big, formal lounge that is also quite comfortable in the manner of 1940s hotel interiors. People gather here—in the clubhouse drawing room—

before disappearing into the private parterre boxes or one of the restaurants.

The Haskell Invitational Handicap

In 1968 the Monmouth Park board of directors honored the memory of Amory L. Haskell, founder of the park, with a race for older horses. It is a 1⅛-mile invitational (horses are entered by invitation only) for the nation's top 3 year olds, run every August. In 1997, the purse was raised to $1 million, making it the richest invitational event in North America.

The Haskell is a favorite race for New York City dwellers who do not go to Saratoga. They can wrap up

The Haskell in 1995, won by Serena's Song—the only filly ever to win the race.

the summer season by seeing some of the best horses from the big spring events closer to home. In 1994, Holy Bull (owned by W. Croll Jr.), that year's champion 3-year-old colt and Horse of the Year, won the race. In 1995, Serena's Song (owned by Robert and Beverly Lewis) became the first filly ever to win the Haskell. In 1996, Skip Away (owned by Carolyn and Sonny Hine), the nation's top 3-year-old colt, took home the purse of $750,000. The following year Touch Gold (owned by Canadian Frank Stronach), that year's Belmont Stakes winner, took the Haskell.

Because these great names have won the race in recent years, and with the relatively new million-dollar purse firmly in place, the Haskell will continue to grow in importance. And with Thoroughbred racing's increasing popularity among the general public, the Haskell will no doubt command more anticipation and deliver more excitement in coming years.

Julie Krone

Jockeying a Thoroughbred horse is not an easy feat. In fact, Thoroughbred jockeys are very fit, well-trained, world-class athletes. And although the role of jockey has been traditionally a man's role, a young female rider named Julie Krone broke many barriers in the 1980s.

Krone was raised on a farm in Michigan where her mother, a dressage rider, introduced her to horses. At the age of three she rode her own pony. At fifteen she got a job galloping horses on the Churchill Downs backstretch. (Too young by the track's standards, her mother altered her birth certificate so that she could procure the job.) Krone returned home to Michigan to finish the school semester and rode races during the summer at local fair grounds. She moved to Florida, lived with her grandmother, and got a chance to ride a horse named Tiny Star at Tampa Bay Downs. She finished second. That race took place on January 30, 1981, and it was the beginning of a famous career.

In 1987, Krone became the first woman to win a riding title at a major racetracks, receiving the honor at Monmouth Park where she rode 130 horses to victory. Add that total to her performance at other tracks around the country that year, and Krone tallied 324 wins to rank sixth in the entire nation.

Touch Gold

Julie Krone, many times the leading rider at Monmouth Park, riding Colonial Affair, on whom she won the Belmont Stakes in 1993.

On March 6, 1988, she became the winningest female rider of all time with 1,205 victories and moved up to rank fourth in the nation among all jockeys for the year. She was the third winningest jockey in the nation in 1989, riding 368 horses to victory. (At that point, she had only been riding regularly at recognized racetracks for eight years.) Her accomplishments were so remarkable that *Sports Illustrated* featured her on the cover. On November 30, however, she suffered a spill at the Meadowlands Racetrack and ended up with a fractured left arm, which had to be set with a plate and seven screws.

In 1991, Krone was back in the saddle again. Then, in 1993, she did something that no other female rider has ever accomplished: she won one of the Triple Crown races—the Belmont Stakes—on Colonial Affair.

Small, of course, but also curvy, blonde, and pretty, she made numerous major television network appearances. She had become nationally recognized and was enjoying a great period in her career when, on August 30, on the last day of the meet at Saratoga, she suffered another riding accident. This time her right ankle was severely fractured and required two plates and fourteen screws for reconstruction. She returned to racing in 1994, but unfortunately suffered another injury. This is not to imply that Krone is more accident prone than any other jockey, however—it is a high-risk business and she is a tough and determined competitor.

After recuperating in 1994, she returned to racing and was the top female rider in the United States in 1995 and 1996. She retired from competition in 1999 as the greatest female jockey in the history of American Thoroughbred racing.

Milestones

1941—Pari-mutuel wagering on racing of Thoroughbred and standardbred horses is legalized in New Jersey.

1946, June 19—A new Monmouth Park opens for racing. Amory L. Haskell, Philip H. Iselin, Reeve Schley, Joseph M. Roebling, Townsend B. Martin, John MacDonald, and James Cox Brady are the owners. More than eighteen thousand people attend opening day festivities. The Monmouth Handicap, a race for older horses which was run at earlier Monmouth racetracks, is revived. Run at a distance of $1\frac{1}{2}$ miles from 1884 to 1893, the race is shortened to $1\frac{1}{8}$ miles. (In 1986, as a tribute to track president and chairman Mr. Iselin, the race is renamed the Philip H. Iselin Handicap.)

1947—The new clubhouse, including the parterre box section, is completed. The Monmouth Park Charity Fund is established by Philip Iselin and his wife, the former Betty Bing.

1948—Dormitories for horsemen are built in the stable area, along with five new barns.

1950—Turf racing begins for the first time in the history of all the Monmouth tracks. Three additional barns are built to increase the stall numbers to 1,200 horses.

1951—Use of a film patrol, first started in Hollywood Park, is adopted. New dining rooms, additional clubhouse seating, and a third tier to the parterre boxes are added.

1954—More parterre boxes are built.

1956—Nashua, ridden by Eddie Arcaro, is televised nationally winning the Monmouth Handicap.

1958—Bold Ruler and jockey Eddie Arcaro win the $1\frac{1}{4}$-mile Monmouth Handicap.

1959—Horse of the Year Sword Dancer, ridden by Willie Shoemaker, captures the $100,000 Monmouth Handicap.

1963—For the eighth time in nine years, season attendance tops one million. Champion 3-year-old filly, Lamb Chop, wins the Monmouth Oaks.

**Nashua winning the 1956
Monmouth Handicap.**

1964—Mrs. Henry Carnegie Phipps's champion 2-year-old filly, Queen Empress, wins the Colleen Stakes.

1965—Closed-circuit televisions and air conditioning are installed in the grandstand.

1966, April 12—Amory L. Haskell, president and chairman of Monmouth Park, dies. Mr. Philip Iselin becomes president and chairman.

1968—The Amory L. Haskell Handicap, a race for older horses, is inaugurated. In 1981, the race would become an invitational for the nation's top 3 year olds and would be run at 1⅛ miles.

1969, June 9—Tuesdee Testa becomes the first woman to ride at Monmouth Park—she finishes second with Verbosity.

1973—Monmouth Park is winterized. Glass windows and doors are installed. The clubhouse dining terrace is enclosed in glass and is equipped with heating and air conditioning.

1976—Track president and chairman Philip Iselin dies.

1980—Spectacular Bid, ridden by Willie Shoemaker, wins the Iselin Handicap after winning the Kentucky Derby and Preakness in 1979, en route to becoming the 1980 Horse of the Year.

1985—Cozzene, winner of the Eclipse Award as outstanding turf horse, captures the Oceanport Handicap. Horse of the Year and Kentucky Derby winner, Spend A Buck, comes in second in the Haskell but wins the $250,000 Monmouth Handicap.

1986—Monmouth Park is bought by the New Jersey Sports and Exposition Authority. Robert E. Mulcahy III is the director. The Monmouth Handicap is renamed the Philip H. Iselin Handicap.

1987—Julie Krone wins the first of her three-straight riding titles at Monmouth Park. She is the top female rider in the United States in 1987, 1988, 1989, 1992, 1995, and 1996. Belmont Stakes winner Bet Twice wins the Haskell. Alysheba, winner of the Kentucky Derby and the Preakness, comes in second.

1987, July 28—Jockey Angel Cordero Jr. wins his 6,000th victory in the Colleen Stakes at Monmouth Park aboard Lost Kitty. He is the fourth rider in racing history to accomplish this feat.

1991—Eclipse Award champion Black Tie Affair wins the Iselin Handicap.

1989—Julie Krone is the third best rider in the nation, with 368 wins (she was fourth in 1988 with 363 and sixth in 1987 with 324).

1994—Holy Bull, the Horse of the Year, is stabled at Monmouth. He wins the $500,000 Haskell Invitational. For the first time, the daily average handle is $3 million.

1995—Serena's Song becomes the first filly to win the prestigious Haskell Invitational. She is ridden by jockey Gary Stevens. The total handle on Haskell day reaches $7 million, a New Jersey record.

1996—Champion 3-year-old Skip Away, ridden by Jose Santos, wins the $750,000 Haskell Invitational—a record $8.1 million is wagered that day.

1997—Belmont Stakes winner Touch Gold, ridden by Chris McCarron, wins the $1 million Haskell. Wagering is $9.7 million.

Woodbine

Etobicoke, Ontario, Canada
(Established 1956)

Although Woodbine as we know it today was built in 1956, there were many events prior to 1956—including the existence of an original Woodbine track at another location—which led directly to the construction of this modern gem. The history that sired the modern Woodbine track offers invaluable knowledge to understanding racing at Woodbine today. It is brimming with fascinating stories of British royalty, grand traditions, successful owners and trainers, and triumphant horses. (Many of the traditions from earlier Canadian tracks, in fact, are upheld by the modern Woodbine). It is a history that dates back as far as Thoroughbred racing in the United States, but one with a decidedly English influence. While Thoroughbred owners, trainers, and racing patrons in the States were generally distancing themselves from English influences, Canadian enthusiasts were embracing their royal connection.

The root of Ontario racing dates from the late 1700s around Niagara's Fort George—the flat grassy plains in the area provided an excellent turf course. There, three-day race meets were accompanied by dinners, parties, and dancing. During the next century, a regal influence was to come upon Thoroughbred racing in Canada. The first Canadian race under royal patronage was run in 1836 at Trois-Rivères, a small village on the St. Lawrence River in the province of Quebec. The race was called the "King's Plate," and was named after King William IV, Britain's reigning monarch.

The English tradition of awarding silver plates to horse racing winners dates back to the seventeenth century, when King Charles II presented the owner of the winning horse at Newmarket—a famous race course in England—with a plate of silver. Typically, the size of the plate indicated the value and importance of the race.

The next monarch, Queen Victoria, in the 1850s was petitioned by the Toronto Turf Club to similarly honor racing in Ontario. She granted the jockey club its request, not because she liked racing, but because Toronto was a rowdy community and she thought a plate race might have a civilizing effect. In 1859, the Queen designated fifty guineas as an annual purse for a race to be called "The Queen's Plate."

The first Queen's Plate was held near Toronto on June 27, 1860, on a little race course in the village of Carleton. After the first race proved successful, politicians from other districts lobbied to have the race relocated to their own areas. During the following

Opposite: **Woodbine is known for grand events.**

twenty-two years, the Queen's Plate was run at tracks across Ontario: Guelph, London, Hamilton, St. Catherines, Toronto, Whitby, Kingston, Ottawa, Barrie, Woodstock, Prescott, and Picton. Finally, the grand race found a permanent home at the old Woodbine Park, in Toronto. Although the date of the race varied from year to year, it was normally held around May 24th—Queen Victoria's birthday.

In 1872, New Yorker W. J. "Jiggs" Howell purchased a tavern on Yonge Street in Toronto called "The Woodbine." Four years later, he and a partner laid out a racetrack next to the tavern. The entire enterprise soon collapsed, however, and Howell ended up selling the inn and track to Joseph Duggan. Here, in 1881, at a roadhouse racetrack called "The Woodbine," the twenty-second running of the Queen's Plate was held. It was a successful event. Getting there was dusty, as usual, but there was a good tram service. A cool breeze swept off Lake Ontario. Bookmakers were present at the track, but everything went smoothly. The following year, the race was held in London, Ontario. After that, for the following seventy-four years it was held in Toronto at the old Woodbine. (From 1956 to present it has been run at the new Woodbine.)

Royalty at the Racetrack

By 1883, the Queen's Plate was back at Woodbine, but racing in Canada—as in the United States—was suffering from a bad reputation. Woodbine needed to

Queen Elizabeth II at Woodbine.

improve its image. One of Queen Victoria's daughters, Princess Louise, was married to the incumbent Governor-General of Canada—the Marquis of Lorne. The Toronto Jockey Club devised a plan to get the Lornes—and especially, the princess—to attend the races at Woodbine. Two of the club's agents went to work: Thomas Patteson (Toronto's courtly postmaster) hatched the plot, and Sir Casimir Gzowski (who had petitioned Queen Victoria back in 1859 for the original Plate race) carried it out.

Gzowski, in his capacity as aide-de-camp—a confidential assistant acting for the Queen—invited the unsuspecting Lornes to be his house guests in Toronto. He craftily timed the invitation to coincide with the racing meeting, and so he accompanied his guests to the races. Her Royal Highness Princess Louise also attended, and Sir Gzowski and Postmaster Patteson got what they wanted for their racetrack—celebrity attendance of the best kind: royalty.

That year, and for years to come, due to the track's royal ties and its beautiful scenery, the Queen's Plate at Woodbine became a society event. *The Toronto Mail and Empire* even sent their fashion reporter. Like the Kentucky Derby, a Cockney spirit was present in the display of brilliant, spirited hats. According to the *Empire*, one "decidedly extraordinary old woman . . . wore a majestic creation of roses, vegetables, jet flies, and horns on her head."

During this period, Waterloo, Ontario, distiller Joseph E. Seagram had the leading stable in Canada. For many years, he dominated the Canadian racing scene, especially the Queen's Plate. In 1898, after his eighth victory in a row (sometimes his horses came in first, second, and third), people started to make jokes about his dominance, popularly renaming the race "The Seagram Plate." From 1891 to 1901, in fact, ten of the eleven winners of the Plate came from Seagram's stable.

In 1901, the year in which Queen Victoria died, the Queen's Plate became the "King's Plate" for the reigns of four consecutive kings. (This distinction lasted until the ascension of Queen Elizabeth II in 1952.) Nevertheless, the race only grew stronger. Each year, the crowds of people attending the race increased. It got so big the trams couldn't handle the riders, and some races went off with many fans outside. In 1913, for the 54th running, the park closed its gates at two o'clock—two thousand people were shut out.

Sir Barton

In 1917, racing was halted in Canada because of World War I. The Plate was still run at Woodbine, but under the auspices of a Red Cross event. In 1917, the major racing stable of Canada, owned by Commander J. K. L. Ross, moved from Canada to Maryland. Ross was the proud owner of Sir Barton, one of the most famous and most talented horses in Thoroughbred history. Sir Barton was Canadian bred, raised, and trained. In 1919, Sir Barton won the Kentucky Derby, the Preakness Stakes, and the Belmont Stakes, making him the first winner of America's Triple Crown. Furthermore, he won these races at a time when they were held only a few days apart—a truly remarkable feat. Sir Barton won the Saratoga Handicap in 1920 against the great Exterminator—one of his top victories. Finally, as a 4 year old, he returned to Canada to run before the Canadian people against the great Man o' War—unfortunately, he suffered from tender feet and lost by seven lengths.

Woodbine reopened after World War I, and going to the old park again became a popular pastime. In 1919, a double-decked members' stand was built—painted white and trimmed with green. The new stand had a dining room where dancing was held each afternoon after the races.

The Plate has been run under six reigning monarchs. They are Victoria, Edward VII, George V, Edward VIII (who renounced the throne in 1937), George VI, and Queen Elizabeth II.

Jockey Mike Smith, receiving the Queen's Plate trophy from Elizabeth II, Queen of England (right), Mr. and Mrs. Frank Stronach in background.

King George VI and Queen Elizabeth (the Queen Mother) attended the King's Plate at Woodbine in 1939. Since then, the royals have attended the race with some regularity. Queen Elizabeth—an avid breeder of racehorses—has appeared six more times after her initial visit with her husband in 1939. She presented the plate in 1962, 1965, 1974, 1979, 1985, and again in 1989. With Elizabeth II, the King's Plate once again became the Queen's Plate. She made her first visit to Woodbine in 1959 for the 100th running, attended the race for the second time in 1973, and again in 1997.

Canada's Mr. Racing

When the Queen visited Woodbine in 1959 for the 100th running of the Queen's Plate, you might say that it was icing on the cake for E. P. Taylor. Taylor had been courting her attendance since 1952 when he purchased and reorganized the Ontario Jockey Club (making him the owner of Woodbine). His successful reorganization of Ontario racing was the foundation for this dream come true. His breeding operations at Windfields Farm and his fine crop of Canadian Thoroughbred yearlings also were a major factor in Woodbine's success.

Old Woodbine was already owned by the Ontario Jockey Club—and therefore, Taylor—but it needed renovations and repairs. A successful corporate businessman, Taylor acquired and absorbed—or closed down—smaller local tracks. His first move, in 1952, was to buy the old Fort Erie track, near Buffalo, from John Cella (who also owned Oaklawn Park). Then, Taylor purchased and closed tracks owned and operated by the Hamilton Jockey Club, the Belleville Driving and Athletic Club, and the Thorncliffe Park Racing and Breeding Association. As racetrack operations, most of these businesses had been losing money, but as developed real estate, they increased the holdings of the Ontario Jockey Club considerably. The acquired assets provided the resources Taylor needed to set about building a new Woodbine.

Old Woodbine—scenic and filled with history—wasn't perfect. The land near the lake didn't drain well. The wind off the lake could be chilly. Much about the move to build a new racetrack had to do with Taylor's way of thinking about things. There is an account of the 1952 running of the Queen's Plate, which was run in the rain and mud, in which two starting gates had to be set up to accommodate all the horses that were running in the race. The eight-stall gate was moved into place but the fourteen-stall gate got stuck in the mud in the infield. It took the crew thirty-five minutes to get it into position. Then, before the jittery horses could enter the starting gates, Taylor's horse, Arcadian, reared up in his starting stall, caught one of his hooves on the front, slipped, and fell onto his back in the mud beneath the gate. The jockey wasn't injured, but he was a mess. They got the horse back onto his feet, and the veterinarian checked him over and pronounced him fit to race. The jockey remounted.

The bell rang out, but the gates did not open. The gate mechanism had broken down. All that horse power pawed the ground, steaming and snorting. The gates had to be opened by hand. Taylor, the breeder and owner of a horse in the race, as well as the functionary of the Ontario Jockey Club, was present through all this. His striped pants, morning coat, and pearl-gray top hat ended up splattered and soaked in mud. Finally, when the race did get underway, Taylor's horse was beaten by a horse that he had bred but no longer owned! In short, he was of the opinion that improving Canadian racing required developing a huge new racetrack.

George Hendrie (left, president of the Ontario Jockey Club), E.P. Taylor, and Ontario's Premier Leslie Frost at the new Woodbine's opening in 1956.

E. P. Taylor and the New Woodbine

An executive committee of the board of the Ontario Jockey Club was formed in 1952 for the purpose of developing a new racetrack. E. P. Taylor was chairman. One of the first things he did was retain a Toronto architect, Earle C. Morgan, who in turn contacted the famous racetrack architect, Arthur Froehlich. By 1956 a new racetrack, made of steel and hung with glass, was built on a parcel of land twenty miles northwest of Toronto. Still standing today, Morgan's grandstand reaches upward toward heaven. Five stories of balconies line the back and overlook the paddock. The front, facing the racetrack, is seven stories high, counting the press box. On major racing days, all the floors are open. The backside of the track features a huge complex of shed row barns built together. Shaped like the letter "U," with a grazing yard in the middle, these are located along long dirt boulevards. The original stables accommodated a thousand horses. Fourteen million dollars was put into this supertrack in 1956.

The 1953 Queen's Plate, first turn. The race is won by Canadiana (white blinkers) one of Canada's greatest Thoroughbreds.

Taylor possessed money and exceptional business skills, and had a strong personal vision regarding racing and breeding Thoroughbred horses. He had wanted to breed good Canadian horses. In less than twenty years, he was the leading Thoroughbred breeder in the world.

As plans for the new racetrack were developing in 1952, Taylor traveled to Newmarket, England, to attend the December breeding stock sales. There he bought Lady Angela, a mare descended from the great stallion Hyperion. Lady Angela was in foal to the famous Italian stallion Nearco (reportedly the only horse to have his own bomb shelter during World War II). Taylor insisted that Lady Angela and Nearco breed a second time. It was an unusual but shrewd request. Undefeated as a European racing champion, Nearco had already sired, among others, Nasrullah (who became the sire of Bold Ruler; and Bold Ruler was the sire of Secretariat). This second mating between Lady Angela and Nearco resulted in a colt named Nearctic.

Meanwhile, Taylor was breeding, racing, and selling other horses. His 2-year-old filly, Canadiana, was an excellent runner and was voted Canada's Horse of the Year in 1952. It is unusual for the Horse of the Year to be a 2 year old, and it's equally unusual for the award to go to a filly. With jockey Eddie Arcaro up, Canadiana won the Queen's Plate in 1953.

In the spring of 1954, Taylor's barns held forty yearlings. He devised a scheme for selling that was indicative of his nerve and generosity. These were the rules: he would offer his entire crop of yearlings at predesignated prices; when half were sold—half of the colts, half of the fillies—the sale would be terminated. This way, Taylor reasoned, no one could claim that he was keeping only the best for himself. And all of Canadian racing would be improved.

In 1956 one of the horses that Taylor bred and sold, Canadian Champ, was voted Horse of the Year. In 1957, he owned and bred another Plate winner, Lyford Cay (his wife's horse, Chopadette, finished second). In the spring of 1958, Nearctic started his racing career as a 2 year old. By the fall he was voted Canada's Horse of the Year.

For his efforts, Taylor was elected an honorary member of the exclusive Jockey Club of New York and the Thoroughbred Club of America. The Kentucky-based Thoroughbred Club also honored Taylor with a dinner featuring dishes named for his champions: the appetizer was a crabmeat cocktail à la Windfields; the main course was filet mignon Major Factor accompanied by Lyford Cay string beans, Canadian Champ baked potato, hearts of lettuce Epic, and coupes St. Jacques Nearctic. The accompanying wine was rose Canadiana. The meal ended with New Providence coffee. (New Providence had just won the Queen's Plate, dashing across the finish line before the royal box at Woodbine in which sat E. P. Taylor, Prince Phillip, and Queen Elizabeth II. That was 1959 and the 100th running of the race.)

However pro-Canada Taylor was, he wanted his horses to be good enough to run anywhere. In 1960 he returned to Kentucky to enter his horse, Victoria Park, in the Blue Grass Stakes at Keeneland. Victoria Park ran second in the Blue Grass, third in the Kentucky Derby, and second in the Preakness. Canadian racing fans swelled with pride over the horse's achievements, but they worried Taylor would forego that season's Queen's Plate and instead enter Victoria Park in the Belmont, scheduled for the same day. Much to their delight, Victoria Park returned home to win the Plate in record time. Victoria Park suffered a bowed tendon soon after and was forced to retire from racing. Around the same time, Taylor was forced to retire Nearctic due to a small crack in his hoof. These were two major blows, but Taylor's luck was about to change.

In 1961, Natalma—a filly Taylor had bought at Saratoga and mated to Nearctic—gave birth to a bay colt so small that the stable hands reportedly joked that he was an Irish setter. This small package blossomed into Northern Dancer.

E.P. Taylor with the legendary Northern Dancer.

Northern Dancer

No warm grasses of Aiken, South Carolina, or Ocala, Florida, for this little darling! Feisty and devilish from the beginning, Northern Dancer cavorted in the deep snow of the paddock and used the walkways for a skating rink. When E. P. Taylor conducted his open yearling sale the next summer, nobody bought Northern Dancer. He was short, at 14 hands, 2½ inches (approximately 4', 10"). He was even perhaps slightly goofy looking, with a white blaze that started at the forelock and ran down the center of his face to below the eyes, where it started to slip off, and then ended up over his left nostril.

Nobody, of course, could see his genetic code.

Northern Dancer's early racing career started off well—he won five out of six races in Canada. Then an ominous quarter crack appeared in his hoof—the same injury that ended the racing career of his sire, Nearctic. But Taylor learned that a California blacksmith had recently developed a plastic patch that anchors the crack until the hoof grows out. With his patched hoof, Northern Dancer spent the winter on the soft sandy paths at Hialeah, winning the Flamingo Stakes, the Florida Derby, and then the Blue Grass Stakes at Keeneland. On the first Saturday in May, 1964, he won the Kentucky Derby, running the mile and a quarter in an unprecedented two minutes flat. (His record stood at Churchill Downs for nearly a decade before it was broken by Secretariat.)

In the winner's circle at Churchill Downs, Taylor declared, "This is a great day for Canada!" This statement, however simple, should not be underestimated. Even nonfans are sometimes moved by a great athletic achievement, just as millions of Americans became interested in ice hockey after the U.S. team upset the Soviets in the 1980 Olympics. Northern Dancer's win electrified all of Canada. People all over Canada crowded around television sets to yell for their Dancer.

Dancer had already won the Preakness, but finished third in the Belmont Stakes (that year held at Aqueduct) to just miss a chance to take home the Triple Crown. Still, he returned home to an adoring Toronto. The mayor wanted to have a ticker tape parade. But Taylor knew his horse—eccentric and shy—and declined. Mayor Lamport instead declared June 8, 1964, "Northern Dancer Day," and awarded the horse the key to the city, carved out of a carrot.

Dancer soon after showed a tendon problem that would end his racing career. Some people speculate that his jockey, William Hartack, kept the reins too tight and was too aggressive with the whip—provocations that allegedly caused negative reactions by the horse. He ran his last race in the Queen's Plate (held on June 20, 1964) restrained through most of the race by Hartack. Finally, when the jockey loosened the reins, the Dancer flew down the backstretch passing all the horses on a strained foreleg. He won his final race in a blaze of glory in front of an adoring home crowd.

Immediately after retiring in 1964 due to a bowed tendon, Northern Dancer went on to an even more illustrious breeding career as a stud. Too short in stature to mount the average mare (on his first attempt at sex, the mare was so disgruntled that she kicked Northern Dancer in the chest), a shallow pit had to be dug for the mares to stand in. With this architecture in place, Dancer went on to become the greatest sire of all time. This statement is no exaggeration. Most winning race horses over the last twenty years in Europe and North America can be traced to Northern Dancer.

He sired 635 foals over twenty-three seasons. Eighty percent of his offspring raced, of which about 80 percent became winners. Of these, 146 were stakes winners and twenty-six were declared national champions in Canada, the United States, England, France, Ireland, and Italy. They, in turn, became magnificent sires and broodmares themselves. Among Northern Dancer's prolific offspring were: Nijinsky II, Northernette, Storm Bird, Fanfreluche, and Sadler's Wells. Yearling sales, stallion syndication and breeding fees soared. Racing changed as well. Million-dollar purses had to be offered to these multimillion-dollar horses. Short, stocky, and well-balanced, they have run well on grass courses as well as dirt. With their unbelievable desire to run faster than any other horse present, the descendants of Northern Dancer are called a "fire line."

Canadian Racing

The walls of Woodbine's grandstand are covered with photographs of Northern Dancer, along with other legends of racing: jockey Ron Turcotte (who guided Secretariat through his Triple Crown races); E. P. Taylor; and jockey Bill Hartack (who rode Northern Dancer in the Kentucky Derby and the Preakness). There are large, framed drawings of all the leading Canadian horses throughout the grandstand.

Woodbine also houses the Canadian Horse Racing Hall of Fame. The hall is a rotunda with trophies and memorabilia: winning tickets, race cards, betting sheets and other things that describe Canadian racing from Sir Barton to the present. There are portraits of leading owners, trainers, and jockeys, and of the famous horses.

Patron friendly, this racetrack also has a day care center. Recently they eliminated all exterior fences and barriers around the racetrack to create a more inviting atmosphere, with free parking and free admissions.

W. Cothran Campbell, president of South Carolina's Dogwood Stable, had stakes-winning horses at Woodbine in 1985 and 1986, and a winning filly who ran in the Breeders' Cup held at Woodbine in 1996. Like most people, he recalls "its gorgeous, elegant walking ring." The large oval paddock, with its walking ring, is dotted with enormous willow trees. The traditional paddock is in complete contrast to the tall, modern, glass-box grandstand. On Queen's Plate day, when the men are dressed in striped pants, pearl gray vests, top hats, and morning coats, it feels like a very important social occasion.

In 1997, all of Toronto found itself in a quandary. Queen Elizabeth II had decided to attend the Plate accompanied by her husband, Prince Philip. Prince Philip made it known that he was going to wear a suit— meaning, lightweight pants and a jacket. Therefore, since nobody could out dress him, of course, they had to leave their high hats and long coattails in the closet! In 1998, with the lieutenant governor (who wore a pale green silk suit and a large, floppy hat) presiding over the event, all formality resumed.

Queen's Plate Day, morning coats are the gentlemen's traditional apparel of the day.

A huge old black carriage—a landau—brought the lieutenant governor (the queen's Canadian representative) along the race course, drawn by horses from the Governor General's Horse Guards (the oldest unit of the Canadian militia), to the Royal Box. Canadian Mounties rode alongside. A contingent of bagpipes played in the infield. After presenting the Queen's Plate trophy, on a red carpet rolled over the big turf course and the dirt track, the queen's Canadian representative left Woodbine in the landau. It is Canada's most prestigious race day and everything was carried out quietly, but in the best possible spirit.

Mr. Campbell testifies to a special ambiance at Woodbine, not necessarily tied to the special Queen's Plate events. "Mostly, I feel there is good spirit, good fel-

Left: **The royal entourage on Queen Plate's Day.**

Right: **The Canadian Mounties are part of dress guard on Plate Day.**

lowship, and a good mood at Woodbine." Recalling one morning in particular, in 1987, after winning back-to-back Rothman stakes races, (with Nassipour and Southjet) he returned to Woodbine. He brought Southjet once more, hoping to win the race for the third year running, he says.

"I remember leaving the barn on the Friday before the race to take the horse to the racetrack for his blowout. As our small entourage walked down the horse path between the barns, it was very moving to me the number of grooms, hot-walkers, and racetrackers who came pouring out of the barns along the way. They came to watch the horse go past and to yell out expressions of encouragement for our quest to win a third straight Rothmans. I can still hear shouts of 'Go get him big boy,' 'Good luck, guys,' et cetera, et cetera . . . with that warmth and hospitality. I'm a pretty strong Woodbine man."

The backstretch at Woodbine is bigger than a good many villages in middle America, and there are thousands of men and women who work there, attending the horses. These horse towns are always called the backstretch, referring to the stretch of land behind the oval track. At Woodbine, it is laid out on a grid with wide boulevards dotted with pine, oak, and willow trees. The street that is closest to the main track is paved but is barricaded during training hours. The others are dirt, and for the horses only, although they are traveled by hay trucks, veterinarians, blacksmiths, grooms, hot-walkers, exercise riders,

Left: **Stables**
Right: **Backstretch tunnel that leads into the track.**

trainers, owners, jockeys' agents, security guards, racing commissioners, track officials, and sundry persons. Woodbine has at least two training tracks, so there is a constant flow of horses and riders coming and going to those tracks or to the main track during the early morning workout hours. Oddly enough, it is busier than many small towns, as well.

There is enough grass along these roadways so that you see horses grazing occasionally. Some of the barn yards are fenced in and have a few animals to keep the horses company. The barns are composed of long shedrows which represent Canadian racing stables: Kinghaven Farms where the trainer Roger Attfield holds court, Frank Stronach's Stronach Stables, E. P. Taylor's Windfields Stable, and many others. Iron jockeys with

The homestretch, the Queen's Plate, June 21, 1998, Archers Bay the winner.

painted silks stand in the yards, window boxes decorate the ledges along the shedrow, and here and there is painted a large maple leaf. The horseman's kitchen, behind the racing secretary's office, is made of plate glass and chrome, with 1950s maroon Naugahyde covering the chairs. It is called a cafe and is as large as any midtown-Manhattan cafeteria. Canadian horsemen mull about wearing wide hats, western style, and some speak of the Canadian West and of breaking horses. These people lived on the backstretch year-round.

The Largest Turf Track in North America

But the pride of the racetrack is its new turf course. It is the largest in North America, measuring a mile and a half. When built a few years ago, it was simply put on the outside of their dirt track—a wide strip of grass that comes up to the edge of the grandstand. On the homestretch, the horses run right in front of the people in the grandstand. The turf course is used for the final race of the Canadian triple crown, the Breeders' Stakes, run in August. Canada's Triple Crown begins with the Queen's Plate at Woodbine in June, at 1¼ miles; followed by the Prince of Wales (run at Fort Erie racetrack) in July, at 1³⁄₁₆ miles; and returns to Woodbine in August for the 1½-mile Breeders' Stakes. For winning all three of these races, Triple Crown winners receive a beautiful gold-sided trophy. Only six 3 year olds have captured this series: New Providence (1959), Canebora ('63), With Approval ('89), Izvestia ('90), Dance Smartly ('91), and Peteski ('93).

Milestones

1860, June 27—The Queen's Plate, the oldest continuously run stakes race in North America, is first run at a racecourse in the village of Carleton, about four miles northwest of Toronto. Don Juan is the winner.

1916, May 20—In an unprecedented sweep, Mandarin, Gala Water, and Gala Day finish first, second, and third, respectively, in the King's Plate at Woodbine for their owner, distiller Joseph Seagram. Three days later, Mandarin and Gala Water again finish one-two, this time in the Breeders' Stakes.

1935, May 18—The Seagram family wins the King's Plate a record twentieth time.

1938, June 26—Nearco ends his career a perfect 14-for-14 by winning the Grand Prix de Paris at Longchamp.

1956, June 12—Opening day of the new Woodbine.

1957, June 8—Jockey Avelino Gomez wins his first Queen's Plate aboard Lyford Cay.

1959, June 30—Queen Elizabeth II makes her first visit to Woodbine to attend the 100th running of the Queen's Plate.

1959—Canada's Triple Crown of Thoroughbred racing is inaugurated. It consists of the Queen's Plate, The Prince of Wales, and The Breeders' Stakes. A horse named New Providence wins the Breeders' Stakes at Woodbine, and in doing so captures the first Canadian Triple Crown.

1960, June 11—Victoria Park returns to Woodbine—after finishing second in the Preakness—to win the Queen's Plate.

1964, June 20—Bill Hartack guides Northern Dancer to a 7½-length victory in the 105th running of the Queen's Plate. It marks the first and only time a horse captures both the Kentucky Derby and Queen's Plate.

1967, May 6—Jockey Richard Grubb wins seven consecutive races in one day. Scoring victories in races two through eight, he accomplishes the most consecutive wins by a jockey ever at Woodbine.

1968, June 24—Waverly Steps crosses the wire first. The win marks the longest priced winner ever at the Toronto track returning $794.20 for a $2 wager.

1968, October 4—Jockey Sandy Hawley wins his first career race aboard Fly Alone at Woodbine. As Canada's top jockey, he goes on to capture 6,449 victories in his career.

1973, October 28—Secretariat wins the $142,700 Canadian International at Woodbine in impressive fashion. The race is the last of his career.

1976—The Sovereign Awards are established.

1980—Woodbine introduces simulcast wagering to allow Fort Erie races to be wagered on at Woodbine. It marks the introduction of simulcast wagering in all of North America.

1989, May 14—E. P. Taylor, born in 1901, owner of Windfields Farm and breeder of Northern Dancer, dies at age 88.

1989, July 18—The last Northern Dancer foal (Northern Park) to be sold at public auction is purchased by Zenya Yoshida for $2.8 million.

1990, November 16—Northern Dancer, born May 27, 1961, dies in Maryland and is brought back to Canada to be buried at Windfields Farm.

1994, September 10—The E. P. Taylor Turf course opens at Woodbine. The 1½-mile oval is hailed as one of the top turf courses ever to be built in North America. Alywow wins the first ever race on the course.

1996, October 26—Woodbine hosts the Breeders' Cup, setting an attendance record of 42,243 fans. Alphabet Soup upsets the overwhelming race favorite Cigar in the Breeders' Cup Classic.

1997, June 29—Queen Elizabeth II visits Woodbine for the Queen's Plate race.

1998, July 1—Jockey Sandy Hawley rides his final career race at Woodbine aboard Terremoto in the Grade III Dominion Day Stakes, finishing third.

Jockey Avelino Gomez

Glossary

The entries below marked with a "CS" are contributions by Cathy Schenck, Librarian, Keeneland Race Course.

Added Money—Money added by the racing association to stake fees paid by subscribers to form the total purse for a stakes race. (CS)

Allowance Race—A race in which published conditions stipulate weight allowances according to previous purse earnings and/or number or types of wins. (CS)

Apron—The paved strip between the front of the grandstand and the track.

Backstretch—The straight part of the racing oval between the two turns at the back of the track. The straightaway in front of the grandstand from the turn to the finish line is the homestretch.

Betting Ring—The portion of the track where wagers are made, more common before the introduction of pari-mutuel betting. (CS)

Bloodline—The genealogy of a Thoroughbred horse.

Bookmaker—A person who quotes odds on various horses, receives bets on those horses, and pays the winning bets. (CS)

Breeders—The owner of the dam of a horse at the time the horse was foaled. (CS)

Breeders' Cup—A championship series of million-dollar races to determine which is the best horse and to stimulate public interest in racing. The Breeders' Cup has been held each fall since 1983 and offers seven races for different age, sex, and distance divisions: 1. Sprint; ¾ mile for 3 year olds and up. 2. Juvenile Fillies; 1¹⁄₁₆ miles for 2-year-old fillies. 3. Distaff; 1⅛ miles for 3-year-old and up fillies and mares. 4. Two-Mile; 1 mile (turf) for 3 year olds and up. 5. Juvenile; ¹⁄₁₆ mile for 2-year-old colts and geldings. 6. Turf; 1½ miles for 3 year olds and up. 7. Classic; 1¼ miles for 3 year olds and up. The Breeders' Cup was conceived by John R. Gaines, founder of Gainesway Farm in Lexington, Kentucky, to provide an international focal point at the end of each racing season. It is held at shifting host racetracks and has initiated major capital improvements at each of the selected tracks.

Caller—The person who calls out the running positions of the horses during the race.

Chute—An extra length of track added to provide a long straight run from the starting gate to the first turn.

Claiming Race—A race in which all horses are entered for a specific price and can be purchased by another owner who has started a horse at the current meeting. Claiming races are used to provide competition between horses of similar value or racing records. (CS)

Classic Races—A series of races for 3-year-old horses that are of set distances and run on the same days every year. The best American examples are the Kentucky Derby, 1¼ miles, run on the first Saturday in May; the Preakness, 1¹⁄₁₆ miles, run two weeks later; and the Belmont Stakes, 1½ miles, run three weeks after the Preakness, in June.

Clerk of Scales—The official who weighs the jockeys before and after each race to ensure that the proper weight was carried. (CS)

Clocker—A person who times the speed of a horse during workouts. Most clockers work for the *Daily Racing Form*, where the times of workouts are published for the racing public. (CS)

Clubhouse—Originally a separate building, the clubhouse is now a section of the main racetrack building reserved for special ticket holders; it usually has the best seats and always contains a restaurant and bar.

Clubhouse Turn—The first bend of the track, at the point where the clubhouse is usually situated.

Color of Thoroughbreds—The official colors of registered Thoroughbreds are bay, brown, chestnut, black gray, and roan. (Ninety percent of Thoroughbreds are bay [reddish-brown], brown, or chestnut [red-hued].) (CS)

Color Room—The room used to store the jackets called silks or colors, worn by the jockeys for various owners. The jackets are usually hung from metal hooks either around the ceiling of the room, as at Oaklawn, or on racks, as at Keeneland. They are managed by the silks man who makes them available to the jockeys' valets, who dress the jockeys before each race.

Colors—Racing silks, jacket, and cap worn by jockeys to denote ownership of a horse. First introduced in England around 1762 when nineteen men registered owners' colors with the Jockey Club. Originally made from silk or satin. (CS)

Course—The racing strip, also called the "track" in America. It can refer to either a dirt or turf course, or be the name of the racetrack itself. The most traditional of the old American racing tracks bear the name, as in Keeneland Race Course. Written as one word in the European manner, "racecourse" connotes an international facility, as in Arlington International Racecourse in Chicago. The racetracks that have always been presented as recreational facilities tend to be called parks, such examples as Hialeah Park, Oaklawn Park, and Santa Anita Park, although there are exceptions.

Daily Racing Form—The racing newspaper, started in Chicago in 1894 by Frank Brunsell, that gives racing charts and past performances of race horses. The *Daily Racing Form* also publishes the times of workouts for the racing public. (CS)

Finish Line—A wire stretched above the track designating the finish; it is attached to a post with a mirror. It is sometimes called "the wire." The term "wire to wire" is used when a horse takes the lead from the start of the race and holds this position until the finish.

Gap—The horse path leading form the paddock to the track, forming the entrance to the track. The term probably derived from the gap between the grandstand and the clubhouse in early racetracks.

Graded Stakes Race—A nonrestricted race with added money of $50,000 or more. Grade race status is conferred by the Thoroughbred Owners and Breeders Association's (TOBA) North American Graded Stakes Committee. (CS) According to Trevor Denman, race commentator at Santa Anita, "Graded races were devised across the country and internationally. The grading is based upon the performances of the field of horses that run in the stakes race and on the performances of those horses in subsequent races; the statistics are compiled to reflect the running history for about five years. The selection panel, composed of a team or racing secretaries from Florida, New York, and California, compiles these statistics and looks at the results retrospectively, determining Grades I, II, and III. For example, if the horses in the field of a particular stakes race went on to win other races, the stakes race would be considered a 'productive race' and could be upgraded from II to I. This method has been employed since about 1971 and is based entirely on cold facts."

Grandstand—The main building of the racetrack, used primarily for spectators to view and place bets on the races.

Handicap Race—A race in which compensations (weight carried) are given to different horses to equalize the chances of winning. The criteria for compensation include past performances, weight carried, track conditions, jockey, and distance of the race, among others. The *American Heritage Dictionary* states that the origin is from "hand in cap," a lottery game in which players held forfeits in a cap.

Hot Walker—A person who walks a horse after a workout to cool the horse down.

Infield—The part of the track surrounded by the racing oval. It is usually an open, landscaped area, sometimes containing a lake.

Jockey—A professional rider of race horses.

Jockey Club, The—An organization started in 1894 that maintains the *American Stud Book* and approves Thoroughbred names and registry. Also the governing body responsible for the standardization of the rules of racing. (CS)

Jockey's Quarters—A group of rooms for jockeys, usually consisting of a steam room, a room where the jockey dresses, and another room where the jockey either relaxes or waits for the race he is to ride.

Maiden Race—A race for horses that have not yet won a race (this includes both male and female horses).

Owner—Any person who holds, in whole or in part, any right, title, or interest in a horse.

Paddock—Where the horses are saddled and kept before proceeding to the track. In the paddock the owner has the last moment with the jockey and trainer, and the patrons are able to see the horses for the first and only time of the day before making a swift appraisal of their condition and temperament in order to place a bet.

Paddock Judge—The official in charge of all activities in the saddling paddock before each race. (CS)

Pari-Mutuel Betting—1. A system of betting in which the total amount bet on a particular race, less the track's percentage, is divided by the number of winning tickets, thus giving the price each winning ticket pays. This system originated in France and it was first introduced to the United States in the 1870s. 2. The machine that records bets placed under this system. The *American Heritage Dictionary* traces the word to the French *parrier*, to make equal, but in the American racing world it is generally though that the word is derived from the city of Paris.

Patrol Judges—Officials who observe the progress of a race from various vantage points around the running strip. (CS)

Placing Judges—Officials who determine the order of finish of a race. (CS)

Post—The starting gate.

Post Parade—This occurs when the horses leave the gap and parade in front of the grandstand before proceeding to the starting gate.

Post Position—The horse's position in the starting gate, selected from a draw.

Post Time—The designated time for the start of a race.

Purse—The amount of money for which a race is run. The term originated from a custom in the late 1800s of hanging a silk purse containing the race money in front of the judges' stand. (CS)

Race Meeting—The established number of racing days and fixed number of races that are held at each particular race track.

Racing Commission—A commission designated in each state to regulate racing within that state.

Racing Secretary—The official responsible for writing the conditions for the races of a meeting. The conditions—purse money, claiming prize, weight, sex, and earnings—are published in a condition book that is distributed to trainers. (CS)

Rail—The fence that separates the racing strips, as between the dirt track and the inner turf track, and both from the infield. There is an inside rail, where the horses run, and an outside rail, which acts as a barrier.

Receiving Barn—A barn that houses horses shipped in for a certain race. It is sometimes called an isolation barn or, in the case of international horses, a quarantine barn.

Silks—The name of the shirt worn by the jockey identifying the stable for which he is riding. (see "Colors")

Stable—The building where horses are housed. It also refers to a group of horses under an ownership.

Stakes Race—Any race in which entries are made at least seventy-two hours in advance and which require payment of subscription, entry, and starting fees by the owners. (CS)

Starter—The official who gives the signal for the horses to begin a race. (CS)

Starting Gate—A metal structure with partitions for horses which have gates on each side. The horses are loaded into the partitions for a few moments until the starter opens the gates in front of them, thus starting the race.

Stewards—Officials who supervise the conduct of a racing meeting. They interpret and enforce the rules of racing, and their authority supersedes that of the racing association. (CS)

Stretch—The straight portion of the racetrack between the final turn and the finish line.

Stud Book—The registry and record of the breeding of Thoroughbreds.

Stud Farm—A farm that houses stallions that are used for breeding.

Thoroughbred—A distinctive breed of horse tracing its genealogy back to horses registered in the *English General Stud Book* (1791), the *American Stud Book* (1896), *the French Stud Book* (1838), or a stud book of another country. By 1700 the English had long been aware of the speed of Arabian horses; they had some horses that were spoils of war and started breeding them to English mares. Racing and breeding records were private until the eighteenth century, when several volumes were compiled. The first was a record of all English races valued ten pounds or more, published in 1727; this was continued under the name *Sporting Calendar* with the addition of pedigrees in 1743. It soon became clear that the horses that performed well could be traced back to Eastern, Arab, Barbary, or Turk descent. The first English stud book, titled the *General Stud Book*, was published in 1791 and was a listing of horses with good racing performances and their pedigrees. This was not a book about bloodlines per se, but a book about racing bloodlines. This particular book is recognized as documenting the beginning of a new breed of horse, the Thoroughbred—a racing horse that combined mostly Arab, Barbary, or Turkish blood with English stamina and strength. Originally the book merely listed horses that raced and proved to be winning horses. Now the *General Stud Book* has become the racing bible because only horses with a bloodline that can be traced back to it can be entered in Thoroughbred races. Thoroughbreds are horses descended from ancestors bred and trained for racing; the best among them are selected to breed in order to improve and carry on the line. Americans developed the sport concurrently with the English and French.

Thoroughbred Industry—The business of breeding and racing Thoroughbred horses. (CS)

Timer—The official who records the length of time in which a race is run. (CS)

Tote Board—An electronic panel that displays such information as post time and time of day. Recently, the tote board has included digital pictures of the leading horses from the starting gate to the ⅛-mile pole.

Trainer—The person responsible for proper care, health, conditioning, racing strategy, and safety of horses in his charge. (CS)

True Race—A race with as little as possible left to chance—this usually refers to longer oval courses and straight, English-style courses.

Turf Course—A grass racing strip.

Valet—The person who attends to the jockey, keeps equipment in order, acts as a dresser, and helps saddle the horse in the paddock.

Walking Ring—The circular or oval path in the paddock area where horses and jockeys parade before entering the horse path leading to the track. This is for the benefit of people in the paddock area who want to see the horse and rider before placing a bet. The post parade takes place for the benefit of those in the grandstand.

Whip—The jockey's crop or stick, which he or she uses to inspire the horse to run faster.

Windows—The site where bets are placed at a racetrack.

Winner's Circle—A small area where the jockey brings the horse after winning a race, to weigh in, meet with the owner or trainer, and be photographed.

Workout—A training exercise during which the horse is timed for speed over a specified distance.

Photography Credits

Index